Winged Bull

The Extraordinary Life of Henry Layard, the Adventurer Who Discovered the Lost City of Nineveh

Jeff Pearce

Prometheus Books

Guilford, Connecticut

Ⓟ Prometheus Books

An imprint of The Rowman & Littlefield Publishing Group, Inc.
4501 Forbes Boulevard, Suite 200, Lanham, Maryland 20706
www.rowman.com

Distributed by NATIONAL BOOK NETWORK

British Library Cataloguing in Publication Information Available

Library of Congress Cataloging-in-Publication Data

Names: Pearce, Jeff, 1963– author.
Title: Winged bull : the extraordinary life of Henry Layard, the adventurer
  who discovered the lost city of Nineveh / Jeff Pearce.
Other titles: Extraordinary life of Henry Layard, the adventurer who
  discovered the lost city of Nineveh
Description: Lanham, MD : Prometheus Books, an imprint of the Rowman &
  Littlefield Publishing Group, Inc., [2021] | Includes bibliographical
  references and index. | Summary: "Real-life Indiana Jones meets Lawrence
  of Arabia in Winged Bull, the first biography in half a century to tell
  the story of Henry Layard and his daring adventures. While you may not
  know his name, you likely have seen his work. The winged bulls, lions
  and priceless treasures of art and jewelry that he found make up
  permanent collections in institutions such as the British Museum,
  Britain's National Gallery and New York's Metropolitan Museum of Art"—
  Provided by publisher.
Identifiers: LCCN 2020048528 (print) | LCCN 2020048529 (ebook) | ISBN
  9781633886995 (cloth) | ISBN 9781633887008 (ebook)
Subjects: LCSH: Layard, Austen Henry, 1817-1894. | Assyriologists—Great
  Britain—Biography. | Diplomats—Great Britain—19th century—Biography.
  | Archaeologists—Great Britain—Biography. | Art collectors—Great
  Britain—19th century—Biography.
Classification: LCC DS70.88.L3 P43 2021 (print) | LCC DS70.88.L3 (ebook)
  | DDC 935/.4 [B]—dc23
LC record available at https://lccn.loc.gov/2020048528
LC ebook record available at https://lccn.loc.gov/2020048529

On a corner of London, twenty-five years ago,
a beautiful young woman says to a stranger,
"Is there a big bookstore around here?"
And then a walk to Foyles and so many laughs and
stories, conveyed and continued even with an ocean
in the way and with so many life changes.

This book is dedicated to my beloved friend Paola Orfei.

Contents

A Quick Note on Names and Places

The reader may notice some minor inconsistencies throughout in the spellings and use of Middle Eastern names for persons and locales. Rather than try to shoehorn names into today's conventions of transliteration into English, I have opted sometimes to render them as Layard or others of his era identified them so that they can be found more easily in his original texts. The goal was readability and the reader's convenience.

In the same vein, I feel no need to be cravenly tied to British titles. Some historical figures remain well known by their peerages, such as Aberdeen or Raglan, so *Winged Bull* is still lousy with lords. But you won't find its pages littered with "Sir So-and-So" or much attention paid to the tedious minutiae of who was baron or earl of what. Traditionalists are free to grumble over my Canadian impertinence.

As well, to help today's general reader, I often use modern name equivalents wherever possible for locales, such as *Istanbul*, not "Constantinople," and *Mumbai*, not "Bombay," except for in quoted texts. In chapter 14, I have opted to honor my hosts in Kurdistan and rely on Kurdish names rather than their Arabic ones, hence *Suleimani*, not "Sulaymaniyah." When in Rome, etc.

Hopefully, the reader will forgive me my trespasses.

Introduction

One Man against a Mob

He had been told it was foolish, reckless—so dangerous that no one expected him to come back alive. His own traveling companion refused to go with him. But the young Englishman decided to go on his own, into the remote areas east of the Dead Sea in what today is modern Jordan.

Back in 1840, the region was supposed to be under Egyptian control, but it was anything but. It was a countryside filled with hostile tribes and bandit raiders who would expect to be paid at every stop for passage through their territory, and if they didn't get what they wanted through bribes, they would draw their swords, wield their clubs, and merely strip away the coins from a dead body or a live victim who was beaten senseless. The young Englishman didn't have a lot of cash. He didn't know these lands. He didn't even speak Arabic. All he had was his obstinate will, plus a desire to go see for himself what were said to be fabulous ruins, what remained of the ancient city of Petra.

He was only twenty-three years old, and his name was Henry Layard.

There were no embassies where Layard was going. No official would intervene on his behalf or could. No one even had a clue about his route. No telephones, no mail. Today, teenagers and university students from the United States, Britain, Europe, and Australia strap on backpacks with a national flag sewn on a patch of denim, and they catch a flight to tourist spots waiting for them with clean hotels and high ratings from a *Lonely Planet* guide. For them, this is adventure. After all, Cairo or Istanbul is still exotic, even if these destinations come with Wi-Fi. For Henry Layard, there would be no such luxuries. He was a son of the 1800s who would be riding a camel even farther back in time. For out in the gorges and the dunes of red sand, the fourteenth century kept a fierce grip on life, and white men were still called "Franks"—as if the age of the Crusades had never ended.

Westerners didn't regularly go to Petra. They couldn't, not normally. But Layard wouldn't be the first—a Swiss explorer named Burckhardt had "discovered" the ruins in 1812, and he still had to trick his way into seeing them. Outsiders were few and far between. It would take a hundred years after Layard was born for Lawrence of Arabia to show up, mustering rebels at Petra to fight the Turks in World War I. This brash young man in 1840 didn't have an army backing him up, but he was determined to go anyway. In fact, he fully expected to get there despite the incredible dangers and his own lack of funds and experience.

From different paintings and drawings made during these early years of adventure, Layard was a lanky figure with brown hair, pensive eyes hooded by slightly thick eyebrows, and a somewhat weak chin covered at the time with a full beard, which wouldn't succeed very often in disguising his youth. He made his goodbye to his travel companion, promising to meet his friend weeks later in either Damascus or Aleppo. Then he set off. He had a couple of mules, a secondhand tent bought from an Egyptian soldier and a carpet, as well as saddlebags stuffed with medicines, a small supply of food, his maps and notebooks, a compass, and changes of clothes.

Along for the ride was Antonio, a young Arab he had hired to be his servant and interpreter—not that Antonio was fluent in anything besides his own native tongue. Antonio wasn't even his actual name; Italian friars had offered it to him when they gave him an education and had made him a convert to Christianity, and the boy had, as Layard put it later, "acquired a smattering of that mongrel Italian known as 'Lingua Franca.'" Layard's only real protection was a double-barreled pistol and a couple of rifles.

On his first stop in Hebron, he learned just how cruel and unforgiving life could be in this frontier. Locals who didn't pay their taxes were dragged in chains before an official and tortured with *bastinado*—the soles of the feet whipped. "I felt too much disgusted and horrified with these barbarous proceedings to continue to witness them," Layard wrote later. After denial comes bargaining, and the young Englishman stubbornly haggled with the local sheikh to safely escort him through his lands with two camels. Then the sheikh didn't show up for the journey's start, and though he arranged for the animals to be delivered, they didn't even belong to him. Worse, Layard, Antonio, and the camel herder soon got lost for several hours.

Riding a camel looks easy. Layard soon discovered it isn't, and the results were comical. He'd been trying to get his animal to pick up the pace, and his mount decided to do just that by going down a steep hill, taking off "in a kind of awkward gallop." When he pulled on the halter, the camel whipped its head around and glared at him but didn't stop. "My saddle-bags first fell off, my carpet followed, and losing my balance, I slipped over the tail of the animal and came full length to the ground." Layard wasn't hurt, but now he had to chase after his ride. He eventually got the hang of it.

An evening meal was often rice and boiled mutton, rancid butter over pasty balls of flour, or bread. Nights were frigidly cold. The absent sheikh made an appearance at last, claiming he was delayed because of business with the governor of Hebron and yet nagging for more money. On top of the austere conditions, Layard had a toothache. It was so painful that he finally entrusted himself to the local dentist, who cut at his gums with a knife, then braced Layard's head between his knees, and, believe it or not, used an awl—yes, an actual woodworking tool—on the tooth. And it *slipped*. Layard was left with a nasty gash in his palate. Incredibly, he let the man try again, and his dentist only managed to break off a piece of the tooth. That was when the patient reached his limits.

Meanwhile, the sheikh kept nagging him for cash. Maybe this was why the man still didn't deliver—his overhead wasn't covered. He was supposed to provide his own brother to ensure protection; instead, there were only two Arab guards with rifles. The small band set out, crossing hills, navigating sandy plains south of the Dead Sea, and working their way up mountains. Under clear blue sky, Layard climbed up a peak on foot to have a look around. "The scene was wonderful, and magnificent from its savage desolation. Range after range of barren, naked hills of the most varied and fantastic shapes, like the waves of a sea which had been suddenly arrested when breaking and curling, stretched before me." And then after passing through a long, narrow gorge, his party reached its goal: Petra.

Pillars and friezes carved out of the reddish-brown stone were waiting for him. There were tombs and facades, an amphitheater, and temples—all offering testimony to the era of the Nabateans who lived hundreds of years before Christ, right up to the epochs of the ancient Romans and the Byzantines. Petra is so amazing that today it's a symbol of Jordan and a beloved UNESCO World Heritage Site. Even in our modern age, it's not easy to get to, with infrequent public transport. If you want to reach it by car, you better know how to haggle. But tourists still come in droves. Layard came before all of them.

After he and his group entered the Wadi Musa, the Valley of Moses, he happily pitched his tent and spread out his carpet. He thought everything was fine. When curious Arabs showed up, he even asked them for some bread and milk, which people gave, and his servant, Antonio, kept busy, setting up breakfast. The atmosphere was tense, but not ugly—yet. Then at last, the English tourist was ready to go check out the ruins, and that was when all hell broke loose.

The onlookers, who were apparently "known to be treacherous and bloodthirsty," expected a hefty toll. There was yelling back and forth with the two guides, the metallic *zing* of swords being drawn, while others tried to swipe Layard's belongings. He was told in no uncertain terms that he wouldn't be leaving alive unless he paid. The menacing crowd grew bigger, nastier. Both men and women joined its ranks, slipping out of the tombs "like rabbits from a warren." And then a man grabbed a rifle away from one of the guides.

Layard could have lost his life then and there. He had Antonio inform the mob that he was under the personal protection of the sheikh, who had vouched for his safety to the governor of Hebron, who in turn had to answer to Ibrahim Pasha, the feared commander of the Egyptian army at the time. If anything happened to Layard, the Egyptian government wouldn't be satisfied until each and every one of his attackers was exterminated. It was a phenomenal bluff—and it worked.

Now anyone else after a grim standoff would have packed his saddlebags and gotten the hell out of there. But Henry Layard had come to see ruins, and by God, he was going to see ruins. Even with the tension diffused a little and the mob broken up, a chieftain of the tribe tried to bargain for payment, showing up to negotiate through intimidation with pistols and a rifle (though the man's followers only had spears). Layard still wouldn't back down. He told his men to bring the camels after they were finished loading them up and started off for the valley to see the sights.

And in another confrontation that would fit right into an old black-and-white adventure movie, the tribal chieftain, frustrated and angry at this foreigner getting the better of him, snapped, "As a dog you came, as a dog, you go away."

Layard offered the traditional Arab salutation and contemptuously threw a silver coin at the man as payment for the morning's milk and bread. His nervous team pleaded now and then to leave, but he took his time, soaking up the vision of monuments, enjoying the views.

Not too long after their visit to Petra, Layard's party ran into some bandits who tried to con the group into dropping its guard, but he and his men stayed vigilant. As the leader of the robbers tagged along on the journey and tried to lure them into an ambush at a ravine, Layard grabbed him and pointed his pistol at the man's head. Convinced that this foreigner would blow his head off, the man ordered his gang of thieves to fall back. The bandits threw stones and hurled a spear, and though Layard kept a steely grip on his hostage, the robbers still made off with a good portion of his belongings.

But there was a bizarre final act to this showdown.

When Layard and his men tracked down the camp of the bandit leader, he didn't hold out much hope of getting his things back, "for I had never set eyes upon a more ferocious, forbidding set of ruffians than those who were glaring at me." The robber-in-charge first told his side of the story. Then Layard told his version of what happened. But the bandits' leader had made the ultimate *faux pas* in his world, and his colleagues rounded on him: "Why did you not tell us that you had eaten bread with this Frank, instead of joining with us in robbing him?"

So there *was* honor among thieves. Stealing was permissible, of course, but you don't share a meal with your victim before you rip him off. Layard was considered the injured party. People in the camp brought back his saddle-bags and other belongings and served him a meal. A young fool had poked around in Layard's medicine chest and sampled one of the bottles, thinking he was drinking liquor; he got sick, and the locals persuaded Layard to try to cure him. Layard gave the youth an emetic to induce vomiting. He had rescued the thief, "but I inwardly rejoiced that the fellow had been well punished."

★   ★   ★

Indiana Jones is fictional, but if you take away the Nazis, the fedora, and the supernatural elements, you have Henry Layard, who had Indiana-like adventures while he made discoveries along the way.

T. E. Lawrence was very real indeed, living and fighting at the Bedouins' side. If you take away his narcissism mixed with masochism and self-doubt, you have a more confident hero: Henry Layard.

Here was a young man who befriended Arabs but with no political or military agenda to cloud his motivations. He lived and rode among the Bakhtiari people of Persia and wore their clothing. Later, when he did represent the interests of the British Crown, he still championed the cause of Turks coming out of the restrictive bonds of the Ottoman Empire. And he would always be the man who discovered priceless Assyrian artifacts and ruins.

To appreciate just what he accomplished and his place in the world, you have to keep in mind the colorful early chapters of archaeology. Today, we stroll into museums, and we take the white sculpted marbles of the Greeks and the mummies of Egypt for granted. They're simply *there*. We don't even need to leave home to learn every detail about them. But they were handed down to us from a field inhabited once by hobbyists where any amateur, if he had the time and money, could join the scavenger hunt. The Scottish peer William Hamilton had enough spare hours when he was a diplomat in Naples to collect Greek vases; his friend Thomas Bruce, better known as Lord Elgin, used bribes to sneak treasures of the Parthenon out of Greece. Layard was different; he sought formal *permission* from the Ottoman authorities, and he acted as an agent of his government back home and the British Museum.

Visit the Metropolitan Museum of Art in New York, and you see his legacy. The museum has a substantial collection of Assyrian treasures that Layard found. Walk into the British Museum in London, and if you turn left and go down the corridor past the coat check, your mouth will open over the dark stone winged bulls that loom over you. Layard brought them back all the way from Nineveh. Then stroll up Tottenham Court Road, make your way to Trafalgar Square, and head into the National Gallery. On its walls are some of the priceless Italian works of art that Layard collected.

Archaeologist, adventurer, art historian, diplomat, politician—he was all these things, and his life was long and full. He was famous in his own lifetime for his discoveries—and his status as a best-selling author. This is how Layard opened the first chapter of his two-volume work on his excavations at Nineveh, and with crackling prose like this, it's no wonder that Victorians snapped it up from bookshops: "During the autumn of 1839 and winter of 1840, I had been wandering through Asia Minor and Syria, scarcely leaving untrod one spot hallowed by tradition, or unvisited one ruin consecrated by history. I was accompanied by one no less curious and enthusiastic than myself. We were both equally careless of comfort and unmindful of danger. We rode alone; our arms were our only protection; a valise behind our saddles was our wardrobe, and we tended our own horses except when relieved from the duty by the hospitable inhabitants of a Turcoman village or an Arab tent."

In the late 1990s, there was a peculiar resurgence of interest in Nineveh, with two brilliant books published on the excavations and finds: Mogens Trolle Larsen's excellent *The Conquest of Assyria* and John Malcolm Russell's *From Nineveh to New York*. But there has been only one comprehensive and full biography of Henry Layard himself, written by a British journalist, Gordon Waterfield, and published more than half a century ago.

That brings us to a pressing question: *why* Layard? Why should we care about him and consider him important?

Let's put aside for the moment his substantial contribution to the museums and art galleries. After all, archaeologists *find things*—that's what they do. Today's archaeologists don't lead particularly dramatic lives, with battles or chases on horseback, and after they're finished digging up whatever they become noted for, that's when the drama usually ends. Howard Carter introduced the world to King Tut and soon retired. Heinrich Schliemann had already made a fortune and had retired, and *then* he went looking for Troy. But the most dramatic thing Schliemann ever got up to was smuggling golden treasures out of Turkey. It's not unreasonable to expect Henry Layard's story climaxes with his great finds at Nineveh, and that's all there is to him.

But it didn't, and it isn't. There is so much more. In 2013, for example, Britain's Prime Minister David Cameron visited India and placed a wreath at the memorial for the Amritsar Massacre of 1919, but in a controversial stand, he refused to deliver an official apology. British newspapers thought it worth pointing out that Cameron's great-great grandfather was a British cavalryman who helped suppress the Indian Mutiny. As it happens, it was Henry Layard who went off to India while the mutiny was still on to investigate its causes, and his progressive views and criticisms of British rule earned him the lasting admiration of many Indians who knew the cruel realities of the Raj.

As this book was started in 2014, Viktor Yanukovych fell from power, and Ukraine was in the middle of an uprising; then Russia stepped in, and a controversial referendum was held that delivered Crimea back into Moscow's hands. Now consider that Henry Layard got to witness some of the most important battles of the Crimean War, including the infamous Charge of the Light Brigade.

We live in an era when activists and commentators are still trying to figure out how democracy can function with capitalism. Henry Layard—a man whom Karl Marx paid attention to, a man supported by his admiring friend Charles Dickens—would enrage the powerful British aristocracy when he called for more citizens to get the vote. At that same time, he helped found one of Turkey's oldest banks and usher the nation into international finance. And he traveled and recorded life in fractured, close-to-lawless regions of what today is Iraq and Syria.

★   ★   ★

I feel it's necessary to state clearly what this book isn't. It is *not* a book about archaeology.

Yes, of course, attention is paid to Layard's discoveries and contributions in the field, and his work here was the defining experience of his career. But these breakthroughs were part of the larger tapestry of his life. For those who need more on Assyriology, there is a long list of scholarly volumes and an ever-growing collection of articles widely available, and I would never delude myself that this book has new revelations on the subject or could presume to contribute in that area. I wanted to tell the unknown story of an amazing man, that's all. This is a book for the general reader and not the scholar. So those who think history or biography should be presented in a stuffy, overly formal or pedantic manner should look elsewhere. Layard himself would never want the tale of his life offered in a turgid chronicle.

And as we'll discover, he refreshingly defies our expectations and clichés of the Victorian man and even the Edwardian one who followed. In a time when the English could cheerfully use every racial epithet under the sun, not only in the street but in private clubs over snifters of brandy, Layard actually *apologized* in an introduction to one of his travel memoirs for his old descriptions of Persians and Arabs: "The character that I have given of them will not be considered a favorable one. It is possible that since the time of my residence among them—now more than forty-five years ago—a change may have taken place, and that the misgovernment, oppression and cruelty which I have denounced, especially in the rulers of Persia, and the vices of all classes of the people which shocked me so greatly, are no longer what they were." He hoped that "I may not be giving offence to any modern Persian."

Imagine Winston Churchill or Kitchener or Jan Christian Smuts having this capacity to revise their old opinions!

Layard was, in fact, more tolerant than he gave himself credit for. He understood then what is still true today: we hardwire our presumptions about a foreign people through news reports and often through the most limited and casual contact. Here is a quick note he inserts about Arabs later: "The same man who at one moment would be grasping, deceitful, treacherous and cruel would show himself at another generous, faithful, trustworthy and humane." With the Victorians, we expect—almost by reflex—that we must pick our way through all the freight of racial bigotries and imperial biases at the time. But we do this far less with Layard, making his observations both more compelling and arguably more reliable than other writers of his era.

And let's remember: his books are still around. They are still a rich resource of detail on life in the Ottoman Empire in the nineteenth century and on the thinking and personalities of great men making decisions in London, Washington, Paris, and Istanbul. Staying in print for close to two centuries? Most writers would be very happy indeed with a legacy like that.

I left for last perhaps the best reason of all for examining his life, and it's simply this: it makes for a thrilling yarn, a wonderful story. Facing bandits and uncovering lost treasures, there are bound to be whiffs of the kind of Orientalism that would make Edward W. Said groan. This often can't be helped. Today, the word "exotic" has almost become pejorative because of its rude use in multicultural contexts. But for many Europeans of the nineteenth century, the Middle East was exotic in the true sense of the word, and so the Europeans wrote about it this way. As we'll discover, Ottoman citizens often felt Western Europeans were just alien and peculiar.

Luckily, our intrepid hero noticed the good with the bad, was often unflinching over his own foibles and mistakes, and cared about these lands and their peoples—an adventurer with a conscience.

The backdrops to the amazing movie of his life will shift rapidly. Sometimes the villains will stampede over the hill, but there will be moments, too, when we're blindsided and left with nothing but rags under the sun along a desolate stretch. We'll need to keep our wits about us. And there will be danger of a kind on the floor of the House of Commons just as on a battlefield in distant Ukraine. But our guide is never helpless, always resourceful. So hold the reins tight because young Henry Layard is galloping hell-for-leather toward his destiny, and he expects us to keep up.

• 1 •

Victorian Slacker

*H*enry Layard came into the world in 1817, and it seems fitting that he was born not in a house but in a hotel on the Left Bank of Paris.

The infant's timing was good. Though English, he was born safely away from England. Europe was in the middle of a lull, relatively speaking. Napoleon had been packed off to St. Helena, where he'd spend the rest of his days, but the French, the Italians, the Belgians, and the other peoples on the continent were all still feeling the aftereffects of the Little Corporal's convulsive wars. Britain had won, but it didn't feel like a winner. It had a massive hangover debt and high unemployment. Luddites were smashing the mechanical guts of textile factories, trying to turn back time and reverse the industrial revolution. And Englishmen had other things to gripe about, demanding voter reform.

What gets glossed over in all the gilt-frame pageantry of the cannon fire and battles, the white waistcoat of Napoleon and Tchaikovsky's *1812 Overture* soaring in volume, is that the wars were also about *ideas*. As much as the French emperor could be depicted as a tyrant in *The Times* of London, there was that nagging contradiction that the Napoleonic Code had a few good notions in it. After all, it encouraged greater religious tolerance, it gave civil service jobs to qualified candidates instead of the old boys' club, it introduced a revamped criminal code—all these reforms were bound to find their way to every capital across continental Europe in one shape or another, and they would even jump the English Channel. Britain's prime minister in 1817, Lord Liverpool, fretted about radical groups and had habeas corpus suspended.

None of these issues at the time, however, were on the mind of Henry's father. Peter Layard, a mild-mannered civil servant, had brought his young wife to Paris to have a look around postwar France, and Peter wanted to check

1

out what was left of the battlefield of Waterloo. He probably would have been astonished at the idea that 60,000 spectators would come out in 2015 on the battle's bicentenary to watch an extravagant and expensive reenactment, complete with 300 horses and 100 cannons, or that Belgium's prime minister would use the occasion to call for European unity. If Peter Layard worried about the condition of Europe at all, he soon had other concerns.

Marianne gave birth to a son on March 5 in their hotel in the Rue Neuve des Petits Champs. So it can be accurately said that Henry Layard was literally born a tourist.

And the whole course of his life was set early because of travel. His father had picked up asthma from years of working in Ceylon (today Sri Lanka), and after coming back to his old hometown of Ramsgate—one of Britain's prettiest seaside towns—he still wasn't comfortable. But he could afford to retire and live on a pension, and at least his return to England had earned him a wife. He would confide to his son years later that even as a boy, he was determined to marry his childhood playmate, Marianne Austen, the son of a banker—assuming, of course, she was still single when he got back. She was, and the two were a reasonably good match.

Peter Layard, whose own father had been an austere, cold presence, was determined to treat his children more decently. He enjoyed literature and the arts, and the Layards kept a modest salon for creative types and travelers at their home. Marianne was twenty-eight when she had Henry, and she would give birth to several more boys, his brothers, Arthur, Frederick, and Edgar. While high strung, she was bookish like her husband, devoted to her children, and had liberal sentiments. Henry wrote almost a lifetime later, "She was the kindest, the most unselfish and the most generous of women."

Though the couple tried living in Bath, it wouldn't do, so Peter took a doctor's advice, pulled up stakes, and moved the family to Italy. At three years old, Henry's earliest memories were of the journey across Europe. In Paris, someone thought it was a good idea in the Jardins des Plantes to let the Layard children near a lioness and her cub. Little Henry hugged the animal, while his brother, Frederick, cried out in fear. When they got to Geneva, Henry witnessed an eclipse of the sun by looking through a piece of smoked glass, with the image reflected in a bucket of water. In Italy, they hoped Peter would find relief for his lungs in Pisa, but the only place where he was unaffected by his condition was in Florence, and if the father ever roamed far, his asthma would flare up again.

As for Henry, his earliest companion was an old veteran of Napoleon's army named Pachot, who had been taken prisoner at Waterloo, only to be discovered and hired years later in Brussels by Peter Layard as his servant. Pachot, gentle and loyal, walked the little boy to school. If it was dark, the family's equally faithful black poodle, Mouche, would trot along with a lantern clamped between his teeth. Pachot was a fixture in the Layard household for decades, retiring to Brussels only when he was too old to carry out his duties, while his daughter ended up becoming a "reader" to the Queen of Belgium.

The Layards' firstborn was a bundle of contradictions. He was considered "good natured and amiable," but Henry himself remembered being sent to a corner quite often because of his bad temper and for making trouble. He liked the outdoors. He liked wandering hills with a nurse or gathering flowers. He also enjoyed birds, but his mother put a stop to his keeping any when she discovered a horrific practice common among locals and being used by one of the family's servants: the eyes were plucked out to keep the birds singing.

It sounds very much like the boy had an idyllic early childhood. His father brought him along whenever he went to visit museums and art galleries, and it wasn't long before he was explaining to his son just what made the paintings worthwhile or even important. Peter Layard had to have been a gifted and charismatic teacher because Henry considered that his lessons were responsible for "his ardent love for Italy and the Fine Arts which I have preserved through life, and which to me has been the source of much enjoyment and happiness."

The Layards were happy, frugal, comfortable—what more could you want? Nothing, at least for a while. But a few members of the clan never quite got over their spot on the social ladder. They were descendants of Huguenots, and the family legend went that once upon a time, they had titles and money and were related to three wealthy, respected French brothers named Raymond. Henry's great grandfather, a doctor (a thoroughly middle-class profession to the British), tried to make a claim to a baronetcy in Staffordshire. He spent so much of his hard-earned money trying to prove it that he infuriated his son, an army general, who destroyed as many of the accumulated documents as he could. He wanted future Layards to drop the whole thing, only his tactic didn't work.

While Peter Layard was still at his job in Ceylon, he happened to read an ad one day in a London newspaper; a Frenchman was looking for descendants of the Raymonds. There was more than just genealogy on the line—there was an actual fortune at stake. But in those days, it took ages for newspapers and the mail to travel from London all the way to the frontiers of the British Empire, and by the time Peter could enlist relatives back home to make contact, the man who had placed the ad died. The fellow left his wealthy estate to a tradesman on Bond Street. Being so close to peerage and fortune kept having a psychological roll-over effect. One of Henry's younger brothers would devote his spare time to tracking down all the details about the family tree and its history. No doubt his ancestor, the old army general, would have been thoroughly disgusted.

Along with Peter's living on a modest pension, maybe this explains why the Layard family caved in on a frequent basis to relatives, especially relatives who had more money. Marianne's side of the family hated the idea that her sons would be educated in a foreign country, so they browbeat an already nervous young woman who in turn had to persuade her husband. Peter Layard didn't think his health could take another sampling of English weather, but he relented anyway. Back the family went to Ramsgate, where Henry was stuck in a red brick house of a prep school on the main street of Putney. It wasn't long, however, before Peter's asthma acted up again, and his doctor recommended he move to Moulins in the center of France.

By now, Henry was eight years old. Amazingly, one of his uncles on his mother's side who was supposed to look after him thought this was old enough for the boy to make the journey on his own. The eldest Layard son was passed from train coach porters to a relative in Ramsgate to the boat leaving for Calais just "like a parcel." There wasn't even a familiar face to greet him when the little boy stepped off the train in Paris. Instead, a Frenchman who knew Peter had agreed to go collect his son, and he took Henry around to a hotel near the Tuileries.

Today, it would be unthinkable at least in the Western world to send a child this young on his own ten blocks away let alone to a foreign country. And most children probably would be terrified at the prospect. But Henry did what he wanted when he wanted, an attitude that never really left him. The landlady of the hotel took a shine to him, and he played with the woman's daughter, who must have been about his age, and slept beside the girl in the same bed. They took in the sights, including watching the guards on parade outside the Royal Palace. At one point, Henry asked for a bottle of champagne—which was a shock to his father when it turned up on his hotel bill.

Then it was off to Moulins in a stagecoach, with Henry fascinated by all he saw along the way. The coach arrived late in the evening, and as the passengers disembarked and the steaming horses were led away to their stables, Peter Layard stood in a small crowd waiting for him.

While it was good to be back with his family, Henry was promptly deposited in another school where he was soon miserable. Peter and Marianne must have underestimated the bitter resentment French people felt over Wellington clobbering Napoleon and wiping out the country's status as a superpower. In the classroom, little Henry was not just a foreigner, he was an *English* foreigner. He was a Protestant—by definition, a heretic. The bullying came not only from his classmates but from his teachers as well.

One tactic was to try to force him to kiss a cross drawn in white chalk on the filthy floor. Henry refused. The other boys grabbed him, beat him with their shoes, and rubbed his face in the chalk. Henry wouldn't give in. One time when a religious procession went by, he didn't kneel as was customary for Catholics, so the boys chased him through the street, eventually caught him, and were hell-bent on tossing him into the river nearby. Fortunately, a passing stranger intervened, and Henry was saved from drowning. When another boy managed to cut Henry's face with the stiff leather rim of his cap, Peter finally pulled his son out of the school. Peter's asthma was defeating him anyway in Moulins, so the family tried Geneva.

Henry was highly intelligent for his age but still rebellious, and his escapades sometimes had comical results. With his pocket money, he found a way to buy a small amount of gunpowder, which he and his friends wanted to use in a set of toy cannons. They were far from demolition experts, and when the powder went off, it singed Henry's eyebrows and almost hurt a classmate. But this was the era when "boys will be boys," and if your stunt was clever, your headmaster was just as likely to give you a hint of grudging admiration. Today, a boy might even be sent off for psychiatric counseling. Henry appears to have got a lecture, and that was the end of it.

His father liked to retell an anecdote that gives an impression of his son at this time. One day, Henry went wandering across a suspension bridge and paid the toll with the only coin he had on him. He was shocked to discover that when he wanted to go home, he needed to pay for another crossing—but he had no more money. He didn't know what to do until an old man approached the bridge. The boy went over to him and asked, "Will you lend me a *sous*? I am Henry Layard. Everyone knows me."

The old man was so surprised at the boy's confidence that he lent him the coin, and because Henry had given him his address, he went to visit the father. To a surprised and delighted Peter Layard, the old man declared, "*Ce garçon-là ira loin!*" (That boy will go far!).

★ ★ ★

For the time being, however, Henry was only going back to Florence. The Layards took the whole first floor in the Palazzo Ruccellai, a fifteenth-century town house in the Via della Vigna Nuova, a short walk from the River Arno.[1] The Ruccellai family dated back to the greatness of the Renaissance but had fallen on hard times and were happy to rent out most of the building, living on their limited income on the upper stories.

Henry was instantly enchanted by the family's new apartment with its carved frames and silk curtains, which Peter Layard had managed to get cheap. The boy also flourished at his new school, where he had a few other English natives as classmates. But he was still strong willed, refusing to kiss the ring of the head priest. "It appeared to me a degrading ceremony to which an Englishman ought not to submit."

Like all educated English boys of the nineteenth century, he was immersed in ancient Greek and Latin. His father liked the Elizabethans, so the son learned to appreciate Shakespeare and Spenser. At ages twelve and thirteen, he naturally enjoyed Walter Scott's escapist adventures with the same enthusiasm we have today for superhero movies and action films; British readers loved *Ivanhoe* and *Rob Roy*. But the book that captured the boy's imagination and never let go was *Arabian Nights*. "I was accustomed to spend hours stretched upon the floor, under a great gilded Florentine table, poring over this enchanting volume." Henry got so carried away by *jinns* and storybook adventure that he created a fantasy romance with himself, of course, as the hero and the sister of one of his English schoolmates as his beloved princess. It led to an ugly quarrel. The boys studied fencing at the time, and someone got the idiotic idea to remove the buttons from their foils for a duel. Someone else—a teacher or an adult—must have intervened and put a stop to the whole thing.

The puppy love over the girl faded. The love for *Arabian Nights* never did. In old age, Layard wrote, "I can read them even now with almost as much delight as I read them when a boy. They have had no little influence upon my life and career; for to them I attribute that love of travel and adventure which took me to the East and led me to the discovery of the ruins of Nineveh." Even more telling perhaps is that he found "the truest, the most lively and the most interesting picture of manners and customs which still exist amongst Turks, Persians and Arabs when I first mixed with them." To a child, the book was fiction. To the grown-up and the lifelong fan, the book was an anthropological study.

Competing for his interest was another passion: art. Peter Layard was back to haunting galleries, and his son took in all his father's critiques of the Italian Grand Masters. Soon, Henry knew every important work in the Uffizi, and he could identify a major painter's work at a glance. Peter was also a collector, and in Henry's room above his bed hung an altarpiece by the fifteenth-century master Filippino Lippi. Layard later donated the work to the National Gallery, but it still had a mark of damage; when Henry had a quarrel with one of his siblings, he flung his shoe at his brother—and missed.

The father could only blame himself when young Henry announced he wanted to be a painter. Peter had the good sense to let his son put his ambition to a few tests of talent. In a cell of a convent, an Italian hack of an artist, "poor and indifferent," gave the boy a few drawing lessons. Henry would never become a painter, but it was something he hardly regretted; years later, in fact, he concluded that he probably wouldn't have been very successful at it. And he was already showing an interest in poking around ruins. When the family regularly made a trip to Lake Trasimeno, he was eager to see Etruscan excavation sites and the ancient battlefield where Hannibal bested a Roman general.

Peter Layard expected his son to abide by his wishes and eventually go into law, and yet he unconsciously did everything to steer Henry toward the arts. The Layard family visited the villas of friends and spent summers in the country. Henry was introduced to and acquired a taste for opera. And father and son were keen collectors of antiquarian works, especially about Florentine history. "It was my delight to return home in triumph with a soiled and torn engraving, representing some Italian worthy whose name I had found in them [*sic*], and which I had 'picked up' at a book-stall for a fraction." Painters and engravers, poets and novelists, regularly dropped by the Layard household.

How could a young man exposed to all these influences possibly dream of donning a wig and black robes and *practicing law*?

Layard himself noted the irony later. "My boyish life was a very happy one; but the tastes I was acquiring and the education, such as it was, that I was receiving were not calculated to fit me for the career for which I was destined by my parents." Peter and Marianne might have been more open to Henry carving out a path for himself—if Marianne's brother hadn't stomped in and thrown his weight around like a second-act villain in a Dickens novel.

This was Benjamin Austen. He was a lawyer and a successful one, rich enough that he felt entitled to exert his influence. Austen clearly wanted an heir he could mold in his own image, so he browbeat Peter and Marianne into shipping Henry, as well as his younger brother, Frederic, back to a school in Richmond, Surrey, in 1829. The master plan was that Henry, who was also the uncle's godson, would eventually become an articling clerk in Austen's practice. He would then graduate to partner and some day—if he proved himself—take over the business. Henry, of course, didn't have a say in this at all.

This meant another few gloomy years of English schoolboy sadism, simply because he was fluent in French and Italian (which earned him the nickname "organ grinder").

Once again, the grand plan to convert Henry into an obedient, middle-class Englishman failed. In the summer, while other boys went home, he stayed in his school lodgings. This meant he could do what he liked. He read. He fished the Thames. His Uncle Benjamin gave him a copy of Blackstone's *Commentaries*, one of the most influential works in English law. It bored Henry silly. He used the age-old fake-out of hiding a travel book or novel behind its covers.

By the autumn of 1833, he was out of school, feeling that he had learned nothing. The real tragedy was that at heart he was a scholar, but his parents had never had the money to send him on to Eton and to university. Benjamin Austen led the boy's father into believing that he held keys to Henry's future and that he would "do something for him." Peter Layard could afford to send his son only £8 a month to get by, but Austen never bothered to add to it except on special occasions for a present. He seemed concerned only with his own posterity, and he persuaded his young nephew to reverse the order of his Christian names. The boy had been christened "Henry Austen Layard," but now he would legally be "Austen Henry Layard." It didn't matter. No friend or family member ever called him anything but Henry.

With his father's paltry £8 a month, he had to feed, clothe, and house himself. He got a second-floor apartment on London's Sidmouth Street, a brief walk to his new place of work, the Raymond Buildings in Gray's Inn, still used today as posh law offices or "chambers" as British solicitors prefer to call them. Walk along by those Georgian buildings near a green and pleasant park square, and you get some sense of what it must have been like. Save for a black cab and the occasional bit of summer construction, it can be unbelievably quiet, a little rarefied world unto itself in the din and daily chaos of London.

From nine in the morning, he needed to be in his uncle's office, copying out briefs, tagging along on errands with the senior clerks, and generally applying himself to his fledgling career. Off the clock, he was expected to read, breathe, eat, sleep, and think law. This was hell for a youth who had tunneled his way through Gibbon's *Rise and Fall of the Roman Empire* and would have preferred the latest best-selling novel. Once he made the mistake of admitting to Austen that when he was supposed to be thinking about a dry, boring legal text, his mind wandered to Boccaccio and Petrarch. His uncle was predictably horrified.

Maybe Austen reacted that way because history seemed to be repeating itself. Henry wasn't his first failed protégé. There was a time when Benjamin Disraeli had also gone the articling route (and at around the same age) and had even wanted to spend time in Austen's office since Austen was a family friend. The old lawyer helped Disraeli and then ratted on him to his father, reporting that he "took books on other subjects with him to chambers"—Austen had caught him reading Chaucer.

To young Layard, Disraeli cut a dashing figure early on. When Henry was six years old, he had traveled with his mother to an address in Bloomsbury, where Disraeli had breezed into the drawing room, still wearing boxing gloves from a workout. He ended up visiting the Layards later in Italy after he suffered exhaustion from writing his first novel, *Vivian Grey*. Now Disraeli came into Henry's life again, a regular fixture at Austen's house as a guest. With his Bohemian poses, the young author wore the most outrageous fashions: waistcoats with loud colors and gold embroidery, velvet pantaloons, and shoes with red rose accents.

He was also building up quite an ego. When Henry asked him a polite question about his writing on Corfu, Disraeli offered only a mocking laugh and replied that he didn't remember what he wrote. He also didn't have a clue how he was putting others off with his attitudes. After reciting one of his "turgid and now forgotten" poems in "a bombastic manner," Disraeli left the room, and another guest—the lawyer and minor novelist Samuel Warren—jumped up and put the rest of the room in hysterical laughter by doing a wicked, bang-on imitation of him and his pompous style.

Disraeli, however, wasn't completely delusional about his own gifts. During social visits with the Austens, he would casually tell them, "When I am Prime Minister . . ." Others laughed. Disraeli didn't take this well. After enough chuckling at his expense, he finally lost his temper one time and hit the mantelpiece in the room with his fist, declaring, "Laugh as you may, I *shall* be Prime Minister."

In time, of course, he was. He would drift out of the creative, artistic orbit of Bloomsbury and the Austen house to the power-broker set in Mayfair. But a teenage Henry witnessed many times when his uncle had to drop everything or left in the middle of the night because "Ben has got into another scrape." These episodes filled Henry with such a neurotic dread of debtor's prison or financial risk that he made sure that for the rest of his life, he never owed anything he couldn't pay. As an adult, he knew Disraeli when both were members of Parliament—from the opposite side of the aisle.

⋆   ⋆   ⋆

At eighteen, Henry often went without meals so he could spend what little money he had on books (he thought he might try to write a history of Italy, and like many a book lover, he could justify his favorite purchases by considering them "research"). If he did buy himself dinner, he'd swing around to a cheap tavern on Holborn or Fleet Street where he could buy a chop for a sixpence. There was no beer for his meal—he could afford only water. He wanted to learn German, so he hired a Polish refugee to teach him the language. Soon, a circle of other Polish refugees, all fleeing Russian expansion—miserable, destitute, and disenfranchised—were having animated political discussions in Henry's apartment. They confirmed for him his own budding radical views.

Life itself, the example of his own hand-to-mouth existence and the crushing poverty of the Poles, taught Henry Layard new truths and experiences he would never pick up in his uncle's chambers. But Austen thought he could still turn his nephew into a solicitor if he exiled him to an office. He expected him to work twelve to thirteen hours a day. Henry did as he pleased.

He had his meal, then regularly went home to pursue his own interests, a Victorian slacker. He joined small debating societies where young men like himself, including Irish radicals, were trying to carve places for themselves in the world. He tried his hand at journalism, writing a few articles for a new but marginal London magazine that inevitably folded—anything but law.

His father, having tried to live in Aylesbury despite his health problems, finally succumbed to his asthma and died in 1834. It was a shock to Henry, who must have watched his father wheeze on for years, but all fathers seem indestructible to their sons. His own health was beginning to suffer from the long hours spent hunched over a desk in a stuffy solicitor's office. Fortunately, a friend stepped forward to rescue him. This was William Brockedon, a skilled portrait painter who also wrote and illustrated alpine travel books and who put his busy mind to a wide array of inventions that were eclectic, to say the least. He came up with new manufacturing methods for lozenges, for lead pencils, and for wadding in firearms. Brockedon was willing to take a miserable, frustrated youth along on his travels through France, Switzerland, and Italy in 1837.

It was on these excursions that Henry's political sympathies probably became set, almost invariably allied with the underdog. He made a lifelong friend in Turin with a young Cavour (Camillo Benso), the statesman who would become the first prime minister of a united Italy. The two had in common the experience of detesting educational discipline.

Having developed tastes in Italian literature and art, Henry was obviously going to side with those who resisted Austrian rule, and one day, he was invited by a group of Piedmont refugees in Lyon to a secret meeting. It turned out to be one for revolutionaries. "Their agents had on many occasions," Layard wrote decades later, "been guilty of acts of bloody vengeance upon the oppressors of their country, which had brought them to the scaffold." Henry, however, got caught up in revolutionary fervor and was ready to help them.

He made no excuses or regrets in his autobiography, defending them to the last: "Although these young men were as conspirators odious to, and persecuted by, all continental governments, they were, for the most part, honest and sincere patriots in the truest sense of the word—ready to make every sacrifice, even that of life, for the freedom and independence of their country, and for what they believed to be its welfare. . . . If they were irrepressible conspirators, shrinking from no crime, even that of assassination, it was the wickedness and tyranny of governments that made them so."

Henry went to the meetings, enjoying the secret thrill that he was risking prison and feeling "well pleased" when he managed to slip safely back to his hotel. But rubbing shoulders with terrorists on the continent was a short-lived adventure, and soon he was back to the mind-numbing tedium of the law office. In 1838, he was able to take another long vacation where he got to see Stockholm and St. Petersburg, but no sooner was he back home than the Austens and the Layard clan were all wondering, what are we going to do with this boy?

Henry wondered what he was going to do as well. He was in despair, reaching for even the dimmest prospect, thinking he might support himself through writing. "I was so harassed by these thoughts," he wrote in his autobiography, "and by family matters, and my mind became so unsettled that I was unable to apply myself seriously to any occupation." His uncertain future was making him a nervous wreck.

This time, his savior wasn't a new acquaintance in arts or literature but, surprisingly, one of the family. Another uncle, Charles Layard, was visiting from Ceylon, where he worked in the civil service just as Peter once did. Even though Henry hadn't been called to the bar yet in England, Charles explained that he could do well as a barrister in Ceylon. The opportunities were there. The family connections were there. And even if he failed, well, there was always running a coffee plantation or something else, right? Henry made up his mind—he would go. Benjamin Austen was "sincerely grieved" over the news but recognized that his nephew was never going to cut it in his world. He would let the young man leave, with, of course, a parting lecture on how Henry was taking a great risk going to a faraway land "without even the means of subsistence."

Henry's love of adventure would be his chief motivation for going, but tantalizingly, he felt he had another good reason to leave England. He genuinely thought he would get into trouble with his politics.

His relatives were all "staunch and bigoted Tories of the old school," and he knew that his more liberal views would be just one more thing to make Austen pass him over for partner: "With people of his class, to accuse a man of being 'a radical' was in those days to believe him capable of committing almost any crime." To be fair to Austen, Henry's complete lack of interest in the profession hammered the nails in that coffin far sooner than any disagreements over what went on in Parliament.

It was true, however, that Henry flirted with risks. These were the days when the hottest, most controversial issue was the Corn Laws. On first blush, the debate looks complicated (and excruciatingly dull), involving protective trade tariffs on grain imports, food prices, and the wages for a growing population of new industrial factory workers. Look deeper, and we find ourselves on familiar ground. Rich landowners portrayed themselves as the backbone of the country and needed special privileges—and protective tariffs, even when parts of England and Ireland suffered famine. It's not quite equivalent to our modern "Occupy Wall Street" debates, but it's not difficult to imagine that young Henry Layard would think himself as one of the "99 percent."

He had written to one of the top opponents of the Corn Laws, and he was sure that if he had stayed in London, he likely would have joined a group of agitators. Better that he take that impetuous feeling and occasional quick temper and see other parts of the world again.

So in June 1839, Henry went through the motions of taking his law exam. By his own account, it wasn't "very severe," even though there were sections of law he hadn't learned yet. He was now, at least on paper, a solicitor of Her Majesty's Court of Queen's Bench at Westminster. He would never be formally called to the bar, which would have allowed him to argue a case in court. In fact, he would never practice law anywhere, not in England and not in Ceylon. It wasn't the destination that would change the course of his life; it was the mode of transport itself.

It was all because his traveling companion hated the idea of going by sea—to an island.

Edward Mitford was a friend of Henry's Uncle Charles. He was a full ten years older than Henry, and when he finally wrote his own personal memoirs of his travels, he says next to nothing personal about his travel companion except to comment that he was "somewhat taken aback by his youthful appearance." Still, the two must have warmed up to each other. Having been in business in Morocco, Mitford wanted to try his hand at growing coffee in one of the jewels of the British Empire. Getting there was Mitford's dilemma. The prospect of spending long days on a ship and getting repeatedly nauseous was unbearable to him, and a conventional voyage involving sea travel would take months anyway.

Instead, Mitford suggested a detailed, elaborate overland route that would cross Europe, Central Asia, and India. Henry's enthusiasm was automatic—and the objections of his family were predictable. They thought the plan was insane. Henry was determined to go anyway.

He couldn't have had a better partner for the epic journey. Mitford was mature, and though he had a sense of adventure himself, he was a seasoned traveler, sensible and certainly more cautious than his young companion. One of his passions was ornithology; he knew taxidermy, and he gave Henry a few lessons in how to stuff birds.

Meanwhile, to prepare for the trip, Henry threw himself into studies with a zeal he never showed over dusty statutes and precedents. He found a professor to teach him how to use a sextant and the basics of trigonometry. He pored through pamphlets on the different countries they planned to visit, and he and Mitford went to consult the Royal Geographic Society. Henry also went knocking on the doors of the Scottish travel writer Baillie Fraser, who could tell him about Persia, and John McNeill, the surgeon and diplomat who had just served as Britain's minister in Tehran (its ambassador). Even the disapproving Austen was still useful because he often had as a dinner guest Charles Fellows, the archaeologist who found the ruins of the capital for the ancient region of Lycia.

Fellows and McNeill were particularly full of helpful hints, lighting Layard's imagination. There were hopes of visiting Palestine on the way to Baghdad, of venturing into Kandahar and entering India by way of Afghanistan. Persia might be a problem since diplomatic relations had been broken off recently with Britain. But there would be other routes, and the veterans advising Henry had their "must see" lists. McNeill, for instance, urged Layard and Mitford to check out an island on a lake in Persia that was "supposed to be inhabited by a colony of Fire-Worshippers."

The two would travel on the cheap—no extraneous luggage and only enough clothes as they needed. If they required more, they would buy it along the way and wear native dress when they could to blend in. Henry brought along a collection of instruments, too—a pocket sextant, compass, barometer, and thermometers—and he painted his silver watch black to avoid its attracting attention. As for his finances, he deposited £300 with Coutts bank and carried its letter of credit so that he could draw on this sum. His passport, which would soon be creased and weathered by his travels, was issued on July 5, written in French for travel on the continent under the authority of "Vicomte" Palmerston.

The publisher Smith, Elder & Company had also heard about the trip and in a nice deal that would make any writer envious, offered Layard and Mitford an advance of £200 for the journals they intended to keep along the way, deliverable six months after they reached Ceylon. If a book was forthcoming, the publisher would take out the profits from the advance; "in the event of the advance being more than covered, we were then to receive two thirds of the surplus." Not many first-time authors swing a deal like that today. Of course, if it got turned down, the pair staked their honor on repaying the publisher the advance plus interest.

Henry's mother came down to see him off, and on July 10, 1839, he and Mitford boarded a steamer headed for Ostend, Belgium. Henry was twenty-two years old. As the ship chugged its way down the Thames, he felt a mix of emotions: "I had an unknown future before me. . . . My plans were, after all, vague and somewhat wild. If I failed in the object of my journey, and the means of supporting myself were wanting, what was to become of me?" Even decades later, his contradictory feelings over the law betrayed themselves within a single paragraph. On the one hand, he wrote, "My chances of success on the new career I had chosen for myself were doubtful"—which either suggests he'd try law in Ceylon or he was already thinking of something that involved antiquities and archaeology. Only a couple of lines or so later, however, he remembers that he "experienced a happy sensation of relief at leaving England and abandoning a pursuit which was odious to me." So much for the wig and the black gown after all.

"I was now independent, and no more exposed to the vexatious interference and control to which I had hitherto been subjected and greatly resented." The phrasing is Victorian, but the sentiment will be recognized by any twenty-something today clutching the keys to a new apartment. By July 11, he had landed at Ostend, checking out Bruges, Ghent, and Brussels, where he met up with Mitford on July 14. After a happy reunion with the retired family servant Pachot, Henry did a favor for some old friends in London and delivered a letter to a Polish radical who didn't trust the mail.

Then it was a trip to Coblenz by steamer on the Rhine and various stops in Germany, taking in different museums and galleries. Moving on to Italy, Henry spent only two days in Venice, but he was instantly "enchanted." He didn't know it, but he would see far more of the city in the future.

Another steamboat carried Layard and Mitford to Trieste, where they set out for a rugged trip through Dalmatia. Though they were still in Europe as we know it today, they were heading into a countryside that few British travelers visited. They were eager and enthusiastic. They felt themselves ready. They were "now about to leave the realms of civilisation, and to embark upon our adventurous and perilous journey."

★   ★   ★

Today, the town is called Rijeka in what is now modern Croatia. But in August 1839, it was called Fiume, a German name for a spot under the thumb of the Austro-Hungarian Empire, though this port on an inlet of the Adriatic Sea had changed hands many times. The Romans came here. So had the Franks of Charlemagne and the Venetians on a looting spree. And so now had Layard and Mitford. This was their real starting point, a town of Renaissance and Baroque towers. They managed to get letters of introduction to help them with the authorities they would need to deal with along the way.

They were now in a region beyond the technology of trains or trams where you relied on a system of what were called "post-houses," inns at which you could exchange horses and get a bed in rather spartan furnishings for a night or two. On their first day on the road, the pair encountered "a barren and desolate country. Rocks of varied and fantastic shapes rose in wild confusion around us when we were on the high land." The coastal areas offered figs and pomegranates, and Layard noticed how the peasants wore clothes that were less European, more Ottoman in style: red skullcaps with "elegant patterns in black silk" for the men, while the women had ones decorated with gold and colored thread. Both sexes sported embroidered jackets and styled their hair in long plaits down the back. In Dalmatia, the turban was fashionable.

Getting by in Italian when they interacted with the locals, Layard and Mitford—two pale and distinctly English nomads—couldn't help attracting attention. In the small town of Gospich, the woman who ran the post-house was curious where they were going and when told their destination was Istanbul, assumed they were religious pilgrims. In the town of Obrovazzo, they got a less warm reception from the prefect, who demanded to know what they did for a living. Were they merchants? No. Soldiers? No. Then they must be aristocrats? No. It was inconceivable to him that two young middle-class men would want to wander a countryside without purpose. Finally, he screamed at his secretary, "Write: *Two English noblemen!*" Layard and Mitford got moving before he could change his mind.

They carried on to the Republic of Ragusa, what is today the region of Dubrovnik flanking the Adriatic Sea. Layard described it well as a territory in the Ottoman Empire that, "dreading Venetian encroachments on its possessions, made over to the Turks a strip of land extending from Bosnia to the sea coast . . . completely isolated and separated from its ambitious neighbors." But not invulnerable. Near the coast, they passed the charred ruins of houses burned by Montenegrins during the Napoleonic occupation. The people hadn't bothered to rebuild. Layard nearly ended up a charred ruin himself. At one point while staying at an inn during a severe thunderstorm, watching the rain through a window, a bolt of lightning hit the house, and he was "almost thrown to the ground and remained stunned for a short time."

To get to Istanbul, the pair needed to pass through Montenegro. Montenegrins at this time were fiercely tribal, set on keeping their independence yet happy to invite incursions by attacking their neighbors, burning villages and mutilating and killing women and children during their raids. Layard and Mitford sent a messenger with letters of introduction to its *vladika*, its bishop-prince, cooling their heels in the meantime in the town of Cattaro (today Kotor).

After some time, they got a response. Sure, the prince was willing to see them at his capital, Cetinje, and he would send them a military escort. Until it showed up, they explored the town's old castle, and Henry found it remarkable that this fortress—the people's one major defense—had been allowed to fall into a derelict state, its "Lion of St. Mark, much battered and broken," and guns that were "lying about" from the old Venetian foundries.

At four o'clock in the morning, their escort turned up with mules for the pair to ride plus a horse to carry baggage: "Four savage but fine-looking fellows, dressed in short white woolen petticoats and a long outer dress or cloak of the same material and color and small black skull turbans" who "each carried a long gun, and were armed to the teeth with pistols, *yatagans* [Ottoman sabers], and knives."

It took hours through craggy mountains, thick woods, and another treeless plain to reach Cetinje, a disappointing village of shabby huts. Layard and Mitford were temporarily put up in a house where—as he wrote home to his mother—rough characters were "intruding with the greatest coolness into our room, where they place themselves on the bed, smoking their pipes with the utmost indifference; there are two in the room while I write, quietly watching our movements."[2] As for the "palace" of the vladika, it was no more than a one-story nondescript building with a round tower. But as the mules ambled along, bringing the Englishmen ever closer to the turret, they couldn't help but notice the poles at the top. . . . Poles on which were mounted heads. The heads of slain Turkish soldiers.

• 2 •

Debating Bloodlust with a Giant

*L*ayard and Mitford were led into a simple room of the palace, the crowd of fighters around them "armed as usual to the teeth." White-bearded chieftains sat on the floor, puffing away on their long pipes, and the travelers had to wait while their host finished a meal. Then they were ushered in to meet the vladika. He was a giant at seven and a half feet tall, dressed in the black robes and round cap of a Greek Orthodox priest. Layard called him Danilo in his autobiography, but he was, in fact, Petar Petrovic Njegos, who is still considered today a national and cultural hero to Montenegrins as well as many Serbs.

Njegos spoke with Layard and Mitford in French and clearly wasn't as rough and uncouth as his men. He wrote poetry, was a good shot, and was well traveled. At about twenty-seven or twenty-eight years old (scholars disagree on his birth date but have settled at around 1813), he was young enough to be able to relate to his guests, and he had held his position for only just under a decade, ousting opponents of a rival clan, consolidating his power, and doing his best to forge tribal alliances. His uncle and predecessor, Petar I, had warned him to "pray to God and hold on to Russia." It was advice Njegos took seriously, traveling to St. Petersburg in 1833 to win over Tsar Nicholas I. The story goes that as the young vladika stood next to the tsar during a speech, Nicholas remarked, "My word, you're bigger than I am."

Njegos had the good tact to reply, "Only God is bigger than the Russian Tsar!"[1]

He returned home to Montenegro with 36,000 rubles, books, and icons for his capital's monastery and the knowledge that he had secured a powerful ally. The Russians didn't always like how Njegos's behavior was less than expected of a pious bishop, but they still supported him. Njegos, in turn, observed carefully how Russia was more advanced than his rugged domain, and he wanted to modernize his country.

Now Layard and Mitford had their chance to sample the vladika's wit and sincerity. As Njegos and his guests chatted, there was a touch of surreal humor to the scene. The vladika didn't like how he was being portrayed in German newspapers. There had been a story in the press, for instance, about a visit by the King of Saxony in which there was supposed to have been an embarrassing diplomatic incident over dinner when no one had a knife available to cut up a roasted sheep. Not true! Every Montenegrin always carries his blade, he insisted. Njegos had lots to complain about, too, over his people's traditional enemies, the Austrians and the Turks. Things seemed to be going well for the visit. The vladika showed off captured muskets and other confiscated items, and he and his guests played several games on his billiards table, shipped in all the way from Trieste.

Days passed. The three went riding. Then as cues were cracking the ivory balls one day, they heard shouting and guns fired outside the palace. Some of Njegos's men had raided the Turkish region of Scutari, which today is part of Istanbul. With a supportive, cheering crowd behind them, the soldiers strutted their way proudly up to their leader and unloaded a makeshift cloth bag: bloody heads fell to the ground, not just ones of enemy soldiers but of civilians. "Amongst these were those apparently of mere children," noted Layard. "Covered with gore, they were a hideous and ghastly spectacle."

He couldn't hide his disgust and railed on Njegos on the spot; the two had discussed how the vladika wanted to civilize his people, and yet "he permitted them to commit acts so revolting to humanity and so much opposed to the feelings and habits of all Christian nations." Njegos conceded that it was a barbarous practice but argued that it was necessary to maintain the "warlike spirit of his people." He needed his men to always have their blood up and journey out on raids; otherwise they'd let their guard down, and their land would be conquered.

His only modern biographer, Milovan Dilas, wrote, "That mountain swagger and quick temper, that Montenegrin self-indulgent pride and personal touchiness, as well as resistance to order and discipline, were all to the good as long as the struggle against the Turks did not also require a denial of personal and clan contumacy or autonomy. [Njegos] wished to preserve the Montenegrin as he was, and yet rule him according to his own rule."[2]

He portrayed himself as a reformer. Njegos claimed that for the previous two years, the annual murder rate in his territory had been 400 people; this was an improvement—it used to be 600. In trying to introduce reforms and set up schools, the vladika earned the young Englishman's grudging respect. But having seen the bishop's marauders close-up, it amused Layard years later

The only known photograph of Petar Petrovic Njegos, taken by Serbian photography pioneer Anastas Jovanovic in 1851.

when Europe extolled Montenegrins "as the bulwark of Christianity and civilisation" against the Islamic "wave" of the Ottoman Empire.

Njegos would live on as a controversial hero to Montenegrins and Serbs because of his epic poem *The Mountain Wreath*, published only a few years after he met Layard. In the poem, Montenegrin renegades who have converted to Islam are given the chance to switch back to Christianity, but when they refuse, they're put "all unto the sword. All those who would not be baptiz'd." In his landmark history *The Serbs*, Tim Judah wrote, "It is hard to underestimate the influence of *The Mountain Wreath*. It is still celebrated as one of the pinnacles of Serbian literary achievement. . . . It helps explain how the Serbian national consciousness has been molded and how ideas of national liberation are inextricably linked with killing your neighbor and burning his village."[3]

If Njegos was a philosophical architect for Balkan ethnic cleansing, it's even more remarkable that Layard not only casually met this leader but engaged in ethical debates with him over conduct in war and barbarism versus civilization. Though young and inexperienced, he was an impromptu representative for the modern Western conscience, and while he likely couldn't imagine the scale of the Bosnian genocide, the horrors of the Kosovo War, and the ruthlessness of a Slobodan Milošević, his basic decency made him a voice not only for his time but for our own as well.

★   ★   ★

When Layard and Mitford reached what today is Erdine in East Thrace, they were forced to undergo a strange kind of nineteenth-century hazmat drill. Guards at the city limits ordered them to dismount and, as Layard recalled, "enter into a kind of sentry-box, but completely closed, and to stand on a grating, beneath which was a large pan of sulphur, rosin and other materials, which when heated, sent forth a dense and stifling smoke. When we had been duly fumigated, we were released, half suffocated and gasping for breath." It was the city's way of trying to prevent plague. As Layard noted, it was hardly scientific since their baggage went through no such decontamination procedure.

They didn't bother to stay in the city long. After two and a half months on the road, on September 13, they reached Istanbul—to Europe, still Constantinople. "With this place, I am much delighted," Layard wrote to his aunt. "It even exceeds any description I have seen. The imagination could not picture a site more beautiful as that occupied by Constantinople. In the hands of any other European power it would have been the strongest city in the world; in the hands of the Turks, it has become the most picturesque."[4]

It was a city in transition. On the shore of the Bosporus, there was yet to be the Dolmabahçe Palace, the imposing seat for sultans and, one day, the final home for a dying Atatürk, and it would be a few more years before the city generously borrowed stylings from the *Belle Époque*. But just as today, Layard could take in the grandeur of the Hagia Sophia, Emperor Justinian's great Byzantine basilica, while standing opposite the famous Blue Mosque.

The Ottoman Empire, having lasted more than 500 years, now had less than seventy years left and was sputtering toward its decline, earning the title the "sick man of Europe." In our age, we casually equate the word "Ottoman" with "Turk," but there was no sense of nationalism across the empire. It was a patchwork quilt of multiple ethnicities and different languages, with the bureaucracy ruling its subjects according to their religion. It had taken until 1727 for a Hungarian Muslim convert to bring Istanbul its first printing press, and even then, the technology was suppressed for several years.

Henry Layard visited just as the Ottoman regime was on the eve of the *Tanzimat* (the word literally means "reorganization"). It was an astonishing period of modernist reform in which the first paper banknotes and proper post offices were introduced, the criminal code was overhauled, and the first national census would soon be organized. But the empire had started far too late to catch up to Western Europe.

No sooner had Layard arrived than he barely got to see any of Istanbul or discern any significant social changes because he was suffering from malaria. He had been feverish as he and Mitford traveled through the rice fields of Philippopolis, and now he was miserable in bed, being treated by a young Armenian doctor. The good news was that the Armenian had got his education in Edinburgh, arguably the place with the best medical schools in the world at that time. The bad news was that the good Dr. Zohrab believed in bloodletting, sometimes applying as many as fifty leeches on Layard's stomach.

As Layard's condition worsened, a Dr. Julius Millingen, another bloodletting advocate was brought in to consult. Millingen had also helped treat Byron but later was haunted by the poet's death in 1824, recognizing in hindsight that he had horribly misdiagnosed his famous patient and helped speed his end. Fortunately for Layard, Millingen and Zohrab also gave him quinine, which probably saved his life, though he would be stricken with recurrent bouts of malaria for many years.

★   ★   ★

As Layard and Mitford traveled on, there was a serious chance they would wander into a shooting gallery. The region was at war, and Britain and the other powers of Europe were meddling enough in the whole mess that Layard and Mitford might not pass at all for disinterested tourists.

The background requires some explanation. For decades, the viceroy of Egypt, Mehmet Ali, had been consolidating his power and testing Ottoman strength. Albanian by birth, he had worked his way up from tobacco trader and tax collector to fighting Napoleon for the Ottomans in Syria. Once he was head of the Albanian military force in Egypt, he cunningly manipulated the Mamluks into raising taxes to pay his soldiers, only so that ordinary people in Cairo would riot, then he cut the taxes to gain populist support and pushed the Mamluks out. When the Turks saw what he was up to, they tried to get rid of him, but Mehmet Ali orchestrated another riot and manipulated events to set himself up as pasha. In time, his regime would become infamous for its heavy tax grabs, but he started small, first making sure he stayed popular by raiding the accounts of the Coptic Christians. He achieved his ultimate victory over the Mamluks in 1811 by tricking their leaders to a celebration at the Cairo Citadel and promptly massacring them in a narrow passage; he then sent a bag of their ears to Sultan Mahmud II.[5]

But by 1839, Mehmet Ali was more reformer than butcher. There were irrigation projects and navy projects, a military machine to build up, and a navy to expand. "In your country you must have a great many hands to move the machine of state," he once told a visiting British member of Parliament, "I move it with my own. I do not always exactly see what is best to be done; but when I do see it, I compel prompt obedience to my wishes, and what is seemingly best is done."[6]

With piercing eyes and a full white beard, he cut an impressive figure in his short jacket, cashmere sash, and pantaloons, hardly ever without his scimitar sword. The man who readily admitted to not learning how to read and write until he was forty-seven years old authorized the establishment of several schools, often ones with a French curriculum. If you're in Paris, you can easily find an example of Mehmet Ali's respect for the French. In the Place de la Concorde rests the Egyptian obelisk that stands seventy-five feet high, a gift from the pasha to France in 1829.

Mehmet Ali had a Western-trained army, so when the Greeks rebelled and wanted independence, it only made sense for the sultan to enlist his help. For his trouble, he was supposed to get Crete and the Peloponnese, but he wanted Syria instead. When he wasn't rewarded with it, he sent an army headed by his son, Ibrahim Pasha, who hammered the sultan's forces again and again, quickly capturing Gaza, Jerusalem, and Acre and taking his men all the way up to Bursa. This meant he was within range of taking Istanbul itself and pulling down the whole foundations of the Ottoman Empire.

Panicking, the Turks asked the British for help. London said no. The Turks then appealed to their old enemy, the Russians. This was quite amazing given that the Ottomans had closed the strait of Dardanelles back when the Russians sided with the Orthodox Christian Greeks and the two empires had gone to war. But the Turks had got the worst of it and, in a treaty in 1829, made the Black Sea virtually a Russian lake. So, of course, the Russians were happy to send thousands of troops in.

Now, it was one thing for Egypt's Ibrahim Pasha to knock out poorly armed and disheartened Turkish soldiers and quite another to confront fresh troops, courtesy of the tsar. Still, Ibrahim was in a good enough position of strength that in a newly worked-out deal, his father got Syria, plus he kept many of the gains made by his son. The catch was that Ibrahim didn't have a guarantee to inherit them. And there was more trouble.

The British, first refusing to help the Turks, soon realized their mistake that put the Ottoman welcome mat out for the Russians, and now they petulantly demanded the Turks show them the door. They even teamed up with France to broker the peace agreement, but the sultan made his own side deal with the Russians, allowing them to sail their warships through the Turkish

Straits, and if another appropriate crisis ever broke out, they could mobilize their forces on Ottoman territory.

Then things got worse. The whole debacle was too much for the sultan, who wanted his territory back. So in 1839, he sent land and naval forces off to recapture Syria. It was an unmitigated disaster. Ottoman soldiers deserted in droves, their pockets stuffed with Egyptian bribes, while the commander of the Turkish fleet promptly sailed to Alexandria, defected, and made a gift of his ships to Mehmet Ali. As if that weren't enough, in late June of that year, under a boiling sun as camels and horses lay dead on the dusty Syrian plain, the miserable army of the sultan—many of the soldiers restless and insubordinate Kurdish conscripts—faced Ibrahim Pasha's forces near a small village called Nezib.

The Ottomans had no will to fight; in fact, they had no will to even move. One of their advisers was Helmuth von Moltke, a Prussian officer who would one day be a field marshal and a military legend for Germany. Von Moltke coined the motto, "No plan survives contact with the enemy," and here was his aphorism given an example. He knew the sultan's army had to adapt and react to the Egyptian deployment. He first recommended an attack and then, exasperated by a superior who paid rapt attention to the whispers of mullahs, pleaded for a discreet withdrawal.

"I urged Hafiz Pasha not to pay any attention to people like the mullahs who didn't understand military matters and reminded him that tomorrow, when the sun sank behind the mountain, he would probably be without an army."[7] His estimate was off by only one day. The Egyptian artillery guns first mauled the Ottomans, and Ibrahim's infantry only had to finish the job. As for von Moltke, he went back in disgust to Istanbul and then home to Berlin.

His patron, Sultan Mahmud II, never had to cope with the humiliation of Nezib. He died—leaving the Ottoman Empire in the hands of a sixteen-year-old boy. But as teenage leaders go, young Abdulmecid did rather well. He believed in reforms, he liked literature and music, and he would even listen to the public on special occasions. And he was lucky. That's because the European powers were about to save his reign for him, partly by squabbling among themselves.

London certainly didn't want to see the Russians coming back into the picture, so the British were determined to settle things once and for all. Austria and Prussia got involved. The French, having got a taste of Egypt decades before thanks to Napoleon's peculiar invasion and collection of artifacts, decided this time to side with Mehmet Ali, who, after all, had given them such a lovely granite column for decorating Paris. The Russians were back in the game, only they chose to play the conciliatory, noble power this time around and were willing to give up the Dardanelles.

While European statesmen adjusted pins on a map, Egyptian and Turkish armies advanced and retreated in the Syrian dust, and ordinary shopkeepers and tradespeople in the cobbled streets of Brussels and Frankfurt wondered if they might be dragged into a widening conflict.

What did all this mean for two English travelers wandering across the deserts and mountains in 1839? The world was in flux. Different peoples had taken advantage of Ottoman laxness for some time, but now genuine opportunities emerged for individual regions to decide their own destinies. For the time being, however, Britain was propping up "the Sick Man of Europe." Never mind that "Franks" earned suspicion and hostility in the Middle East—to be British could be an added risk.

It was a strange panorama the pair encountered on their journey. They followed a route where rocks could be fashioned into a sarcophagus, where inscriptions could be pagan or early Christian, while in other spots, they followed in the footsteps of the Crusaders. The war sometimes rudely intruded. One day, they passed several groups of Turkish farmers and peasants who had migrated to Egyptian-controlled territory, thinking they'd have a better lot in life, "but finding the taxes heavier than they could bear, they were now returning to their homes."

At a village under Egyptian rule, Layard asked the locals if the taxes were too much and how they were levied. The people told him they didn't know how the assessments worked, and they hardly cared whether the taxman was Egyptian or Ottoman: "We understand nothing of the matter. All we know is that when our corn is cut, a pasha arrives and carries off as much as he thinks proper. When our barley is ready, he comes again and does the like. When our fruit is ripe, he appears for the third time and the same happens to us. How then can we complain?" Layard concluded that Mehmet Ali, if left in charge, would have governed Syria far more wisely than the Turks.

He and Mitford had gone months without seeing a London newspaper, but they got the sense of the big picture by being in the thick of the areas up for grabs. By the time they reached Tarsus with its "filthy, muddy streets," the town had changed hands and was now under the thumb of the Egyptians. Layard noted how Turkish soldiers, looking shabby in their red fezzes and uniforms, had been replaced with smart-dressed Egyptians who seemed better disciplined and whose drilling and exercise seemed to go on all day.

They got their chance to glimpse both the low- and the highborn. Mixed-race women of European and Middle Eastern descent lounged around on divans, smoking *shisha*; their voices "were drowned in the bubbling noise of these water-pipes and the atmosphere was dense with their somewhat sickly fumes." The women gossiped in Arabic about scandals, the men talked about prices in the bazaars or news about the Egyptian army. In Lebanon, he discovered many of the famous cedars had been cut down for the construction of soldiers' barracks.

Layard, picking up various scraps of information, concluded that Ibrahim Pasha's rule in Syria was stern but just. But those he spoke to said Ibrahim "had neither the genius nor the abilities of his father." Yes, the man was apparently brave, but he lacked coolness under fire, and he knew next to nothing about military logistics and tactics. There was gossip that he was a notorious gambler and had even fallen down drunk in front of his officers. No, the real commander behind the scenes was a curious personality, a man as self-made as Ibrahim Pasha's father. A sailor turned soldier, he had the unusual distinction of serving at the two greatest defeats of the Napoleonic forces Trafalgar *and* Waterloo. Not even Turk or Albanian, let alone Egyptian, this Frenchman now ran the Egyptian army, and Layard was about to meet this fantastic character.

★　★　★

He was born Joseph Anthelme Sève in Lyon, and the way he told his story, he had gone from being a common sailor in the French navy to serving in the cavalry and artillery of the *Grand Armée* in some of Napoleon's most crucial battles. He must have adjusted his biography according to the person he spoke to because in one version he rose to the rank of lieutenant after fourteen years, then abandoned the military after Waterloo. The truth was that he made it only as far as corporal before he was kicked out for insubordination.[8]

Then he went into business, where he seems to have been a spectacular failure despite bankrolling enterprises with his wife's money. Running a service of horse-drawn carriages in Paris didn't work out. Neither did joining an expedition to find coal in Egypt, especially since Egypt has no coal—in fact, to this day, there are regular controversies over the country importing the stuff. The whole venture was ridiculous, but once he was back in Cairo, he managed to impress Mehmet Ali, who made him a military instructor.

The pasha already had one French general running his army, but that man had balked at attacking Christians when the Greeks fought for their independence. Sève didn't have a problem with it at all. Given that the highest ranks were open only to Muslims, he promptly converted, and "Colonel" Joseph Sève became Suleiman Pasha al-Fransawi, "the Frenchman." From the beginning, his conversion was an empty gesture for show. "He was never seen to say his appointed prayers or to enter a mosque," Layard reported years later. "He drank wine and spirits, perhaps more freely." But he did marry an Egyptian woman, and his children, who spoke only Arabic and whom Layard got to meet, were brought up to be strict Muslims. One of his descendants would be Nazli Sabri, the beautiful and unhappy second wife of King Fuad I and mother of King Farouq.[9]

After getting drenched in a heavy rainstorm, Layard arrived in Sidon and called on Suleiman Pasha, who insisted he stick around for the rest of the day and have dinner with him and his other guest, a fellow French veteran staying at his house named Clément. By 1840, Sève-Suleiman was in his early fifties, a short and talkative, somewhat excitable man who at least dressed his part as an Egyptian general: a waistcoat buttoned up to his throat, a signature red fez on his head, and, on his feet, the red shoes that curved up at the toes. As he lounged on a divan, smoking his hookah pipe, he "condemned in strong terms the policy of England and the European Powers" trying to keep the sultan in charge. France, he maintained, "was pursuing a wiser and more generous policy in supporting an enlightened and successful ruler, who was introducing great reforms into the East."

But the justness of the claim hardly mattered. Sève expected Mehmet Ali "would blow up Alexandria and Cairo and retire with a few troops into the remotest part of Upper Egypt rather than submit to dictation. . . . If the Powers did not interfere, Ibrahim Pasha would have no difficulty in making himself master of Asia Minor, and ultimately of Constantinople." He was making this argument just as the Turks were thoroughly beaten at Nezib, and Layard didn't doubt he was right. After the battle, "the panic which ensued had opened the road to the capital."

Layard posed an interesting counterargument. What if the Russians came to the Turks' aid and mobilized their troops right along the coast to defend Istanbul? "If she were to do so, we should not be discouraged," replied Sève. "We should avoid giving them battle, for although the Egyptians are ten times better soldiers than the Russians, we are greatly deficient in good officers. But I will make them wear out a deal of shoe leather. An Egyptian soldier can march sixteen hours a day without serious inconvenience, living upon nothing but a little bread and water. No Russian could overtake him." He thought it impossible to find more docile, obedient, and orderly troops than the Egyptians, and he was prepared to lead them anywhere.

Here is what's remarkable about this friendly debate. Layard had quite literally knocked on the door of the man in charge of the Egyptian army, and considering the tensions going on between London and Cairo, he could have been tossed in jail, suspected of espionage. But Sève was a gracious host. He may have thought the young man was an operative in an informal role sent by the British government. Then again, he may have taken Layard at face value, an inquisitive young traveler. Layard thought he was in many ways a typical French officer, no doubt brilliant at his command, honest, and straightforward but still a bit of a boaster.

After a hardy meal and good wines, the dinner party went to smoke and drink coffee in the private study, a room that was a modest shrine to Napoleon, with portraits of him and the Bonaparte family on the walls; "a kind of trophy had been constructed of gold-embroidered, silken Turkish flags, and of various arms and trumpets, the spoils of Nezib, which was surmounted by a bust of Napoleon." Layard was inwardly amused as the crusty old vets discussed their campaigns of long ago, "fighting their battles over again. . . . These were intermingled with repeated toasts in champagne and brandy to the heroes of the great war and the victories of their immortal chief." Sève was convinced that Bonaparte lost at Waterloo only because the English, in cahoots with Bourbons, had bought off certain generals.

Before Layard moved on, Sève gave him some useful notes on certain ancient monuments he had found himself during his campaigns in Syria and Asia Minor. And in time, Layard discovered the general was right about Mehmet Ali; it would take force to make him back down.

It happened like this. The European powers met in London in the middle of July 1840 and worked out a tidy arrangement they called the "Convention for the Pacification of the Levant." If Egypt pulled out of Syria and gave the new teenage sultan back his ships, Mehmet Ali would be declared pasha of Egypt (which he pretty much already was) and pasha of Syria (which he already was except in title). It shouldn't have surprised anyone that he said no.

The British grew tired of talking. Take the deal, they basically told him, or Egypt and Syria will face the wrath of three European nations. The Royal Navy came out and aimed its cannons at Beirut and when it was finished destroying the fort there, teamed up with the Austrians to blow Acre's defenses to bits. While the French huffed and puffed, threatening to go to war with Britain (but in the end backing down), the two navies bore down on Alexandria, and Egypt's pasha wisely reopened negotiations.

As for Sève, the old upstart from Lyon achieved a modest form of immortality. For years in Cairo, a street known today as Talaat Harb was referred to as Suleiman Pasha. There was even a statue of him. When Gamal Nasser came to power, a street named for a European was politically unacceptable, so the name was changed and the statue moved. You can now see it outside the Military Museum at the Cairo Citadel.

★   ★   ★

Mehmet Ali and Ibrahim Pasha had left their own marks on Jerusalem. Only six years before, at his father's bidding, Ibrahim Pasha had taken the city, making himself at home on a European-style throne in King David's Tomb.[10] He did, in fact, lighten restrictions on Christians and Jews, but he and his father apparently had nothing but contempt for Arabs; to Mehmet Ali, they were "wild beasts."[11] Ibrahim didn't hesitate either to ruthlessly put down a rebellion with indiscriminate slaughter. But by 1839, he and the new young sultan in Istanbul, Abdulmecid, were both issuing decrees for Jerusalem, ones really aimed at the nations of Europe to win their support.

Yet Jerusalem was an unremarkable backwater when Layard and Mitford first arrived at the Damascus Gate in February. Layard estimated that the city probably only had about 20,000 people at the time, one where the finances were run by "ignorant and truculent" Greek and Armenian officials "who cared for little but enriching themselves" and Turkish soldiers and bureaucrats "who had no consideration for the population, and who were corrupt and brutal." Mitford wrote that the troops garrisoned in the city had been sent to Jerusalem as punishment for mutinous behavior.

There was only one European diplomat residing in Jerusalem, and that was the British consul, William Turner Young. The Russian consul was in Jaffa, but Layard wrote that this didn't stop him from constant intriguing, and the official had managed to replace the Greek Orthodox patriarch and the chief rabbi with individuals who were more susceptible to his political will. French citizens were temporarily under the protection of Suleiman Pasha, but the coffeehouses and bazaars were filled with chatter about the machinations going on between the Russians and the Roman Catholic authorities and other Christian sects over who controlled specific sacred sites.

Then as now, religious rivalries were bitter and intense. The previous Easter, Egyptian soldiers used bayonets to drive out feuding pilgrim mobs from the Church of the Holy Sepulchre; several people were killed.

Layard and Mitford, though often agreeing on what they saw, had very different reactions to the city. Mitford was a Christian and a believer: "I feel nearer heaven as I stand on that ground which once my Saviour trod."[12] There were, however, all kinds of scams and misrepresentations going on, and fortunately, he wasn't completely credulous. "On the Via Dolorosa, by which Jesus is supposed to have proceeded to Mount Calvary," he wrote, "they actually show a dent in the wall, against which he is said to have leaned his cross!"[13] The idea, of course, was ridiculous; the building was only about 600 years old.

Besides exuberance over walking in the supposed footsteps of Christ, Mitford felt more than anything else a deep compassion for Jews in the city. He thought they were abominably treated by the local authorities, and in 1845, he drafted a pamphlet calling for the creation of an independent Jewish state in Palestine but one that would be under British protection. It was a theme he picked up in his own account of his travels, and one passage is worth noting with hindsight: "The Jews have, through the lapse of ages, kept their attention fixed on Palestine, to which they never doubt of returning, and their gratitude to their liberators and restorers would be unbounded, at the same time that they could not by any possibility gain by turning against us."

For Layard, any interest in Jerusalem was almost purely archaeological and historical, and while he had the opportunity to visit many sites thanks to the help of a Protestant missionary, he was disgusted by the religious infighting, by the "degrading superstitions and practices which have been nourished by priest-craft and ignorance, and of the ignoble and shameful contests between rival Christians which have desecrated and stained with blood even the spot where the Christian faith—the faith of peace, brotherhood and love—had its birth. I was not sorry when the time came for me to leave it."

On another destination, he and Mitford couldn't be more far apart: Petra. Layard wanted to see it, proposing they reach their scheduled stop of Damascus through the desert instead of the usual route, allowing them to see the ruins. Mitford pointed out they were in the middle of winter and would have to sleep out in the open when the weather was at its worst, with cold temperatures and frequent rains. They would need formal protection from some sheikh plus an armed escort: both would come at a hefty price.

Years later, an older, wiser Layard admitted, "My companion's objections to my proposal were no doubt well founded, and had my experience been greater and had I been less headstrong, they would have prevailed with me." But he was determined to go. The English consul also tried to talk him out of it, calling his trip "foolhardy and impracticable"—he wouldn't be held responsible. But the consul was willing to provide letters of introduction for Egyptian authorities to help.

If you want to see Petra in the twenty-first century, your surest method is to ride a bus or car on the main highway, and it takes three hours across a stark, forbidding waste—it makes the accomplishment of the trip by camel, let alone one made by a foreigner practically out of his depth, even more amazing. And once modern tourists hand over their ticket and pass through the gate of the park, they trudge along a stretch of rock and dust under the punishing sun for about ten minutes before they reach the opening of the *Siq*. This is the twelve-kilometer-long rocky enclosure that's a beautiful present from the tectonic plates violently shifting about. Walls of rosy rock, light brown and red stone seem to have been caressed by giant hands. Then human ones came along and sculpted inscriptions and images.

And then you turn the last winding curve and glimpse the Treasury, the spectacular, columned portico of sandstone. The name is a misnomer; there were no riches here, the Greek-style pillars and plinths were a front for a tomb.

Petra wasn't built by the Greeks or Romans. The city was the work of another people who unfortunately don't get a mention in school textbooks. The Nabateans, the descendants of ancient Arabian tribes, had managed to elbow their way into the strategic spice trades from India and China, allowing them to carve out an impressive empire of their own. The Romans eventually took them over, but Nabatean architecture shows a fascinating fusion of Egyptian, Greek, Roman, and Mesopotamian styles.

After coming all this way, after sleepless watches in the night and meals of bread cakes cooked in ashes and boiled rice, after the painful misadventure in dentistry, this was the view Layard claimed as his prize. "The scenery of Petra made a deep impression upon me, from its extreme desolation and its savage character," he wrote. "The rocks of friable limestone, worn by the weather into forms of endless variety, some of which could scarcely be distinguished from the remains of ancient buildings; the solitary columns rising here and there amidst the shapeless heaps of masonry; the gigantic flights of steps, cut in the rocks, leading to the tombs."

The natural wonder of the stones was impressive, but nothing could live up to the hype for him, those lofty descriptions he had found in books. He felt disappointed. "I thought the architecture debased and wanting both in elegance and grandeur. It is of a bad period and of a corrupt style." This was unfair. Petra boasts the impressive remains of a theater, a colonnaded street, temples, and tombs, and the "Monastery"—not quite as stunning as the Treasury yet an elegant feat of architecture nonetheless—is positioned high in the mountain, accessible after more than 800 brutal and rough steps.

To his credit, Layard still appreciated the "impressive number of excavations in the mountainsides. It is astonishing that a people should, with infinite labor, have carved the living rock into temples, theatres, public and private buildings, and tombs, and have thus constructed a city on the borders of the desert, in a waterless, inhospitable region, destitute of all that is necessary for the sustenance of man—a fit dwelling-place for the wild and savage robber tribes that now seek shelter in its remains."

With incredible luck and guile, he had managed to reach his goal unscathed. Then came the adventure of the robbery and its dramatic reversal. He would certainly have a few colorful tales to offer Mitford when they met up again! His older friend had been so concerned, predicting certain doom, and look what he had accomplished. Henry Layard—brash and willful, clever and curious—had no idea that it was *after* Petra, after his saddlebags were stuffed again with his belongings, that he would be in the most danger.

But first, there was a comical episode in which one of the tribal chiefs sold Layard off without his knowledge to a local sheik, promising that the Englishman would pay big to see those useless heaps of stones in the countryside. When Layard's "buyer" found out that his hostage hadn't brought any large fortune along for protection money, he didn't believe it and led the Englishman hither and yon, trying to nag money out of him. Layard didn't care. He was having a great time, discovering new sites of ruins and aqueducts. The sheik, however, got bored and finally gave up, no doubt happy to see the back of him.

His solo travels seemed to be going well. One morning, he left before daylight to explore the ruins of Jerash. "I was enchanted by the wonderful beauty of the scene and surprised at the extent and magnificence of the remains. On all sides, I saw long avenues of graceful columns leading to temples, theatres, baths, and public edifices, constructed of marble, to which time had given a bright pinkish-yellow tint." Jerash still delights tourists to this day.

But his luck didn't hold. In trying to cross a rain-swollen tributary, he and a hired mule-wrangler guide were attacked by a group of Egyptian army deserters who had turned to robbery. As the wrangler fled to hide in the hills, the soldiers surrounded Layard, grabbed him, and threatened to shoot him if he didn't cough up some money. They rummaged through his saddlebags, took his tobacco, made him strip off his best clothing, and tore the belt from his waist. He was left in only his trousers and his shirt, with his Arab cloak "almost in tatters and not worth taking." Fortunately, they had no interest in his books, his notes, his compass, or his medicines. But now he had no money, scarcely any clothes or practical supplies, and he had to find his way into Damascus past the cordon for the plague quarantine.

With the help of his mule wrangler and others, he eventually arrived at the city gates. He could have easily been turned away, but he found a single gold Turkish coin deep in his saddlebag to bribe a guard. Staggering into Damascus with a crowd of peasants who brought their goods to market, he blended in with the poor and navigated his way through "numberless narrow-winding streets enclosed by the naked walls of mud-built houses."

At the British legation, the consul was shocked by his appearance. Here was this apparent beggar "almost shoeless" and in rags, filthy with dust and tanned after long days in the Arab sun, but who addressed him in the familiar vowels of an educated person. Layard was a wreck, exhausted. The consul did what any good Englishman does in a crisis. He served Layard a cup of tea.

• 3 •

Camping Near Desolation

"*I* now felt an irresistible desire," Layard wrote in the opening chapter of *Nineveh and Its Remains*, "to penetrate to the regions beyond the Euphrates, to which history and tradition point as the birthplace of the wisdom of the West. Most travelers, after a journey through the usually frequented parts of the East, have the same longing to cross the great river, and to explore those lands which are separated on the map from the confines of Syria by a vast blank stretching from Aleppo to the banks of the Tigris. A deep mystery hangs over Assyria, Babylonia, and Chaldea. With these names are linked great nations and great cities dimly shadowed forth in history; mighty ruins, in the midst of deserts, defying, by their very desolation and lack of definite form, the description of the traveller; the remnants of mighty races still roving over the land; the fulfilling and fulfilment of prophecies; the plains to which the Jew and the Gentile alike look as the cradle of their race."

Layard wasn't using a poetic metaphor when he wrote "vast blank"—there certainly was a massive deficit both on the maps and in the scholarship over these parts of the Middle East. What the Victorians knew of Assyria amounted to a few references in the Bible, chiefly the book of Isaiah, and in the works of the Greek historians. All were more myth than history. Byron wrote a popular poem first published in 1815, *The Destruction of Sennacherib*, which he based on an account of an Assyrian siege of Jerusalem found in the biblical book of Kings. You can still find an older generation in Britain that recognizes these lines:

> The Assyrian came down like the wolf on the fold,
> And his cohorts were gleaming in purple and gold;
> And the sheen of their spears was like stars on the sea,
> When the blue wave rolls nightly on deep Galilee.

In the poem, the Assyrians lose. But according to the chronicles left by the Assyrians, the wolf got to chomp down on his prize and capture Jerusalem. We wouldn't know of the Assyrians' claim at all if not for Henry Austen Layard, who must have read Byron's couplets, never knowing as he traveled east that his greatest accomplishments would serve to contradict them.

He and Mitford had a listless, unremarkable journey through the desert until they reached the Kurdish hills, where they had to skirt the plundering tribes taking advantage of the war going on between the Ottomans and Egyptians. In some parts, they came across tents that only an hour before had been robbed. Finally, on April 10, they reached Mosul, where they visited the ruins east of the river. At the time, it held about 50,000 people, a mix of Muslims, Chaldean Christians, Jews, and Syrian Catholics.

"The town, with its walls and minarets and gardens, stretching along the right bank of the Tigris," recalled Layard, "has the appearance of a considerable city. It was only when we entered it that we realized the condition of ruin and decay to which it had been reduced by long misgovernment and neglect." Many of the city residents lived in hovels. "In front of us were the vast mounds that marked the site of ancient Nineveh. . . . I was deeply moved and impressed by their desolate and solitary grandeur."

For two weeks, they lingered, the sites capturing Layard's imagination. He got help in his study from a genuine modern Assyrian. We can't forget there really is a descendant people—predominantly Christian and who speak Eastern Aramaic dialects—that has survived into our modern age, though persecution by Mongols, Persians, and Ottomans has done much to scatter and reduce their numbers. (And the recent war in Iraq has added to that heritage of misery.) The vice-consul for Britain in the area was Christian Rassam, a man whose father was from Mosul and whose mother was from Aleppo.

He was the perfect guide, knowing how to talk to the locals and how to navigate his way around the harsh terrain. Rassam was eager to check out for himself the nearby Parthian ruins of Hatra, taking along an English engineer named Ainsworth for his inspection, and the more the merrier. Layard was racked with another bout of delirium from malaria, but fortunately, he bounced back in time to come along.

Hatra was once a small Assyrian village that evolved into an impressive fortified city in the era of the Roman emperors Trajan and Septimius Severus. Like Palmyra and Petra, it was a major stop on the spice and silk roads, and it blended Greco-Roman architectural styles with Eastern touches in its elegant columns. Layard wrote how near a "magnificent pile of buildings" were "scattered flocks of sheep and innumerable camels, and on all sides we could see the black tents of the Bedouin. . . . This picturesque and striking scene thus suddenly disclosed to us filled me with wonder and delight." But even Hatra isn't what impressed Layard most. There were other structures that would haunt him.

On the group's very first night out, it camped near a small village called Hammum Ali, a place where there were sulfur springs, and they had lit a large fire to drive off, believe it or not, lions, which still lived in the remaining sections of jungle along the Tigris. The men had a good view across the plain, and the landscape had "a line of lofty mounds" with a ziggurat, ones where Layard envisioned that 10,000 soldiers for Xenophon had camped centuries before. Nineveh, he knew, had been ancient even in the Greek general's age. In these complexes of ruins near the village of Nimrud, "desolation meets desolation; a feeling of awe succeeds to wonder; for there is nothing to relieve the mind, to lead to hope, or to tell of what has gone by."

He roamed around the heaps of soil and stone and brick, happily exploring. "These huge mounds of Assyria made a deeper impression upon me, gave rise to more serious thought and more earnest reflection than the temples of Balbec or the theatres of Ionia." This was the turning point, the defining moment of his life. Layard didn't know it yet, but he was stepping into his future.

★   ★   ★

Only there were a few more miles to cross with Mitford first, and maybe it took a little while for Layard to realize the purpose of his journey had changed. Mitford probably reminded his companion that they should move on to Baghdad, and the easiest way to get there was to hire a *kelek*, a raft of inflatable sheepskins, and float south down the Tigris.

With the thick smell of orange groves on the banks, Layard was at first excited by what he thought was the city "rising majestically" with its "innumerable painted domes and minarets, its lofty walls and towers, its palaces and painted kiosks." The boy who loved the *Arabian Nights* was now a man coming face-to-face with the fairy tale. Baghdad, however, wasn't so appealing to him close-up. He found it "an assemblage of mean, mud-built dwellings under a heap of ruins." The city was recovering from years of flood and plague.

Not everyone shared his assessment. The Scottish writer and painter Baillie Fraser had checked out Baghdad around this same time and was taken by some of the architecture. He wasn't that impressed with the bazaars, but he was "struck with the singularly wild attire of the Arabs and the brilliant costumes of the Kurds." Fraser, however, hated the noise of the place. In addition to Bedouins shouting in "stentorian voices," there were the "Jew and Armenian merchants, the camel and mule drivers, the boys, the women—nay, the very ladies upon their donkeys, all seem to vie with each other in loud vociferation."[1]

Others studied the city with different motives than plain sightseeing. An Irish naval lieutenant took a steamship along the Tigris for the Royal Geographical Society while his captain did the same on the Euphrates; he concluded in 1839 that "there could be no difficulty in marching armies along these rivers."[2] Queen Victoria's empire had definite intentions to keep a high profile here, and about a decade later, a commander of the Indian navy had a secret and detailed map of the city drawn up—secret because officials for the Ottoman Empire didn't like a foreign power knowing the exact outline of Baghdad's streets.[3]

Not long before Layard and Mitford drifted down the Tigris, the sultan introduced a new system of provincial government. The last governor, a Daoud Pasha, had a favorite punishment for criminals: they were placed on stakes at the ends of a bridge of boats as a warning to new arrivals in the city. But the new governor from Istanbul, Ali Pasha, brought a collection of toadies and officials with him who were each determined to line his own pockets. Layard noticed how the population of Baghdad was in decline while its fertile land was being lost to either desert or marshes. The roads weren't safe, with caravans falling easy prey to either Bedouin or Kurdish bandits. And inhabitants of nearby villages regularly fled into the countryside to escape conscription into the Ottoman army.

Perhaps one day, Layard thought, Baghdad might be a great city again, but it would need a great change plus "a considerable period of time must elapse before the havoc and devastation caused by oppression, misgovernment and neglect can be repaired. I trust that it may be the destiny of England to bring about that change, of such vast importance and of such incalculable benefit to peace, commerce and civilisation." He was, of course, proved half right. In less than a century, Britain would have a mandate over a new country it created by redrawing lines on a map; the world still waits, however, for Iraq to prove its incalculable benefit to peace.

Layard and Mitford intended to visit the British Residency, its formal legation, and knowing they would meet many of their fellow countrymen and European expatriates, they had the ferryman take them to shore before they arrived. They washed, tidied themselves up, and redressed in Western suits. But no sooner had Layard made himself presentable than he slipped while trying to get back on the raft . . . and plunged into the river. He had nothing else to wear and would have to go as he was; he "trusted that my character as an adventurous traveler with small means would furnish me with a suitable excuse for my forlorn and somewhat wretched plight."

So the kelek drifted along until it came to the bank of the Tigris, where a large building flew the Union Jack. These were the last monopolistic years of the East India Company, when the corporation's interests were considered virtually identical to those of the Foreign Office. At its outposts, a political agent for the company could live like a king. Layard and Mitford walked through a vaulted entrance, with one of the sepoys standing guard from the household's own Indian detachment, and Layard saw several balconies, terraces, and doors to rooms as well as a collection of attendants, all wearing different outfits. The Resident in Baghdad was a Colonel Taylor, a "slight and wizened man" who warmed to Layard's interest in archaeology and other cultures and let the pair use his small guesthouse—complete with garden. Here, Layard and Mitford did their homework for the Persian leg of their trip. Taylor was an Eastern scholar himself, and he had an impressive library of Arabic and Persian manuscripts, particularly ones of early Arabian geographers.

The young travelers also did a bit of socializing. After so long mixing in exotic cultures, they were only too glad to rub shoulders with the "agreeable and intelligent society of the small English colony." At dawn, Taylor's friends and family members rode horses along the palm groves of the Tigris. On these trips, the English women could switch to the comfortable riding outfits they wore back home, but if they wanted to explore Baghdad's streets at all, they had to don Arab dress, complete with horsehair veils. The first English lady who tried to wear European clothes in public was the immediate victim of catcalling, hooting, and insults, including the yell of "Mother of the dirt basket!"

Layard and Mitford spent two happy, restful months in this insular cocoon of the expatriate world. At breakfast, an Indian officer offered a snappy salute and announced in Hindustani, "All is well." Arab and Indian servants moved noiselessly on bare feet to bring dishes to the English seated around the table, and when the meal was done, "an army of attendants" brought in hookahs, which were especially popular with the English ladies. In the evening, people spent time relaxing on the Residence's flat roof or, if it was too hot, sprawled out on silk-covered divans in a domed chamber inlaid with ivory, fine woods, and elaborate glasswork.

One day, Taylor brought the young men to call on Ali Pasha. The formal visit involved a fair amount of pomp and pageantry, and the new governor sent gold-embroidered riding gear for their horses. The head dragoman of the Residency, wearing a turban and cashmere shawl, accompanied the group, which had a mounted escort of the governor's soldiers carrying silver-headed maces while runners trotted along with staves. Added to that was Taylor's sepoys. The whole procession muscled its way through the crowded bazaar, scattering the sellers and women with baskets of fruit and bowls of curds, causing a lot of commotion and whispered epithets. At last, the group reached the palace and were ushered into a courtyard and finally an opulent apartment.

To Layard, Ali Pasha was a repulsive figure, "disgustingly obese." Like a bloated walrus, he was sunk low on one of the rich divans, and because he wasn't used to the heat, he wore only a *shalwar*, a pair of traditional baggy trousers, and a light linen jacket that did little to cover his naked chest, its ripples of fat on display. He took his fez off time after time to mop his sweaty forehead with a handkerchief. The conversation between official and guests was a stilted one; no surprise questions and all the perfunctory expected compliments. Layard thought this man, already known for a local regime fetid with corruption, was a perfect example of why there was so much misery and poverty in the Ottoman Empire.

While at Baghdad, Layard had the chance to make two visits to satisfy his appetite for yet more ruins. He explored the Palace of the Sasanian Empire at Ctesiphon, and he rode to another site that would have an irresistible hold on him and shape his future. "I shall never forget the effect produced upon me by the long lines and vast masses of mounds which mark the site of ancient Babylon, as they appeared in the distance one morning as the day broke behind them. The desolation, the solitude, those shapeless heaps, all that remain of a great and renowned city, are well calculated to impress and excite the imagination. As when I first beheld the mounds of Nineveh, a longing came over me to learn what was hidden within them, and a kind of presentiment that I should one day seek to clear up the mystery."

★   ★   ★

He and Mitford didn't have much longer together. They complemented each other as travel companions but were very different men, and Layard no longer needed an older-brother figure. He had already demonstrated that when his impetuous mind was set on a goal, no argument could sway him. Mitford could be equally stubborn in his fusty way. In May 1840, as they prepared to journey into Persia, the advice given was that they should wear local dress to attract less attention. Shia Muslims apparently disapproved of European clothing as indecent.

With his coloring and English features, Layard certainly couldn't pass up close for a Bedouin, a Turk, or a Persian, but his youthful face was now covered with a beard, and his disguise of native costuming might work at a distance. He sported a long robe cinched by a shawl, a black lambskin hat, and ashalwar. Mitford wouldn't play this game; he always insisted on English clothes for himself, "as any disguise would have exposed me to danger and detention; disguise should never be resorted to but in cases of extreme emergency, and quitted as soon as its purpose has been answered." But there's a big difference between affecting the local clothes and giving the impression you're up to something and riding about in a Western suit blares your presence from yards away.

They tagged along with a scruffy caravan of poor pilgrims and their wives led by a couple of Turks, but as infidels, they were hardly welcome.

As they made their way into what is now Iran's Kermanshah Province, the pilgrims shunned them and refused to share their water, and at one point, the Englishmen had to beat back the more aggressive ones with the butt ends of their rifles. They managed to see Bisotun, where Darius the Great had crucial inscriptions about his rise to power carved into the mountain rock. Because the cuneiform message was written in ancient Persian, Babylonian, and the language of another ancient people, the Elamites, it's virtually the equivalent of the Rosetta Stone and just as important. Only part of the text had been translated a couple of years before—by a man who would be one of Henry Layard's archaeological mentors.

Layard had heard there were fabulous ruins in Sistan, the region that sprawled across eastern Persia and Afghanistan. He was also curious to learn more about its inhabitants since this area was supposed to be where the Zoroastrian religion began. It would be quite a lengthy trek, but first he and Mitford needed the permission of Vizier Meerza Aghassi. Their timing was terrible. The vizier was leaning toward the idea of taking the Persian army and invading Mesopotamia. At the same time, relations between Britain and Persia were extremely tense. Nevertheless, the pair would try. When they caught up to the army at a town near Hamadan, Layard was appalled at the destruction it left behind: "The country and the villages they pass through are left a desert, the crops destroyed, and the trees uprooted."

Days passed before Meerza Aghassi granted them an audience. The vizier turned out to be another vulgar and mercurial official who had a reputation for being "a fanatical hater of Christians." In his own memoir of the journey, Mitford wrote that he was "a little shrivelled old man, very ignorant, but shrewd and cunning, with a shrill loud voice." He kept knocking his black cap from one side of his head to the other as he became agitated, eating a tray of fruit and ice while petitioners and attendants sat sullenly against a wall. Layard and Mitford needed a *firman*, an imperial decree, that would give them permission to travel through Isfahan and via Yezd to reach Kandahar and then carry on down to India.

The vizier was already suspicious, thinking they might be spies, and his men rolled out lurid tales to scare them about how dangerous the countryside was. This wasn't going to work, not after all the pair had been through. So the vizier tried another tack; if anything happened to them, it might spark an international incident with Britain. Layard and Mitford offered to sign a waiver that would release him from all responsibility, and while the vizier at first agreed, he kept them waiting and then turned them down. Mitford couldn't help commenting in his memoir that if they *were* spies, the Persians were stupid to keep them detained *here*, allowing them to learn all the goings-on and principal players at court.

The wait dragged on for a month. Layard and Mitford shuttled between the prime minister and the foreign minister at their offices in Hamadan, always told to come back the next day. A ride through the camp outside the city could mean stones thrown at them and shouts of "Infidel!" and "Dog!" Layard, however, wasn't going to take this abuse—ever. One time when a sentry threw a rock that struck his horse, he promised to take the matter up with the shah; the guard was punished with the bastinado. And the wait went on. With their cash and supplies running low and no friendly reception in the encampment, Mitford's patience was especially wearing thin. He was disgusted that Meerza Aghassi, having confiscated their passports, lied to a Russian diplomat who was trying to help the Englishmen, given that they carried no other papers of identification.

Mitford was anxious as well to reach Ceylon. To Layard, Ceylon could wait—if he bothered to think that far ahead at all. He was determined to press on with or without the Persian government's official permission, and now the companions knew they had to obtain separate firmans. Mitford decided to take a northern route towards Mashad, Afghanistan. At last, the paperwork came through, with permission from the shah himself.

On August 8, 1840, Layard and Mitford rode together as far as the village of Shaverin and said their goodbyes. In his own memoir, Mitford barely tells anything of this parting of the ways, only that it was "regretful." By the time his book was out, decades had passed, and Layard had become famous. Was it mild envy and resentment that kept Mitford from sparing so few words on his travel companion? Or had they left each other in bitter disagreement over the risks? We simply don't know.

In leaving Mitford behind, Layard took the high road: "We had been together for above a year," he wrote in *Early Adventures*, "and I much regretted that we had to part. He had proved an excellent fellow-traveller, never complaining, ready to meet difficulties or hardships, and making the best of everything."

★   ★   ★

The firman from the shah granted Layard the privilege of traveling at public expense, which from the very beginning made him uncomfortable. He would be given a specified number of horses, and at every place he stopped, the locals would have to supply him with chickens, beef, eggs, rice, bread, sugar, as well as a bounty of other supplies—enough for eight people. And then there was the feed and straw for his mounts. The terms were lavishly generous, and Layard would be accompanied by a *mehmander*, an officer for the shah who would supply village headmen with receipts and make sure they coughed up the goods. What bothered Layard was that he would be living off the charity of locals who could hardly afford this largess.

After his first night on the road, he tried to pay for his lodgings and entertainment, but the shah's official, a man named Imaum Verdi Beg, insisted the firman had to be obeyed and none of the villagers would accept any reimbursement. Soon, Layard discovered the petty officer was extorting the locals along the route far in excess of what either of them needed, and he complained that he would have none of it. Imaum Verdi argued that if he didn't squeeze the peasants this way, they would be charged for the goods and horses anyway, and, besides, there were a few unscrupulous types who always hiked their prices. Layard was trying to practice what we'd call "socially responsible tourism," but the official was too good at intimidating the different innkeepers and headmen.

All along the way to Isfahan, Layard complained and protested as Imaum Verdi blackmailed and bullied and filled his own pockets. At one point, the official pushed his luck too far and threatened his own charge: pay up a big sum, or he'd abandon the Englishman in open country. Layard promptly told him he would send a messenger off to the shah, complaining about this behavior—and oh, by the way, the last fellow who tried this stunt had lost his head. Imaum Verdi quickly changed his tune, begging him to forget the whole thing, but his contrition went only so far. He still went on strong-arming the locals to extort goods. Since he hung on to the actual document of the firman, Layard could never really force the issue.

He came to a point in his journey when he no longer needed Imaum Verdi's services, though the official chose to follow anyway. The final days Layard spent on his way to Isfahan were miserable, as he suffered bouts of dysentery and fever again because of the malaria. One night after a thunderstorm, he came across a group of shoemakers who had made camp in old castle ruins. Soaked through and ravenously hungry, Layard plunked himself down and helped himself to their cauldron of broth without even waiting for an invitation. Later, he passed through Tehran, where fruit and vegetable groves seemed to grow in "an almost uninterrupted line to Isfahan."

At last he reached his destination, where old friends and new allies waited. A visiting English merchant, Edward Burgess, learned of his arrival and offered help. And the French artist Eugène Flandin was also in town, as was the French architect and artist Pascal Coste. At one point, Layard suggested to Coste that he sketch a particularly fine drawing of the Sassanian period. Coste "rode off at once to do so." Coste seemed to have been a man of extraordinary concentration; as he drew, he had his horse's reins looped around his arm. When he finally looked up from his drawing, he discovered a thief had cleverly removed his mount, leaving Coste with only the reins in his hand.

Edward Burgess suggested that he and Layard call on Manucher Khan, the governor of Isfahan whose domain included the constantly rebellious Lur and Bakhtiari tribes. The governor was a larger-than-life sadist of almost cartoonish proportions. A Georgian eunuch with a high, shrill voice and flabby features, dressed in the finest cashmere tunic with a jewel-handled, curved dagger in the shawl wrapped around his waist, he enjoyed being creative in his cruelties. He'd ordered men to pull the teeth of a horse thief and then hammer them into the soles of the man's feet like shoes for a horse. He ordered a tower built near Shiraz with 300 rebels stacked and mortared into a living wall.

When Layard met the governor, he didn't hesitate to complain about Imaum Verdi Beg. Manucher Khan promised the official would be punished, and "he was good as his word." It was only after the wretched thug suffered the agonies of the bastinado that Layard felt any regret or pity. Imaum Verdi, brutish and corrupt, still had the spirit to scold the young Englishman for denouncing him. "What good, sir, has the stick that I have eaten done you?" he asked. "Who has profited by it? You and I might have divided the money and the supplies that as the Shah's servant, I was entitled by his firman to obtain for you on our way. The villagers would have been none the worse, as they would have deducted the amount from their taxes. Do you think that they will get back their horses or their donkeys?"

To be fair, Layard sought a small spiteful revenge, but he also genuinely wanted to see the victims get compensation; his fault was in his naïveté in ever expecting Manucher Khan to arrange compensation or practice any restraint in his sentencing.

If Manucher Khan ever entertained the notion of letting the Englishman go on his merry way to Kandahar, he wouldn't allow it now. This was the time when the Cold War between Russia and the West really began, only in this age, the British called it the "Great Game." They had long feared the Russians might try to invade India, and so Cabinet ministers in Whitehall looked on with dread as their counterparts for the tsar orchestrated an alliance with Persia. Perhaps inevitably, Afghanistan became the site of the proxy war between the nineteenth-century superpowers. The British Empire soon found an excuse to send in an army of more than 20,000 men so that a pro-London puppet, in this case a governor of Herat and Peshawar named Shuja Shah Durrani, could proclaim himself "King of Afghanistan."

The fractured kingdoms of Central Asia, always ripe with rebellion, could only become more restless with this conflict that threatened to spill into their domains, and Isfahan was abuzz with rumors. They included one that Britain was helping a large force headed by the Aga Khan against Persia. It wasn't true, but it made life difficult for Layard nonetheless. He was granted permission to wander about the Bakhtiari lands but no further for the time being. This was something Layard wanted, to explore the life and country of the tribesmen, and, as usual, he was indifferent to the risks. It wouldn't be the shooting gallery of Kabul or Kandahar, but it was dangerous enough. He had already heard of the Bakhtiari as a nomadic tribe "renowned for its courage and daring and dreaded by the settled inhabitants of the plains. Their *chapaws*, or forays for plundering villages and caravans, were carried on by bodies of horsemen to a great distance. Even the neighborhood of Isfahan was not safe from them. They were everywhere the terror of travelers and of the population."

If Layard traveled among them, he needed to ingratiate himself with Mehmet Taki Khan, one of the most powerful chieftains of the Chahar Lang clan of the Bakhtiari. He was a larger-than-life figure "famed throughout Persia as well as in his mountains as a dauntless warrior, a most expert swordsman, an excellent shot and an unrivalled horseman." More than a mere brigand, he was also something of a statesman for the Bakhtiari, skilled at dealing in tribal politics. It would help Layard immensely if he could make friends with the man's brother, Ali Naghi Khan, who would soon be taken to Tehran as a hostage to ensure Mehmet wouldn't rebel against Persian rule.

Layard found Ali Naghi on one of the upper floors of a broken-down palace, "indulging in a debauch with four or five friends" while a hypocritical mullah rocked on his knees in a corner, praying loudly and oblivious to the violations of the Koran going on in front of him. Ali Naghi proved an affable host, happy to share his food and curious about England. Things were off to a good start.

But the person Layard really had to persuade was another chieftain, Shefi'a Khan, who was suspicious and kept giving him flimsy excuses for delays. Layard put his time to good use, learning the Persian language and customs, though sometimes there were scenes that could inspire the most outrageous of Orientalist kitsch art.

He was invited one time to dinner at the house of a Lur chieftain and self-proclaimed Sufi. When the night's entertainment moved to the women's apartments, beautiful girls, topless under loose-fitting and open silk jackets, their hands and feet painted with henna, danced gymnastically around the guests. "These contortions soon degenerated into outrageous indecency" because the dancers could help themselves to wine. Layard calls the whole event an orgy, but he's reticent on what else went on. Since both guests and dancing girls slept it off on the carpets until morning (and Layard wouldn't know this unless he stuck around), we can safely assume that if it wasn't an all-out sexual bacchanal, it was at least one hell of a party.

★ ★ ★

At last, on the morning of September 23, Layard could set out. At Shefi'a Khan's suggestion, Layard wore Bakhtiari clothing. He posed later in the costume for a watercolor portrait, which was the basis for an illustration decorating the first edition of his *Early Adventures*. Warned about bandits, he took only a pittance of gold coins, and Shefi'a Khan told him to always keep his pistols handy. The baggage for the trip was carried along on donkeys that were naturally slow and inspired a steady stream of Persian curses—all directed at the animals' original owners. "May your owner eat filth! May his grave be polluted!"

Spending so much time on the road with him, Layard had the chance to assess Shefi'a Khan's character and judged him more liberal and enlightened in his opinions than other Bakhtiari chieftains. He was an educated man who could read and write, understand a map and how to work a compass, and who had even served for a while in a Persian army unit run by English military advisers. Layard was always careful not to make notes or take compass readings in front of the chieftain's men, but as he and Shefi'a Khan rode along, they began to loosen up around each other. Shefi'a Khan would recite verses of Persian poetry, and when Layard wanted to know something, he was happy to give him information on the territory.

He also learned the Bakhtiari were nothing like their bloodthirsty image. He was treated again and again in villages with hospitality, though the simple tribespeople were as curious about him as if he were an alien stepping out of a UFO. At the town of Lurdagon up in the mountains, people assumed that as "a Frank," he must be a skilled physician, and they visited him with trays of food, hoping he could cure their ailments. At night, Shefi'a Khan pulled out a beautifully illustrated manuscript of the celebrated Persian poet Nizami Ganjavi, and Layard watched in fascination as wild-looking warriors stood around in a circle, leaning on their flintlocks, calmed by verses—which told a love story.

Sightseeing was harder out here, as the road forward was treacherous. Exhausted horses and mules struggled to pick their way over loose stones. The women in the group could also barely keep up. A night's rest was ruined when the caravan woke to discover they had been robbed, thieves having taken shoes, caps, and other provisions. On another morning, Layard woke to find his quilt stolen, no small loss at the beginning of October with the nights turning chilly. They soldiered on, higher into the mountains, until Shefi'a Khan stood on a slope and pointed out a speck on the horizon—their destination, Kala Tul, the name for the castle and its nearby village where they would meet the powerful Mehmet Taki Khan.

Only they didn't. As it happened, the khan was away on some administrative business. Layard was welcomed cordially enough by others, and it wasn't long before he was implored again to act as a doctor. This time, however, he ended up with a very important patient whose fate could decide his own. He was led to a spacious cabin made of tree boughs where the Bakhtiari chieftain's first wife was at the bedside of one of her children, a ten-year-old boy, sick with fever. Mehmet's wife was Khatun-jan, which meant "Lady of my soul." She was a "tall, graceful woman, still young and singularly handsome," and she greeted Layard with elegant manners. "She entreated me with tears to save the boy as he was her eldest son and greatly beloved by his father."

Layard offered doses of quinine. But the mother made the mistake of listening to the tribal physicians, who called this foreign visitor's medicine "dangerous." They had every reason to malign his efforts given that if they worked at all, the Englishman would show them up. A mullah was consulted. He opened the pages of a Koran at random, as was the practice, and he soon came down on the side of the local physicians—no surprise. The boy, however, was getting worse, and a messenger was sent to bring his father home.

Soon, Mehmet Taki Khan returned, riding his magnificent Arab pure-bred up to the main entrance of the castle. Though corpulent and of average height, he had a natural charisma, his handsome face marred by an old battle wound—an iron mace had broken his nose. He packed a rifle with a stock inlaid with ivory and gold, a scimitar of the finest Khorassan steel, a jeweled dagger, and a long, elaborately decorated pistol tucked into his belt. That didn't end the inventory of weapons; strapped to his saddle, decorated with red silk tassels, was a second sword and an iron mace.

Here was a man whose whole life had been forged by blood feud. His father, Ali, got on the wrong side of the Persian government, which used his own brother, Hassan, to betray him. Ali Khan's eyes were put out while Hassan was given his territory. As a child, Mehmet Taki Khan and his brothers were whisked off to safety, hidden in an Armenian village. Once the boys had grown to manhood, they launched their own revenge raid, sneaking into Hassan's castle and assassinating him as he rose from his prayers. The vendetta could have gone on, but Mehmet Taki Khan married his treacherous uncle's daughter and adopted the man's young sons. "His rivals and those who attempted to dispute his authority," wrote Layard, "had one after another been overcome and reduced by him to submission or had been slain in war or by treachery."

Layard says the chieftain had a "winning smile" and "a merry laugh," but as he approached the khan with others, it didn't look like things were getting off to a good start. As he offered his firman and letter of introduction, Mehmet Taki Khan tossed them contemptuously to the ground.

But there was no real cause for alarm. Gesturing for Layard to have a seat, the Bakhtiari leader explained gently that the Englishman didn't need official documents. He had arranged to have Layard checked out, and he'd received good reports from Shefi'a Khan. Layard could stay as long as he liked. Interview over, Mehmet went into the castle, but after a few minutes, Layard was sent for. He found the fearsome warrior sobbing, begging him to save the life of his son. The physicians who had meddled earlier were now begging off, saying there was nothing more they could do—the boy was close to death.

Layard didn't have much choice. If he didn't help, he'd ruin his good impression, and he might even incur the chieftain's wrath. On the other hand, if the boy died, the native doctors would have the perfect scapegoat, and Layard might get cut to pieces by angry tribesmen. He told Mehmet Taki Khan that no one had bothered yet to give the boy *his* remedies. There was another ceremony in which the mullah consulted his holy book for omens, and then finally Layard got down to work. The boy was now in a high fever, and Layard gave him a dose of Dover's powder, a nineteenth-century remedy that was little more than a compound of opium, morphine, and lactose plus a far more useful treatment—quinine.

There was nothing else to do but wait. Layard waited. He stayed with the child through the night, watching—no doubt anxiously hoping—for a change.

· 4 ·

Living among the Bakhtiari

$\mathcal{A}$t around midnight, the fever broke, and the boy experienced violent sweats. The next day, he showed improvement, but Layard kept administering quinine. Soon, it was clear the boy would pull through.

Mehmet Taki Khan and his wife, Khatun-jan Khanum, were delirious with relief, and they lavished displays of their gratitude on the young Englishman. Layard's horse, wounded and suffering, was replaced. Layard was still walking around with great embarrassment in shabby clothes since his shirts had been stolen—Khatun-jan supplied him a new wardrobe. She became a second mother to him, nursing him when he suffered returns of malarial fever, even acting as his banker, guarding his small amount of money in case he lost it to thieves during one of his roaming-for-ruins expeditions, and doling out an allowance when he needed it.

He spent enough time with them that he could write with compelling and eloquent authority on Bakhtiari customs, from the morning routines and ablutions for both genders to how they settled disputes and occasionally indulged in dyeing their hair, hand palms, and nails (Layard put up with the painful weekly ritual of the center of his scalp being shaved—without soap). The women were fond of bracelets and anklets, and both men and women liked to sport necklaces with silver charm cases holding verses of the Koran written on tiny parchments.

He was fascinated by how concepts of modesty were relative. The women often dressed in silk or velvet trousers, embroidered with gold, with "a short chemise of white linen . . . entirely open in front, but fastened with a loop at the neck," topped with an open silk or chintz jacket. He had seen girls on riverbanks raise their shirts to bring it over their heads to hide their faces—leaving themselves topless. But he suspected these same women would be scandalized by the low-cut dresses of their European counterparts.

He was one of the family now. The chieftain's children hung around this entertaining stranger, especially the eldest son, Hussein Kuli. "He was one of those beautiful boys who are constantly seen in Persia," Layard wrote of him, "and especially among the mountain tribes. . . . He became greatly attached to me, and I to him." Layard got to know the brothers of Mehmet Taki Khan well, accompanying them as they took their hawks and greyhounds out to hunt, even moving freely about their wives' *enderuns*, their quarters. Mehmet Taki Khan liked to charge his horse in the castle at a stuffed lion so that his mount would (hopefully) get accustomed to the smell and scent of the wild beast.

He also picked up on the family politics. The chieftain was devout, never drinking liquor. In contrast, his brother Ali Naghi Khan, whom Layard had met back in Isfahan, was the black sheep of the clan. Highborn Persian culture had "spoiled" him, and he wasn't above indulging in an orgy or two as he had while a political hostage.

Layard was accepted by everyone. The Bakhtiari and Lur helped him improve his Persian, though they spoke a dialect of it, and the Englishman later had Persian friends laughing at him because he used Lur words and expressions. At night, as coffee was served and guests played backgammon, Mehmet Taki Khan plied Layard with questions about England. Like Njegos of Montenegro, he wanted his people to advance and his land opened to trade from abroad, but it's clear he had less understanding of what this would mean. Layard was asked to explain railroads and other technological feats of the West, of new findings in astronomy.

The chieftain had a mullah debate these points, perhaps because they sounded so fantastic that he didn't believe them, but maybe with the cunning of a tribal leader, he also wanted to learn if Layard was exaggerating. Since the mullahs invariably fell back on a verse of a Koran to make a flat denial, there was never much of an intelligent debate. One evening, after Layard described the wigs worn by judges and barristers in England, the chieftain burst into a triumphant laugh, declaring, "You see that to make a *Kadi* [judge] in England, it only requires two horses' tails!"

Even Khatun-jan never veiled herself in his presence; neither did her attendants or even the wives of the chieftain's brothers. Layard got into the habit of listening to her stories about the tribes, and he was so familiar a presence that nobody minded if he ate with her. Mehmet Taki Khan teased him that he was introducing European customs to the harem, but he obviously didn't care either. Khatun-jan's sister, Khanumi, was substantially younger and was renowned for her beauty. "Her features were of exquisite delicacy," Layard recalled, "her eyes large, black and almond-shaped, her hair of the darkest hue. She was intelligent and lively."

Mehmet and his wife mentioned on more than one occasion that if Layard would convert to Islam and stay, living as a Bakhtiari, the girl could be his wife. "The inducement was great, but the temptation was resisted." But how strongly was it resisted? Layard was intrigued by a custom called *sigha*, which allowed a man to take a wife for a brief period, even as little as a day. Given that he was accepted so fully into the tribe and the culture, it's possible that the rules were bent for this particular Frank, and he enjoyed the company of Khanumi on a more intimate level. Layard, being a gentleman, wouldn't tell, so we'll never know for sure.

Life in the village and in the castle had to be constantly stimulating for him. He stayed in the upper room of a tower, and one day, Khatun-jan noticed him locking his door with a padlock. She strongly recommended that he secure his window as well. When he laughed at the idea, Khatun-jan turned to one of her handmaidens, and Layard was stunned to see the girl "dragging herself up in the most marvellous way by the mere irregularities of the bricks." He never underestimated the women of the Near East again.

But past the idyllic pastoral scenes and happy nights with his new adopted family, there were reminders that the Bakhtiari were not one united people. "They are constantly at war, either among themselves or with the Persian government, against which they are in chronic rebellion," wrote Layard. Even their games were disguised drills for combat. He watched their spectacular displays of horsemanship, how a man on an Arab mount—hooves pounding the earth at full gallop—could reach down and scoop up a handkerchief. He knew these men were bandits, merciless when they attacked caravans. "But notwithstanding the fierce and truculent appearance of the men, I have never seen together finer specimens of the human race than in a Bakhtiari encampment."

Layard's loyalty to them would soon be put to the test.

★   ★   ★

All this time back in Isfahan, the loathsome governor, Manucher Khan—the Georgian eunuch who rested his considerable bulk on his plush divans—was resenting the fact that a wild Bakhtiari chieftain rode around the mountains, commanding men and power. The authorities in Tehran had never liked it either. This bandit surely needed humbling.

So the governor decided that hefty taxes were owed. That made Mehmet Taki Khan's situation impossible. If he dared to collect taxes from the tribes, he'd have an all-out rebellion on his hands—not that these people had money anyway. What did they need money for? "During the whole time that I was with them," wrote Layard, "I rarely saw a gold or silver coin, except such as were worn as ornaments by the women. They had little or no trade, not sending much of the produce of their mountains and valleys for sale to the settled districts and towns of Persia." Even selling common bread was beneath them and disgraceful. Mehmet Taki Khan had one option: *stall*. Stall for as long as he could.

But it didn't work. The chieftain's hard-drinking, partying brother, Ali Naghi Khan—once more a political hostage in Tehran—sent a letter that explained how the governor had complained to the shah and accused the chieftain of conspiring with exiled princes in Baghdad. With the spring thaw, when the mountain passes were open again, detachments of the Persian army would invade Bakhtiari territory and show who's boss. There were reports that Manucher Khan had already started preparations, mobilizing troops and artillery. The stakes were the very survival of the tribal chieftain and his family. If captured, he faced either prompt execution or to be blinded and kept in chains for the rest of his life while his family languished in prison.

Layard now found himself smack in the middle of the chessboard for the Great Game. Diplomatic relations had been suspended between Persia and Britain, which had called home its diplomatic representative. The chieftain had heard rumors there would be war. "I do not think that Mehmet Taki Khan had entirely divested himself of the suspicion that I was a British political agent entrusted with a secret mission," wrote Layard. "He probably hoped that if war were to break out between England and Persia he might avail himself of the opportunity to proclaim his independence."

It wasn't just the chieftain dreaming of nationhood. Over many nights in front of a fire, Layard got caught up in the idea of helping to forge these loose, lawless clans of wild horsemen into a new country. He pointed out to Mehmet that the province of Khuzistan did have goods Europe wanted, such as cotton and indigo, and he had calculated the prices of various items that could be exported, like wax and different cereals. The chieftain was willing to allow the construction of roads through his territory, ones that could link up to the plains where the Arab tribes dwelled and further on to the Persian Gulf. He begged Layard to go to Karak, an island in the Persian Gulf that today is known as Kharg and belongs to Iran. A large British force had apparently taken the island, and Layard had to find out what exactly was going on and enlist help.

Layard was willing. He might have the chance to get precious medicines that could help one of the chieftain's ailing brothers. It had been ages since he had learned any news of England, and it would be a nice change to spend time among men of his own culture. The mission probably held some small appeal as well to a young man's ego: he would be a courier and intermediary involved in great events.

But the journey to the island was a humbling one; on the last leg of the trip, he endured a storm aboard a rough boat crawling with vermin where the food was awful and the water from a tub was "absolutely repulsive." Kharg was indeed occupied by Indian troops, commanded by a Colonel Hennell who was the Resident for the East India Company in the province of Bushehr. It was a hardship post, with extreme heat in the summer on a "barren rock" and the only water available from the rain collected in reservoirs. But here the British force would stay until the thunderclouds of war had passed.

Layard got his chance to talk with Hennell, who doubted hostilities would break out. Instead, Persia and Britain would sort out their differences at the negotiation table. This was good for London but very bad for Mehmet Taki Khan. War meant the British army would look for allies in the fight, but now it didn't need them. If the chieftain wanted trade and a partner for commercial ventures, that was fine, but the Union Jack wouldn't appear on the horizon when his men clashed with riders for the shah. Hennell sent Layard a letter in September 1841 to reinforce the point that "although the government would have nothing to do with Mehmet Taki Khan's political views, he did not think it was altogether indisposed to meet his commercial projects."

It's important here to note, as scholar Gene Garthwaite has pointed out, that Layard overestimated the power and influence of Mehmet Taki Khan, who "was far from being the all-powerful khan of the Chahar Lang, let alone of the Bakhtiari." The clan and tribal relationships were far more dynamic and complicated. And even if by some miracle the khan won over all the Bakhtiari, it's unlikely he would be able to raise even 15,000 troops for a brief military campaign. But he was the last of his line to wield substantial power.[1] It's understandable that this, along with his progressive views, made him a natural candidate in some British eyes to organize his people.

Layard had little to show for his trip, though he obtained some vaccine for smallpox, which had been decimating the Bakhtiari. He knew he better return as soon as possible to the tribal caravan, but after a frustrating sail with winds against him and then a day of dead calm, he reached his rendezvous point on the mainland only to discover that the band of warrior horsemen had tired of waiting and had moved on. Eventually, Layard found his way back to Kala Tul, but the chieftain was not there, and the word was that the governor was coming for the Bakhtiari.

The governor headed an expedition that would be devoted half to tax collection, the other half spent on ruthless reprisals against anyone who stood up to his administration and the shah's rule. On his list for collecting sums were the cities of Shuster and Dezful. And he forced Ali Naghi Khan, the chieftain's brother, to serve as both hostage and guide to lead him into the untamed mountain lands. The situation was deteriorating fast.

Layard went out with a reconnaissance party to keep an eye on the Persian forces, and one morning, just after dawn, they heard a company of horsemen riding close by. As the Bakhtiari hid behind a rock in a ravine, Layard spotted a European and called out in French. The man turned out to be a Russian baron he'd met before in Hamadan who was on his way to join the governor. Layard warned the tribesmen "of the danger of attacking and robbing a secretary to the Russian embassy." Years later, he met the baron again in London and informed him how close he came to being assassinated and sparking an international incident.

The scouting party returned to the castle, and soon Layard was entrusted by Khatun-jan with two of her sons to take to their father. Mehmet Taki Khan was camped with his best men on a plain not far away, but he still hoped to meet the governor and convince him of his loyalty, slipping out of the net closing around him. With their blades and antique matchlock rifles, however, the tribesmen were eager for war. At night as usual, they huddled around, listening to stories and poetry. Layard had witnessed Mehmet Taki Khan "cry and sob like a child" while listening to his favorite verses. "When I expressed to him my surprise that he, who had seen so much of war and bloodshed, and had himself slain so many enemies, should be thus moved to tears by poetry, he replied, '*Ya, Sahib!* I cannot help it. They burn my heart.'"

In the night, one of the tribesmen played a kind of oboe, which sounded to Layard's ears like a bagpipe. The warriors seemed to enjoy this as much as the poetry recitals. Flames of the campfires popped and crackled, all while the war drum beat monotonously on through the suspenseful night.

★   ★   ★

When the governor and his army emerged from the last of the mountain passes, Mehmet Taki Khan sent two of his boys ahead as a welcoming committee, and as they approached, attendants lifted them from their horses so that the odious eunuch could kiss them in greeting. The chieftain had to step down from his own mount to show deference to the representative of the shah, and the governor was surprised to see Henry Layard among the Bakhtiari. Maybe he assumed Layard had been made quick work of by bandits or had scampered back to his own people. He politely asked about Layard's health, and then the Persian tents were erected directly opposite the camp of the Bakhtiari horsemen. Now would start a long cat-and-mouse game of negotiations that would last forty days.

Layard even had time to go explore sculptures and bas-reliefs at nearby ruins. There was also a short adventure when one of a group of Persian deserters stole his horse. Off he galloped on a fresh mount with a small band of men, and they soon found the culprits cooking their supper. They charged towards them, and as Layard drew his long pistol to blast his attacker, the weapon misfired. In that second's delay, he was struck from behind with an iron mace, and he woke up later with one of the chief's brothers bathing his temples with water. The Bakhtiari were successful, but it sounds like Layard suffered a mild concussion, and he needed several days to recuperate.

Meanwhile, both Bakhtiari and Persian forces jockeyed for position. When both sides moved on to Kala Tul, Mehmet Taki Khan made sure the upper rooms of the castle were packed with fighters to defend him while the governor filled the courtyard and ringed the fort with his own men. But the stalemate was harder on the chieftain, who was required as the host to furnish provisions to his enemy and slowly exhaust his own resources. He was also expected to cough up expensive gifts for the governor: five well-bred Arab horses, twelve mules, an expensive cashmere shawl, an allotment of cash, *and* presents for the governor's men. Everyone assumed this would be enough to satisfy the greed of the governor, Manucher Khan, and that after he and his army collected the taxes from Shuster and Dezful, the Bakhtiari would be rid of them.

But Manucher Khan didn't rise to be governor of Isfahan without a wide streak of cunning treachery. Mehmet's brother, Ali Naghi, had accompanied the Persians on their way to Shuster, and Manucher Khan soon had him and the leader of another tribe thrown into chains. He positioned his army so that it cut off an obvious ally from coming to help, and then he casually demanded Mehmet Taki Khan ride to Shuster. If the chieftain did so, he'd clearly wind up like his brother, and refusing to obey, Mehmet Taki Khan demanded the hostages be released into his custody. The governor now had enough pretext he needed to declare the proud chieftain of the mountains a rebel.

The strategic situation hadn't changed. Mehmet Taki Khan—desperate, knowing he'd been outplayed—thought he might buy his way out of trouble, and so he offered more hostages to prove his loyalty. It was a horrible mistake attempting to placate a sadist. Manucher Khan insisted that the eldest son, Hussein Kuli, be turned over to him—this was the boy whom Layard had saved and nursed back to health. Layard wrote movingly of the sacrifice, "Mehmet Taki Khan was overwhelmed with grief, for he greatly loved his son, and it was long before he could muster sufficient resolution to surrender him. It was with greater difficulty that he could overcome the almost frenzied opposition of his mother. When Hussein Kuli was placed on his horse, ready to leave the castle, she dragged him off again, and clinging to him, refused to let him go. He was at last taken by force from her by the attendants."

Khatun-jan enlisted Layard to go to Shuster to watch over the boy, thinking his presence might keep the governor from indulging his vicious whims. Layard went, but he had little confidence he could keep the child safe. Both parents wept as the small unit of horsemen with a trusted retainer set out, but Hussein Kuli, all of ten years old, "showed no signs of fear." He was dressed in fine robes and armed with beautiful weapons—a jewel-handled dagger, long pistol, saddle bow, and mace—"the very picture of a young warrior." The group collected their other sacrifice, Hussein's cousin, six years older, a teenage boy known for his advanced understanding of the Koran.

The retainer refused to go into Shuster, fearing he might wind up another hostage, and instead, he and his men camped in a village nearby. So it was left to Layard to accompany the boys and their tutor across the bridge and into a fortress built on a cliff. Manucher Khan sat on a carpet of a terrace overlooking the Karun River. The fat eunuch, wrote Layard, "could not conceal the smile of satisfaction and triumph which passed over his bloated and repulsive features when the children stood before him." Layard knew this monster would break his word. But first the beast wanted to play with his mice.

"Why have you not brought your father with you?" taunted the governor in his shrill, thin voice. "Is he not coming to Shuster to see me?"

"No," snapped Hussein Kuli, resting a hand on his pistol.

Manucher Khan motioned to some warriors below engaged in a mock battle. "What if I were to send those soldiers to fetch him?"

"Let them go to Kala Tul," replied Hussein Kuli. "They will all come back naked like this." He put his forefinger in his mouth, drew it out, and held it up. It was an old Bakhtiari gesture that meant stripping a man bare.

Manucher Khan laughed and then adopted a menacing tone. "Has not your father got much gold?"

"I know nothing of such things, as I am a child," answered Hussein Kuli.

"You know, however, the place where he conceals it, and if you do not tell me where it is willingly, I shall have to make you."

If he meant to scare the boy, it didn't work. "It is not likely that my father should have shown me the spot where he hides his money. If I knew, I should not tell you, and if I were compelled to do so, he would not let you have it."

The boys were then taken off to prison. Layard was "astonished at the courage and extraordinary self-possession of Hussein Kuli" and noted how even the Persian officers, so accustomed to Manucher Khan's relentless acts of sadism, showed displays of affection to the boys—safely out of view of their leader.

Layard was smart enough to realize he should make perfunctory courtesies and get the hell out of town. He rode hard back to Kala Tul, where along the way at hospitable villages, he spread the news about the boys and was made to retell the story of Hussein Kuli's courage again and again. He later discovered that the governor's forces had increased: there were two more regiments plus some artillery that had come in from Luristan, and the enemies of Mehmet Taki Khan had provided some riflemen.

At the same time, Manucher Khan sent an ultimatum. If the chieftain didn't surrender, the two boys would be executed. The situation was hopeless, and still Mehmet Taki Khan dithered. Like a Persian Mussolini, Manucher Khan had threatened, promised, extorted, and while his foe hesitated, he bribed and conspired with enemy tribes so that when Mehmet Taki Khan found his will at last, his allies considered the numbers and refused to stand up with him.

Mehmet finally decided to flee while Layard was off exploring more ruins and having some minor adventures. It wasn't until the Englishman was in a bazaar in Fellahiyah that he learned the chieftain had fled to one of the marshes. Hiking past palm groves that surrounded the town, Layard and a guide made their way under a burning sun into marsh water that came up to their armpits, only mud under their feet. He arrived at last—soaked through and covered in mud—to a cluster of black Arab tents and huts constructed of mats and reeds. His old Bakhtiari friends instantly recognized him, shouting, "*Sahab ovaid!*" (The Sahib has come!).

Unusual flooding had prevented the governor's soldiers and horses from chasing down many of the escaping Bakhtiari, but raids had deprived these refugees of most of their provisions. The chieftain urged his followers to head for the mountains while he was "resigned to his fate." Pointing to snowy peaks of a summit on the horizon, he told Layard, "We shall, *in sha Allah* [if God wills], drink snow up there together before the summer is over." The rest of the family was devastated. The chieftain's brother was bitter over the loss of his own son, while Khatun-jan Khanum "was inconsolable for the loss" of Hussein Kuli.

It was an old-fashioned standoff. Mehmet Taki Khan was in a fortress of marsh where the governor's army couldn't penetrate, many of his troops dropping from malaria. But he couldn't escape either. The governor tried threats. He tried intimidating the chieftain's allies. Then he resorted to bribes and promises. Give himself up, and "all would be forgotten and forgiven." The hostages would be returned. He would be named governor of the province of Khuzistan. If he traveled to Tehran, he'd be assured of an escort for his safety, and the shah himself would invest him with a *khilat*, a robe of honor. Mehmet Taki Khan made a trip to Fellahiyah to negotiate, presuming the governor was *sincere*. How on Earth at this point could anyone in the Bakhtiari camp buy what the man was selling?

Khatun-jan certainly didn't. It drove her to exasperation, and when Layard, Mehmet Taki Khan, and the chief's brothers were all bathing down in a nearby canal, she and a group of women turned up to give her husband a thorough tongue-lashing. With Layard looking on, she blasted her husband: "You have taken my son from me, and now you would leave me and your other children without protection. Look at these families; they would not desert you in the hour of danger and will you now desert them? How can you trust to one who has already over and over foresworn himself?"

It didn't work. Mehmet Taki Khan gave himself up the next day to the governor's forces, Layard among those who accompanied him. Perhaps Layard thought—as he had during the incident with the boy, Hussein Kuli—that his presence might deter any ill treatment. If he did, he was wrong. "No sooner were we in the eunuch's presence than, addressing Mehmet Taki Khan in a loud and imperious tone, he accused him of being a rebel to the Shah and ordered him to be put in chains." The chief was dragged away without being allowed to say a word. Even the governor's own envoy, the general, was shocked by this deceit. Layard slipped out of the Persian camp unnoticed and raced back to Fellahiyah to tell his friends what happened.

Back in their camp, the Bakhtiari were cursing the governor as a dog when their enemy sent a message demanding a large sum of money in exchange for the withdrawal of his army. He wanted the rest of Mehmet Taki Khan's family and his followers handed over as well. The Bakhtiari, their Arab allies, and the chieftain's brothers all met in council to debate what to do. But there seemed to be only one sensible thing left that they could do—get Mehmet Taki Khan back.

They would launch a daring night rescue, and Henry Layard would fight right alongside them.

★   ★   ★

A scout was sent ahead to do reconnaissance on the Persian camp, and Ali Naghi Khan took chief command of the raid. Armed with matchlocks, the warriors set out into the darkness, sloshing across a ford in a canal and moving stealthily to get as close as they could to the Persian tents. Layard claimed the "camp of an Eastern army has rarely any proper outposts," which made it easier for the raiders to approach.

Once the raid started, the scene was chaos. Matchlock snipers kept up a continuous fire out of the black night. Their Arab allies had no guns, but they slashed and hacked down anyone they ran into with their swords. "Bakhtiari and Arab horsemen dashed into the encampment, yelling their war cries," wrote Layard. "The horses of the Persians, alarmed by the firing and the shouts, broke from their tethers and galloped wildly about, adding to the general disorder." Layard doesn't write whether he took part in the actual combat.

If he did, he risked starting an international incident, but then his presence alone, if made public, might do that. On the other hand, he never hesitated to defend himself and was fearless against overwhelming odds.

He does tell that he and one of the Bakhtiari chiefs rushed to where the artillery was positioned, and he was so close to the guns that he could hear the Persian general giving orders. He was "almost in front of them when the gunners were commanded to fire grape into a seething crowd, which appeared to be advancing on the [governor's] pavilion." The crowd, in fact, was made up of Persian soldiers who panicked and broke formation, and when the general gave the order, the guns blasted his own men, killing many of them.

Where in all this confusion was the key hostage? The Persians quickly guessed the purpose of the raid, and the governor ordered Mehmet Taki Khan to be dragged out of a tent and brought to him. Surrounded by his attendants, the sinister eunuch promised if the Bakhtiari managed to get close to success, he would have the chieftain put to death on the spot.

But there was no chance. The Bakhtiari kept up the fight as long as possible, but they were no match for the numbers or the guns. There was nothing for the raiders to do but slip back into the night and across the canal. Layard was among them, wading in the ford, "already crowded by the retreating Arabs."

There had been one gain. As the group reached the edge of their marsh, they discovered some Arab soldiers had rescued Mehmet Taki Khan's brother, Au Kerim, rushing him out of a tent, still in chains. Meanwhile, Layard and his friends learned that on the Persian side, Manucher Khan had slipped away with his prize hostage, while the newly appointed puppet governor of the Bakhtiari had been killed in the fighting. The Persians had won the night but suffered many casualties, and though they tried to bridge the canal to exact revenge, the Arabs beat them back. After three days, the Persians quit and left for Shuster.

The raid had failed, and Khatun-jan Khanum "was overwhelmed with despair" over the fate of Mehmet Taki Khan. Layard was deeply affected by the grief of all the Bakhtiari, "reduced from a position of comfort and comparative wealth to absolute want," relying on the Arabs even for their daily food.

Even this wasn't the end of the adventure. Layard joined Au Kerim on one last mission to negotiate for Mehmet Taki Khan's release, but they were taken prisoner by a belligerent chief of the Bahmei tribe. They escaped, but Au Kerim's horse bolted, injuring him, and the wounded warrior urged the Englishman to ride off and save himself. Layard chose to go to Shuster, right into the eunuch's den, to see what he could do. The governor put him under house arrest, but once again, Layard escaped, this time trying for Baghdad. He managed to travel with the postman hired by the Indian government through miles of hostile territory and was robbed twice, finally entering Baghdad with little more than a cloak on his back.

Then he spotted a Dr. John Ross, a surgeon attached to the British legation. "I called to him, and he turned towards me in the greatest surprise when he saw me without cover to my bare head, with naked feet and in my tattered *abba*."

Layard rested in Baghdad, writing letters home and drafting reports for the Royal Geographical Society and the Foreign Office. He hadn't forgotten about Mehmet Taki Khan, and in October 1841, he set out again for Shuster.

It was a huge risk. The governor had given orders that if the Englishman showed his face, he was to be arrested. But Layard took the gamble—after all, relations were thawing between Britain and Persia, so much so that the British government had reestablished its diplomatic mission in Tehran. Better still, when he set foot in Shuster again, he discovered that most of the Persian soldiers had been deployed elsewhere, though the local town folk were still so frightened that the bazaar was partially closed. With the help of an old ally, Layard was escorted through the castle to the small, dark room where Mehmet Taki Khan was in chains, a heavy iron collar around his neck. He put up a brave front for his guest, telling Layard, "Ya sahib! God is great, and we, His creatures, must humbly submit to His decrees. Yesterday I was great; today I am fallen. It was His will, and I must submit to my fate."

Even in this wretched state, Mehmet Taki Khan earned Layard's admiration. He whispered to his young friend how he knew Layard had entrusted some money to Khatun-jan, but because of the tribe's desperate flight and the governor confiscating everything, the sum had been lost. Mehmet handed him a written note that ordered their go-between to give Layard a special cashmere shawl as reimbursement. Layard tore up the note on the spot and told his friend to "think no more of the matter." But Mehmet couldn't lose his despair over what had happened to his people. "All his attempts to improve the country, to develop its resources, to settle the tribes and to introduce good government had thus, he said, been brought to naught."

He had messages for his wife, and Layard had no trouble tracking her down, along with the rest of the family. Khatun-jan and others were living in squalid ruins in Shuster. It was the middle of winter, and the group was without a fire, the women and children huddled together as best they could to conserve body heat. Several of the family were emaciated and suffering from dysentery; Layard noted that Khatun-jan's sister, Khanumi, had lost her beautiful looks.

Despite these horrible conditions, Khatun-jan and the others greeted Layard like a family friend. Layard went back to see them over several days. "Their affectionate gratitude to me in return for my sympathy, which was all I could give them, was most affecting. I found in these poor sufferers qualities and sentiments which would have ennobled Christian women in a civilized country." Mehmet Taki Khan's son, Hussein Kuli, experienced a better fate. He was kept under tight guard, but he was treated with kindness by Shuster nobles who were mostly sympathetic.

Of this second family, Layard wrote, "I had received from them during their prosperity a kindness and hospitality which as a European and a Christian, I could not have expected in a tribe reputed one of the most fanatical, savage and cruel in Asia. I had shared with them their dangers and their privations. I could not forget that even in moments of the greatest peril and of the greatest suffering, almost their first thought was for the safety of me—a stranger. I believed that we should never meet again."

In this, he was right. Decades later, in 1882, he looked through his old notes on his travels and wrote Ronald Thomson, London's representative in Tehran, asking him to make inquiries. For Mehmet Taki Khan, his entire world had shrunk to Tehran. After more time spent in chains, he had eventually been released, though he couldn't leave the city. As the scholar Mogens Trolle Larson put it, he lived "tolerably well" and could even indulge in horse racing. He died in 1851, and Hussein Kuli died only a handful of years later.

As for Khatun-jan, she and what remained of her close family were permitted to settle in a village near Isfahan, while others were granted leave to go back to their native mountains.

Layard would be haunted by their collective miseries for the rest of his life. Even in his memoir on his adventures, their fates were summarized in a long, narrative footnote, while the reader was left with a vivid exit scene to close the chapter. "When I left the wretched abode of the women and children," wrote Layard, "they set up their melancholy wail, beating their breasts and crying, 'Ah, sahib! We shall never see you more. *Wai! Wai!*'"

These mournful voices were the anthem for a dead dream. There would be no national homeland for the Bakhtiari tribes.

• 5 •

A Frantic Gallop through Serbia

$\mathcal{A}$s the calendar changed to 1842, Henry Layard was back in Baghdad and at loose ends. What was he to do with himself now? After all he had seen, all he had done. Becoming a lawyer was out of the question, and he had no interest in going on to Ceylon. Yes, he had a skill set, but it was only good for a narrow spectrum of professions, such as diplomacy or even espionage. He had no firm ideas, let alone a plan, on how to make a living, and it looked like he might have to return home to London.

But he wasn't in a hurry to go home. Maybe a solution would present itself in the interim. In Shuster, he had met with a few eminent locals who were interested in his elaborate ideas on how to expand trade between Khuzistan and Europe and India. Not for a moment did Layard ever see himself as a merchant, ticking off dull lists of legumes or spices, making sure shipments reached the Southampton Docks—he would have died of boredom. But he was already adjusting the vision of his future to at least entertain the notion of a desk.

He also got the chance to meet a kindred spirit who shared his passion for ancient antiquities. This was Paul-Émile Botta, who had just been appointed vice-consul for France in the region. The two liked each other immediately. For Layard, Botta "was a delightful companion." The son of an Italian historian, he had taken French citizenship and had already distinguished himself as a botanist. "He was liberal in his views, large-minded, willing to impart what he knew and ready to acknowledge the merit of others." Botta was an experienced diplomat, having served in China, where he picked up the habit of smoking opium. He urged Layard to try it, but drugs were not the Englishman's thing. One pipe later, Layard had a brutal headache and was miserably nauseous. Botta tried to persuade him that if he only gave opium another chance, he'd really like it. For Layard, once was enough.

The Frenchman had other interests, and he would soon make a name for himself in archaeology. He had initially looked to Mosul, but when sculpted slabs were discovered at Khorsabad, he focused his excavations there.

Meanwhile, it looked as if the sultan would declare war on Persia, and Britain's Resident in Baghdad, Colonel Taylor, was eager to make sure Her Majesty's ambassador to the Ottoman Empire was fully informed on how war might affect the outlying areas. So he asked Layard to start his journey home through Istanbul. Could he play courier for several dispatches? And since he would be in town, why not brief Stratford Canning on the situation? Layard naturally agreed. Here was an opportunity to stand out and be useful to the Foreign Office; maybe he could parlay that into a job.

He arrived in Istanbul tanned, tired, dirty, and unkempt, having braved the elements and choosing to travel in his usual informal style. He changed into what Western clothes were available but must have still looked shabby when he turned up at the British legation. The clerk who accepted his dispatches was a young, smartly dressed Englishman who rudely informed him that the ambassador was too busy to see anyone and then turned on his heel to walk away as Layard tried to respond.

What kind of reception was this? Layard dashed off an indignant letter of complaint to Canning more as an exercise in venting than expecting any result and went on with his preparations to head home. To his surprise, Canning sent a reply; he agreed that Layard had good reason to feel offended, and he was grateful for the dispatches. Could Layard come to see him? Layard, touched by the man's graciousness, didn't feel he could refuse and visited the embassy the next morning.

"I was greatly struck by his appearance," Layard recalled later, "and thought him one of the handsomest men I had ever seen." Layard picked up early how Canning, impressively tall, carried himself with a kind of inflated dignity, which he associated with his office and used to impress foreigners. "His earnest grey eyes seemed to penetrate into one's inner thoughts. His complexion was so fair and transparent that the least emotion—whether of pleasure or anger—was at once shown by its varying tints." As Layard was to discover, Canning felt anger often. For a diplomat, he could be unbelievably tactless and hardheaded. But he happened to be the son of an Irish merchant family that had worked its way up; he got his first job in the Foreign Office thanks to a cousin. Thankfully, he was highly intelligent.

Canning turned on the charm at their first meeting and milked the young adventurer for what he knew about the Turkish–Persian frontier. There's little doubt he recognized Layard's ambition as well as his talent, and he hoped the young man would stay in Istanbul for a few more days so they could talk again. This would have been fine, except Layard was running out of money. He

Stratford Canning, drawing by George Richmond, used as frontispiece for a biography of him.

wrote a tactful note to Canning, didn't hear from him for days, and booked passage on a steamship that would take him across the Black Sea to Galați in what is now Romania. From there, he expected to travel the winding Danube River to Vienna.

But as he stepped out to the wharf for his ship, a messenger—having tracked him down from his hotel—rushed up with a note. The ambassador thought he could use Layard's skills and suggested, "Instead of going away, come and dine here tomorrow, and I will try to arrange a plan with you." What he really had in mind was to enlist Layard on a secret mission.

★ ★ ★

Over the meal, Canning set out his scheme. While Britain and Russia dithered over the details for mediation between Turkey and Persia, Canning thought there was a high chance of a political incident or a flare-up in Bosnia and Serbia—there was already a lot of trouble in the region. He wanted Layard to travel through the area (armed with letters of introduction to Turkish officials and British consular staff) and report on conditions. "It was, however, to be clearly understood that I was to have no official character or mission," remembered Layard. As straightforward as this sounds, he would still get into trouble.

He jumped at the chance to prove himself. He took a steamship after all, only it was the *Maria Dorotea*, which left on August 20 for Salonica. His journey provided another catalog of ways that the Ottoman Empire was rotting from within. In Salonica he discovered European consuls who grew rich from selling passports to local Christians and in Thessaly how bandits preyed on the region so ruthlessly that farmers and villagers had abandoned much of it altogether; "the soil consequently remained uncultivated, and one of the richest districts in European Turkey was reduced to the conditions of a desert."

He arrived in Belgrade on October 8 to find the country in the middle of a revolution. Serbia had never been easy for the Turks to hold, and they would keep it for only twenty-five more years. In that autumn of 1842, the rebellious Serbs had tossed out Prince Mihailo Obrenović, who was considered more of a pawn of Moscow than Istanbul; there were fears Russia might even interfere to put him back in power. While the pasha for the Ottomans kept his garrison of troops in the fortress of Belgrade, his subjects in the National Assembly proclaimed Mihailo's reform-minded adjutant, Aleksandar Karadordević, their new prince.

No one was fooled by Layard's cover story that he was a mere traveler—he had, after all, come into town with letters from the British embassy for three of the top leaders of the revolution. They formed a colorful, motley crew, with a career soldier who sported two huge pistols in his wide leather belt and a lawyer who didn't know English but who had tried anyway to translate Gibbon's *Decline and Fall of the Roman Empire* into Serbian. They were eager to plead their case to a British operative, and Layard, always feeling the pull of liberal biases, felt a measure of private sympathy for them. He wasn't blind, however, to their revolutionary excesses. While accompanying one of the leaders, he saw political opponents being held in an open pit and complained so vehemently that the hostages were taken out and held elsewhere.

He could promise the rebels nothing, but he could take their messages and copies of certain documents back to Canning. He also met with the pasha of Belgrade, who provided him with a horse and escort. It's remarkable that he built up a good rapport so quickly with both sides because the British consul general, Thomas de Fornblanque, happened to be absent. Fornblanque also happened to be an idiot who had left behind a mess.

He was the descendant of a Hugenot family and the brother of a talented newspaper editor back in London. That autumn, he chose to throw out the first rule of diplomacy, which then, as now, is: *don't* make public comments on a country's internal affairs. He came out very publicly against the ousting of Mihailo Obrenović, a move which Layard accurately noted "was deeply resented" by the Serbs. Then he made the situation worse. As "a protest" and without bothering to consult Stratford Canning or Whitehall, he broke off diplomatic relations with the provisional government, lowered the Union Jack at the consulate, and left for Istanbul.

Layard rushed back to Istanbul himself to let Canning know how serious the situation was. The quickest way was by horse, using the reliable system of post stations and mounts, and the pasha of Belgrade was quite willing to provide him with a Tatar guide for much of his route. To weather "the cold in the mountains and bleak plains of Serbia," Layard now switched to Tatar clothing himself, wearing a shalwar and a pair of bulky fur-lined boots. Feeling the urgency of his news, he was once again on a hell-for-leather frantic ride, a trip he considered "one of the most breakneck and fatiguing exercises in which I was ever engaged." He wasn't exaggerating. His progress was an astonishing 100 miles a day.

It was for adventures like this that Layard was at his most compelling in his writing style. In his book *Early Adventures*, he recalled, "The Tatar . . . followed with his long whip, which he used incessantly to keep the animals in front of him to their full speed. I brought up the rear. Notwithstanding the darkness of the night and the state of the tracks, which were deep in the mud and were frequently lost altogether, we galloped as fast as the horses could carry us over rocky hills and through dense forests. I was more than once nearly swept off my saddle by the overhanging boughs and branches. Frequently, my horse stumbled on the stony ground, and my neck was in imminent peril." As they passed through a narrow, crowded bazaar, Layard's horse stumbled, and he flew over the animal's head and landed in the circle of tailors sitting cross-legged on the floor, working in their shop. Luckily, he wasn't hurt, though he probably had apologies to make.

Six days after leaving Belgrade, he reached Istanbul (feeling very proud and sure that he had beaten the record by official messengers). Canning himself could hardly believe the speed his operative had returned. Layard had built up goodwill with the revolutionaries, and he laid the foundation for a British ambassador to open talks with the Serbian provisional government, and Canning could now lobby for more humane treatment of their prisoners.

It was just as well that Layard had interrupted his mission and not moved on to Bosnia because he was about to get his first taste of how dirty politics could get. Without ever meeting him, Layard had made an enemy of Fornblanque, who earned a reprimand from Canning over his unilateral behavior and for abandoning his consulate. Canning's bad temper was legendary, so there must have been a volcanic tongue-lashing before Fornblanque was ordered to get lost and resume his duties in Belgrade. Bitter and having lost a great deal of respect from his boss and officials in Whitehall, he decided to focus all his resentment on Layard.

To be fair, he did have reason for a grudge. Canning had sent in a rank amateur to relay messages and assess *his* brief. But now Fornblanque sent a complaint to Canning and, worse, to Canning's boss in London, Foreign Secretary George Hamilton-Gordon—Lord Aberdeen. It claimed that Layard had misrepresented himself in Belgrade as an official agent of the ambassador's staff and that he carried the ruse so far that he was "promenaded" around the Serbian capital in a state carriage. The last part was fiction, but it had a nice touch of detail to make it plausible. Canning understood the spiteful motivations behind the charges. Aberdeen wasn't so easily mollified, and the bad impression stuck.

Worse, a second blow hammered Layard's reputation about the same time. All through his travels, he had drawn on his funds deposited with Coutts Bank in London, about half of the £300 given to him by his mother. This was done through a letter of credit sent along to Colonel Taylor in Baghdad. Taylor had endorsed it to an official in Isfahan but neglected to notify the bank. This was the nineteenth century, a world without credit cards, let alone automated teller machines, and Layard had needed to rely on the kindness of diplomatic contacts to advance him small sums as he jaunted along.

But Coutts had no idea what paperwork was being done on the account in the Near East, so it refused to honor the bills. Layard was shocked to learn from Canning that he "had been denounced as a swindler." In his memoirs, he recalled that Benjamin Austen apparently had no clue that his gallivanting nephew had some money but, to avoid embarrassment, moved quickly to cover the bills. This seems strange, as how did Austen imagine his nephew was supporting himself?

The humiliation was complete when Layard learned of the whole mess from Canning, who had been warned in letters that he was a crook. "I was overwhelmed with grief," Layard recalled, "and made up my mind that this unfortunate affair would have the effect of destroying his good opinion of me, and of putting an end to the career in the East to which I had looked forward with so much hope." He begged Canning not to rush to judgment while he tried to get explanations from London. It took months, but he was eventually vindicated. Coutts, being a bank, did what banks do: it claimed it had always acted according to its policies, but, *ahem*, Mr. Layard did have ample funds in his account, so the bank really ought to have . . . um . . . honored the bills. Sorry.

If Layard had money then, he didn't anymore. He was surprised that he'd managed to stretch his funds so far in two and a half years. The irony was that despite the cloud hanging over his good name, Canning made it clear he needed Layard's insight from his travels. Stick around, he told the young man in so many words, you could be useful. The carrot offered was that he could put in a good word with Aberdeen to bring Layard on staff—though Layard wouldn't get paid even if he was hired as an official attaché.

What would he live on? He didn't know, and being young, he decided to leave it up to fate. But it was his personality and charm that helped his survival rather than dumb luck. He had made good friends with an Istanbul correspondent for London's *Morning Post*, J. A. Longworth, who arranged for him to stay in the lodging house of an Armenian widow with three attractive daughters.

Through Longworth, Layard came to know one of the most important contacts of his life. This was Ahmed Vefik Pasha, and though he was barely in his twenties back then, he was intelligent, sophisticated, and everyone expected great things of him. The son of the Ottoman *chargé d'affaires* to Paris, he already had a job in the government's foreign affairs department. Longworth, Layard, and Ahmed Vefik would read the works of Gibbon and Hume together and debate issues such as free trade. His two English guests introduced him to Shakespeare's plays and the novels of Dickens, and he was so taken with *Pickwick Papers* that he quoted from the novel for days. This was an era when Europeans couldn't travel around the Golden Horn after sunset, but the rules, just as they are everywhere, bend for those with influence and power. Layard, like Longworth, got into the habit of traveling to the house of Ahmed Vefik's father and staying for a couple of nights.

It's hardly surprising that given his expansive personality, Ahmed Vefik would clash with the irritable Canning. At an embassy dinner, the conversation turned to the arrest in the Galata district of a degenerate who was either Greek or Maltese but who nonetheless had British citizenship. Canning maintained that the Turkish police should have followed bureaucratic formalities—even if these allowed the criminal to escape. As the debate got heated, Canning banged his fist on the table, demanding, "And supposing I went down myself to Galata . . . to effect the release of the prisoner. What would your authorities venture to do?"

Ahmed Vefik wouldn't be intimidated. "Why, they would probably put you . . . in the prison to join him—and they would only be doing their duty!"

Canning then had one of his signature and very undiplomatic tantrums.

Layard had come a long way from when he first showed up at the British legation in poor clothes and the dust of Mesopotamia on his feet. He made lifelong friends with several of the young men on staff, and his first introduction there became a fond inside joke. "We often laughed together over the indignant protest which my offended susceptibility had called forth." These were happy days for Layard, filled with good food and company—sometimes more than he could handle. At a formal Turkish dinner, a whirlwind of forty-two courses was served, while an Armenian wedding lasted for three whole days and nights, with exhausted performers collapsing to sleep on divans and with the *raki*, an anise-flavored alcohol popular in Turkey, still flowing.

He eked out a living, writing articles for different newspapers, such as *The Malta Times*. Canning was shrewd enough to recognize that he could get positive press out of throwing work Layard's way. There would be no objective journalism here, and Layard made it clear to his boss that "I should be able to obtain from [the papers] . . . support, and induce them to write favorably of his policy. . . . I was as good as my word, and for some time I had under my control the Constantinople correspondence of the most influential journals in England and on the continent."

There was danger, too, in the work he took on for the embassy. He acted as an off-the-books liaison to certain reform-minded Turkish statesmen. "Many a night I have spent at Constantinople or on the Bosporus, engaged on these secret missions, sometimes meeting the person to whom I had been sent in out-of-the-way places—sometimes introduced surreptitiously into their harems, where I could see them without risk of interruption or discovery." The cloak-and-dagger atmosphere of these games appealed to his boss, too. "Sir Stratford himself was fond of mystery, and nothing pleased him better than this kind of underground correspondence—not to call it intrigue—which he would carry on with the Ministers or with their opponents through a person not officially connected with the embassy. . . ."

It helped that he thought along the same lines as Canning about the future. Layard was convinced that unless the Ottoman Empire brought in "European institutions," rooted out its massive corruption, and treated its Christian subjects better, it was doomed to fall. These were the years when Turkey was the backdrop for a Cold War between superpowers Britain and Russia. Layard couldn't help but notice the differences in style between the two chess masters at the board: Canning, he judged, was "impetuous and dictatorial," hoping to "inspire them through awe," while his opposite number, Russia's Count Boutanieff, was "crafty, vigilant, far-seeing and unscrupulous," a plotter who hoped to lead "his victims by gentle and persuasive means to their destruction."

What's fascinating and tells us a little more about Layard is that he carefully noted what the *Turks* thought of these men. They appreciated Canning's honesty, but they resented his bullying; they were onto the count's fawning tactics, but "they preferred being led to being driven. In the end, the more cautious and subtle policy of the Russian triumphed."

That was not always a good thing. Layard played a major part in a dispute between Persia and the Ottoman Empire over the Kurdistan mountains and frontier territory close to the Persian Gulf. Britain and Russia were "mediating." Layard pored over the ancient maps and surveys to come up with a fair solution. He thought he found one that sided with Turkey. Back in London, however, Aberdeen didn't care about the specifics but merely wanted to placate Russia and rejected the proposed settlement. Layard came by Canning's office and found his boss "walking up and down his study like a lion in his cage." Canning exploded with rage, ranting about Aberdeen's bias toward Russia and toward Canning personally; in the end, he still had to acquiesce to his Foreign Secretary's wishes.

Layard saw this affair as another example of where Great Britain missed the boat, alienating "an old and faithful ally," one over which it had influence "far greater than that of any other European nation." The smart thing to do, he thought, would have been to side with Turkey, not only because it was ethically right but so that Britain's commerce could invest in development of the wild borderlands and have access to the waterways if they were needed in a time of war.

Here is an early sign that Layard had genuine talent for diplomacy, and he had more vision in terms of geopolitics than scholars often give him credit for.

★   ★   ★

In Istanbul, Layard soon developed a close friendship with Charles Alison, a young man with a similar rebellious streak who was working as the embassy's chief interpreter. Alison knew how to cope with Canning's irritability and bad temper while sticking up for himself and giving blunt opinions. He also had the knack of taking the wind out of the sails of others.

Layard liked to tell the story of how Alison once dealt with a grand vizier who was a notorious bigot. One time, in the middle of negotiations, the vizier excused himself to make his customary prayers, which he always ended by cursing infidels and showing his disgust by spitting over both shoulders. Alison then took a moment, went into a corner, and repeated an improvised prayer in loud Turkish, ending it with curses on the followers of Islam. When the vizier complained, Alison told him "that he had no doubt that the denunciations that they contained against Mohammedans were as much a matter of form, and of as little significance as the curses which His Highness had a short time ago launched against those who professed the Christian faith."

With Alison, Layard had a pal, a fellow expatriate with whom he could go carousing to the brothels and through the streets of Istanbul. They were free, far from home, and they needed to make some noise and lift both their lives out of the sedate office atmosphere into territory that was "reckless and riotous." And "many were the adventures we had together, some amusing, some not without risk and danger." Their standard amusement for Friday afternoons was to visit the "Sweet Waters of Asia"—a fancy name for a district where beautiful Turkish women sat on the grass, sometimes with their children, smoking shisha pipes, snacking on sherbet, and eating sweetmeats.

On one of these trips to check out the local girls, they happened to notice an aristocratic and well-dressed young woman with her attendants on a set of marble steps, about to get into a *caïque*, a traditional boat. Their target noticed these handsome strangers staring at her, and she made a point of rewarding their attention. As she casually dropped her veil to show her face, Layard saw that she was "unsurpassingly lovely." Better still, she signaled they ought to follow. Why not? The only problem was that the boat rowers for the lady were veterans of the strong current on the Bosporus, while Layard and Alison's men didn't put their back into it as much.

When the woman's boat turned towards the district of Eyüp, Layard and Alison expected their vessel to follow, but it hit something, "and a dead body rose to the surface of the water close to us." The rowers took this as an omen and refused to keep the chase going. "The ladies," they told Layard and Alison, "belonged evidently to the harem of a person of high rank, and if we were caught by the police, or were seen following them, we might incur the greatest possible danger." Eyüp was not a safe place then for Europeans, and those who dared to wander around often got a few insults and far worse hurled their way. A good taxi driver lets you know when you're straying into a bad neighborhood, and these rowers knew the turf. There was no convincing them—time to go home.

The twist came the next morning when another Turkish woman, heavily veiled, showed up at Charles Alison's house, and Layard happened to be there. She was one of the attendants for the beautiful lady but refused to give out her employer's name or her own identity. Instead, she had an invitation: the lady would be happy to receive them as guests if they visited a certain garden wicket in a street in Eyüp tomorrow. "Although the adventure was not without peril," wrote Layard, "and it was even possible that a trap might be laid for us, we determined to run the risk."

Come the hour, they were led by another attendant into a beautiful house of classic Turkish architecture, one with gilding, painted ornaments, and a ceiling of delicate mirror glass. As for their host, the lady "was young and singularly beautiful," with large, almond-shaped eyes and a pale complexion, richly dressed in traditional clothing. Alison played interpreter, and she told the pair how she'd acted on an impulsive whim in gesturing for them to follow, and given propriety, she was glad on second thought that they had been forced to turn back. But she was determined to meet these Englishmen, and she had all sorts of questions on different subjects to ask them, including matters of politics.

Everyone had a great time. They talked, they enjoyed shisha and sweetmeats, and the female servants played musical instruments. "The ladies were delighted with Alison," recalled Layard, "who spoke their language perfectly, and laughed uproariously at his jokes and anecdotes." Things even got a bit rambunctious, with the ladies' dancing turning into "a kind of romp in which all the girls took part—pelting each other with [candies] and tumbling over each other on the floor and divans amidst shouts of laughter, to the great amusement of their mistress, who encouraged them in their somewhat boisterous play."

The Englishmen stayed for close to two hours, both smitten, and she in turn made them promise to come see her again. The one problem was that she and her servants had cleverly managed to dodge every attempt to learn her name.

Layard and Alison made it safely out of Eyüp and now were determined to learn the beautiful woman's identity. They had just the source who could tell them: an old Italian matron, known as *La Guiseppina*, who kept a small hotel in what today is the Beyoğlu district of Istanbul and who moved freely in and out of most Turkish harems. Who was this charming, intellectually stimulating and gracious beauty? No problem, La Guiseppina would get back to them by the end of the day. But she returned "with a face pale with terror." Their hostess, she said, was the sister of the sultan! If Layard and Alison ever went back and were discovered, they'd wind up dead; even if word got out that they had visited her today, the scandal would lead to dangerous consequences.

Layard and Alison didn't have to be told twice. They weren't just risking their private necks but a diplomatic nightmare. From here, the story turns tragic. The sultan's sister kept sending a messenger "to reproach us for not having fulfilled our promise to see her again, and to appoint a time for meeting her." This intelligent young woman clearly led a lonely life and was looking for friends, those who could bring the outside world to her and widen her perspectives. But the risk from contact was too great, not just for Layard and Alison but for her as well. Layard subsequently learned that she was something of a proto-feminist, often refusing to wear a veil, her regular trips to the Sweet Waters of Asia acts of rebellion.

"Europeans were led to believe that the princess was a 'strong-minded' person who was seeking to reform the condition of women in Turkey," wrote Layard, "and who was herself setting an example of freedom and independence of the restraints placed upon her sex which would soon be followed by others." She was far ahead of her time, and she was eventually punished for it.

The sultan ordered her to stop appearing in public, and when she absolutely had to, she was forced to wear the thickest of veils.

"She disappeared from the scene," recalled Layard, "her vagaries were soon forgotten, and I do not know what became of her."

· *6* ·

Beginner's Luck

Meanwhile, Layard and Alison drafted up papers, did their research, and went on with their work for Canning at the British embassy. Layard was building up trust with the Great Man while moving further into the circles of the greatest statesmen in the Ottoman Empire. One of these, in fact, was Mustafa Reşid Pasha, whom most westerners won't be familiar with but who is known to Turks as one of the chief architects of constitutional reform in the country, the so-called *Tanzimat* (the word means "reorganization") of the Ottoman Empire. Layard was "constantly passing backwards and forwards" between the embassy and Reşid's house, and the two had long talks about international affairs that went far into the night.

Layard's impression of the man was that he was "morally courageous and resolute, but physically timid and weak." If Istanbul was the bridge between the cultures of Europe and Asia, Reşid squarely looked West. Sophisticated and fluent in French, he was convinced that the future of the Ottoman Empire rested in the diplomatic institutions developed in capitals such as London, Paris, Rome, and Berlin. But Layard knew that many felt Reşid "was going too fast, and that his endeavors to Europeanize the Turks were unwise and dangerous."

Layard was a witness then to the struggle for the Ottoman soul. He could even appreciate the position of the conservatives and their arguments: "I must confess that I was disposed to agree to a great extent in them." It seemed to be a matter of pragmatism for him—he didn't believe you could simply graft democratic liberalism on to a Muslim civilization in the Near East. At the same time, he knew the clock was ticking for this bloated, gradually decomposing empire, and if it didn't hurry up with *some* reforms—such as protecting and politically enfranchising its Christian subjects—it could forget any help from the European powers.

The politics aside, Layard was growing ever more attached to Istanbul. Collaborating with Canning's wife, he also worked on opening schools for children in the poorer districts of the city—ones that wouldn't make a distinction whether a student was Christian, Muslim, or Jewish.

Layard now had a room in the British embassy that overlooked a garden and a view of the Bosporus. He was doing all the work of an attaché, and his boss at least had the decency to give him "a small periodical payment out of a fund at his disposal."

Canning—who had worked in Switzerland, Spain, Russia, and the United States—was evolving into a mentor for Layard, going for rides with the young man into the countryside near the river and the Black Sea and passing along stories about his diplomatic career on missions in different countries. The only problem was that the old man was a night owl, and Layard, having to be at his beck and call, had to listen politely to his employer's bad poetry into the small hours, then settle for a quick bath in the Bosporus and "a nap on a divan" before starting the proper workday. To his credit, Canning realized in time that his subordinates were being far too kind over his verse. He decided to use an experiment to get an objective opinion and asked Layard to read a poem he claimed was written by his daughter's governess. When asked what he truly thought, Layard gave back the poetry, calling it "exceedingly ridiculous"—the young woman ought to spend her leisure time on something else. Canning burst out laughing and admitted his trick, taking it well that the joke was on himself.

But Layard was making no headway in securing a permanent position. Aberdeen, having formed his bad impression, stuck to it and wouldn't even grant him a job as an unpaid attaché. Layard was close to giving up and going home, but Canning kept persuading him to stay on.

His work at the embassy and his continuing adventures probably reminded him that his life must appear quite exotic to friends and family back home. It explains the playful manner he adopted in a correspondence with Cecilia Berkeley, a woman he knew through the Austens. "Of course, you know I have turned Musselman [Muslim]," he teased. "I say my prayers regularly—an improvement, you will say, on my former habits—I have left off wine, gin and all other ardent spirits." Which must have been easy, as there was likely little gin to be found in his part of Turkey. "A beard and a turban [increase] the usual ferocity of my countenance—and as for strangling a few young ladies or depositing them in a sack in the depths of the Bosporus—to these things, I am pretty well accustomed."[1] He would keep trying to scandalize those back home, and he suggested in another letter to Cecilia years later that his new life was "very agreeable, and the privilege of taking four wives, if not abused, that is, if the ladies do not take into their heads to abuse their lord, is a very enviable one."[2]

At the time of his letter, he was living in a small village, Candali, just outside Istanbul, where from the hill behind his cottage he could "trace the windings of the straits from their birth in the Black Sea to their junction with Marmora." When he wandered the nearby hills, he had at his feet "a thousand spots rendered sacred by the most remarkable events of two empires. On these hills, the young Armenian ladies (for my village is inhabited by Armenians) are wont to throw off their veils and sport with unconcealed charms."[3]

He lived more like an impoverished monk than a sheikh. He felt uncertain of his status, confessing to Cecilia that it would be difficult to give her an idea of what he thought he deserved, "but the probability is that I shall settle down somewhere in the East with a government appointment—something between an ambassador and a vice consul's deputy in Turkey, Asia Minor, Persia, Egypt, Syria or Mesopotamia. I cannot furnish you with any more defined ideas of my future prospects."

★   ★   ★

All this time, Paul-Émile Botta had encouraged him to come out to the site of Khorsabad for "a little archaeological fun." Layard, though he wasn't being paid, couldn't get leave from Canning to go. But Botta did pass along to Layard his letters to his superiors in France, which included descriptions of the remains he had found, along with copies of cuneiform inscriptions and drawings of the reliefs in the Palace of Sargon. He also kept his friend regularly updated, and when the time came to go public, Layard was one of the first to announce the Frenchman's achievements, writing about them in *The Malta Times* in January 1845. His stories were carried in several papers across Europe.

As glad as he was for his friend, Layard felt another surge of ambition. What about Nimrud? He should get back to it to find out what was there. Canning would soon go on leave, which would leave him at loose ends and with little to do in Istanbul, still left hanging on whether he could get a paying job at the British legation. So Layard suggested he go on a dig at the Assyrian ruins, "which M. Botta had now abandoned. I was confident that there were other mounds on the supposed site of Nineveh . . . [which] would yield no less important archaeological treasures than those discovered by him at Khorsabad."

Henry Rawlinson—who was Britain's political agent in Baghdad—had heard of Layard, read his articles, and was curious to know what this young man had discovered in his travels. Rawlinson wasn't interested in digging, in rooting around in the dust for artifacts. He was always more interested in "a respectable niche in the temple of fame," that is, literary fame for translating

Old Persian and Assyrian cuneiform. But he fully supported Layard's excavation and encouraged Canning to back him. "It pains me grievously to see the French monopolize the field, for the fruits of Botta's labors . . . are not things to pass away in a day but will constitute a national glory in future ages when perhaps the Turkish empire that we are now struggling so hard to preserve shall be but a matter of history."[4]

Layard had worked out that his excavation should cost—what with the expenses of workmen, a guard, having a tent and a horse—about £150. Canning was willing to fund him for two months, with a possible extension of ten to fourteen days if they were needed. But the money didn't amount to much; only £60, and while he might have sent along "small sums," Layard had to sometimes cover expenses out of his own meager pay and eventually even borrow money from his mother.

The work carried out was a kind of secret mission, and Layard's "cover identity" was to appear to be a casual traveler. Once he left the British legation, he didn't share his plans with anyone. The last thing that he—or the British government for that matter—needed was for the authorities to get curious about what he was up to. Why on Earth should an Englishman be poking about, digging up rocks and inscriptions? He must be up to something else, and if he worked on London's behalf, then what? There was also the matter of competition. A man named Rouet had recently taken over Botta's job as France's vice-consul at Mosul, and he was determined to keep any new glory over Assyrian discoveries for himself and for France. Discretion was essential.

Layard waited for the hot weather to pass, and then in October 1845, he was "anxious to reach the end of his journey" and crossed mountains and great steppes "as fast as post-horses could carry me." Canning sent him other instructions as well. Layard must "keep clear of political and religious questions, and as much as possible of missionaries or native chiefs and tribes regarded with enmity or jealousy by the Turkish authorities" and to "cultivate the goodwill of the pashas and others of the sultan's functionaries by all becoming means."[5] Given all that Layard had accomplished so far, these instructions were terribly patronizing. But the dig had money, it had a schedule, and Layard was on his way. He "descended the high lands into the valley of the Tigris, galloped over the vast plains of Assyria and reached Mosul in twelve days."

Once in Mosul, he quickly enlisted two useful allies. One was Christian Rassam, the ethnic Assyrian who was serving as Britain's vice-consul in the area and whose younger brother would have a greater role in Layard's life. The other was a British merchant named Henry Ross, who immediately connected with Layard and would become another dear friend. "Layard is such a nice fellow," Ross wrote to this sister, "very clever and very amusing."[6] Both men were happy to push the fiction that he was only there just to look around.

Rassam had a building business on the side, so it was easy enough to borrow some tools from his workshops for the dig. Ross, meanwhile, helped spread the word that he and Layard wanted to go hunting for wild boar along the Tigris, so he sent horses and greyhounds ahead twenty miles south to Nimrud. The real obstacle to the whole enterprise was the Ottoman's governor in Mosul, the local pasha, Mohammed Keritli Oglu.

Two days after Layard arrived in Mosul, Rassam got him in to see the governor, who was another villain straight out of the young Englishman's dog-eared copy of *The Arabian Nights*. A short, fat official with a pocked complexion, one eye and one ear, he had a loud voice and vulgar manners. Layard wrote with acid wit, "Nature had placed hypocrisy beyond his reach." When he came to power, he had the three most prominent men in the town strangled and confiscated their property. He often gave free rein to his tax collectors to act like common bandits, destroying and pillaging in their wake. One of his favorite penalties was *dish-parassi*, a tooth tax; the logic behind it was that the governor had trouble chewing the supposedly lousy food he received from the people.

The pasha was civil enough to his guest, but a deeply paranoid and suspicious man, he was anxious to know what Layard was up to. For the time being, however, he had to accept the cover story he was given. Ross and Layard were free to leave for the excavation site on November 8, floating down the Tigris on a raft loaded with their tools.

By sunset, they reached a dam and trudged their way to a village called Naifa. They were resigned to spending the night on the raft "when a glare of a fire lighted up the entrance to a miserable hovel." It was the squalid home of a sheikh and his family of the Jerash tribe, which had been oppressed and scattered by the governor's forces. The sheikh's name was Awad, and as pitiful as the conditions were for his "haggard" women and children, he welcomed them in. Thanks to the pasha's plundering, the local tribes were resorting to bandit raids themselves, almost closing off the roads to Mosul and making it unsafe. Despite all this, Awad volunteered to walk to a nearby village and to Bedouin camps to recruit workmen for the dig. Meanwhile, the two visitors could sleep in his hut.

Layard wrote that he hardly got any sleep that night; he was too excited at the prospects of discovery. "Hopes, long cherished, were now to be realized, or were to end in disappointment. Visions of palaces underground, of gigantic monsters, of sculptured figures and endless inscriptions, floated before me. . . . Exhausted, I was at length sinking into sleep when hearing the voice of Awad, I rose from my carpet and joined him outside the hovel. The day already dawned; he had returned with six Arabs who agreed for a small sum to work under my direction."

They walked for twenty minutes to the ancient mound of Nimrud, once covered with flowers but now "a parched and barren waste," over which a whirlwind dragged a cloud of sand. Like Awad's village, this place, too, was a heap of ruins. But it's important to keep in mind that the ancient city had, in fact, been much larger than its acropolis, where the palaces and temples were located.[7]

Layard had carried so much anxiety over whether there was anything to find. But the minute he stepped on the mound, he spotted fragments of pottery and bricks inscribed with cuneiform. His Arab workers watched with fascinated curiosity as he reacted with surprise and delight over these pieces. It was as if fate had seemingly laid them out for his convenience. Soon, they collected bits for him, and he discovered a marble bas-relief. He knew he was on the right track. Then Awad led him to a piece of alabaster above the ground they couldn't lift, what was clearly part of a large slab. It was time to dig. The workmen spent the morning removing the earth around it and uncovering another block. Then a third. . . . Then ten more. . . . There were inscriptions on the center of each slab. . . .

They had found one of the palaces.

★   ★   ★

Layard decided to put half his work detail on uncovering a fresh wall in the mound's southwest corner, which would turn out to be a separate palace. Unfortunately, the slabs in this spot were too cracked, so damaged by an ancient fire and vulnerable to the elements that they might fall to pieces if the men kept working. When night fell, their labors had to stop, but in a single day, Layard's dream of contributing something substantial to archaeology was a reality. True, they had yet to find any sculptures, but he could afford to be optimistic.

Others were not. Off in Baghdad, Rawlinson dashed off a note expressing his doubts. He thought Nimrud was too far from the mountains to have marble palaces, but on the positive side, he expected to crack the code soon of the Assyrian language. The excavations continued nevertheless, and on the second day, Layard found in the rubbish at the bottom of a chamber several ivory ornaments which had traces of gilding. These were the first group of what would come to be known as the Nimrud Ivories.

Awad, however, still didn't buy that Layard was interested merely in stones and sculptures, and he surreptitiously collected as many pieces of gold leaf as he could find and then drew Layard aside. He thought he knew what the Englishman was really after and warned him, ". . . Don't say anything about it to those Arabs—," meaning the workmen, "for they are asses and cannot hold their tongues. The matter will come to the ears of the pasha."

In an almost roofless hovel—what he called "a very wretched place" that had "more windows than wall"—Layard wrote a letter dated November 10 to his aunt Sara Austen, telling her what he had found. "It appears to be one great palace, principally built of marble, which has been plundered, destroyed as far as possible by fire and has remained ever since under the accumulated dust of the ages."[8] He was convinced it was the great city of Resen mentioned in the Bible's book of Genesis and supposedly built by Noah's grandson Ashur. It was inevitable that word of the discoveries would get back to Mohammed Keritli Oglu, and Layard knew that a showdown of some kind was also inevitable. On November 14, he left early in the morning and rode to Mosul, making the trip in three hours.

Layard arrived to find all of Mosul shuddering over another wave of terror. Only the day before, the pasha had spread rumors that he was on his deathbed and having his servants take care of official inquiries—just so his spies could round up those celebrating the news. Then the governor emerged healthy and triumphant and ordered half the town be tossed in prison. Meanwhile, the local *kadi*, or Islamic judge and administrator, was a fanatic who had heard that Rassam had bought an old building to use as a warehouse, and the man got it into his head that foreigners were trying to buy up "the whole of Turkey." He was busy stirring up a riot with the goal of burning down the British consulate. Into this hornet's nest walked Layard.

First, he congratulated the pasha on his speedy recovery. The pasha smiled in satisfaction—maybe the sarcasm was lost on him. Then the discussion turned to the kadi, who as it turned out was another one of the governor's enemies for whom Mohammed Keritli Oglu had nothing but contempt. Did the kadi think that he could get away with planning a riot in his town? Something like this had been tried in the pasha's previous jurisdiction, but "I took every gravestone and built up the castle walls with them."

As for the dig at Nimrud, the pasha revealed that a commander of irregular troops in a nearby village had been keeping an eye on things. Gold—this is what the pasha thought his guest was after. Since Layard wasn't, he came up with a brilliant tactic to keep the governor's agents out of his hair. He was willing to let an operative "take charge of all the precious metals that might be discovered." Satisfied with this arrangement and thinking he had outfoxed the Englishman, the pasha had no objections to the work; let the Englishman dig around in the dirt as much as he liked.

Layard moved to the half-deserted village of Selamiye, two miles from the excavation site, where he stayed in a mud hut. To escape the winter rains, he crouched in a corner and slept under a rough table he put together. But in this tiny community, he could at least get his hands on valuable staples like eggs, milk, and bread. Each morning before dawn, he rode out to the mounds of Nineveh and didn't return home until after dark.

His workmen, now mostly Nestorians who had fled oppression, were glad to have work, and on November 28, they uncovered a remarkable find: two great slabs with bas-reliefs. The carved scenes are now famous as examples of ancient Assyrian art. Here were helmeted warriors pulling their bows in chariots. And here was a fabulous city under siege from a magnificent army. The first slab, however, was so damaged by fire that Layard considered it "hopeless" to try to remove it. The second slab, too, was badly damaged, defaced in some places, and couldn't be taken away either. But he could at least sketch their scenes.

Layard wrote to his mother that the workers had also probably uncovered more than a hundred cuneiform inscriptions, which would keep him plenty busy in terms of copying. As he was contemplating his latest finds, a man named Daoud Agha, in charge of a unit of soldiers nearby, came into his hut, plunked himself down, and proceeded to give him a long lecture about his duty to the pasha, who in turn had to answer to the sultan. Layard knew where this monologue was going; his friend, Daoud, had been given orders from Mosul with the unenviable task of forcing the excavations to stop by intimidating the workmen. Having just made an important discovery, Layard wasn't about to pack it all in, and he rode to Mosul the next morning.

The pasha liked to play games, and Layard's audience with him was a kind of verbal chess. Now the governor claimed that the mound where Layard was digging was a Muslim burial ground; naturally, the Englishman couldn't disturb graves, and the kadi had already weighed in on the subject. Layard countered that there were no graves at the site, so nothing had been disturbed. The pasha then changed tack. His ruling was to protect Layard from those offended by his alleged grave vandalism: "You are my dearest and most intimate friend. If anything should happen to you, what grief should I suffer! Your life is more valuable than old stones. Besides, the responsibility would fall upon my head."

Layard pretended to go along and made a new small request. Could he have a guard detail keep an eye on the sculptures his men had already uncovered? Layard could at least draw the sculptures and copy the inscriptions. The pasha, thinking he'd won, easily consented.

But after Layard rode back to Selamiye, he was amazed to find his excavation site littered with numerous Islamic gravestones. It was a neat trick—and he got to the bottom of it right away. Daoud had been ordered to use his men for a bit of creative landscaping, swiping the grave markers from distant villages. It was a task the officer deeply resented. "We have destroyed more real tombs of the true believers in making sham ones than you could have defiled between the Zab [River] and Selamiyah. We have killed our horses and ourselves in carrying those accursed stones."

Daoud had little love or loyalty for the pasha. That evening, he and his men fought a group of Arab brigands eager to plunder Layard's cache of discoveries, but the robbers were driven back across the river. These were men who served under one of the region's sheikhs, Abd-ur-rahman, but it's unclear whether the men worked for him or for a plot of the governor.

Fortunately, Layard had a couple of countermeasures of his own. First, he wrote to Canning, who could get a firman for him from the sultan that would allow the excavations to continue. The problem was that lately Canning had his eye on some very different stones miles away.

Back in June 1844, he had sent Charles Alison out on a mission to Syria, with a side trip planned for Bodrum Castle in southwest Turkey. This used to be the site of the Mausoleum of Halicarnassus, one of the famous Seven Wonders of the Ancient World, and Alison's little detour amounted to a shopping expedition for his boss. Canning hoped—and turned out to be right—that there were marble reliefs still in good condition that could be "rescued" from damage or demolition and given to the British Museum. Could he have permission from the Turkish government to cart them away? It took two years of Ottoman bureaucracy, but the sultan would finally make a personal gift of about a dozen reliefs, ones that depicted ancient Greeks battling Amazons. At the time, however, Canning was still waiting for word. He could hardly push his luck and suggest that Layard's Nimrud finds be plucked as well.

In a letter sent about two months later to his wife and after the sultan had made his gift, it's clear where Canning's priorities always lay: "I have at last surmounted all my difficulties about the marbles at Bodrum." He was also worried sick about their transport. "Oh, if they should founder on the way to England! Think of my venturing all at my own expense! Think of the Sultan saying that he won't hear of my paying a sou!" He would be disappointed, in fact, if the latest current events were "not thrown into the shade by these celebrated marbles, which it has cost me nearly three years of patient perseverance to obtain."[9]

As for the finds so far in Nimrud, Rawlinson arranged in Baghdad for a steamship to come up in March and cart away the antiquities so that they could be unloaded in England by autumn. This would beat French efforts to exhibit their own finds, especially since Botta's sculptures still sat in Basra, waiting for transport. "I think we might manage to transmit some sculpture to Europe as soon if not sooner than the French," Layard wrote to Canning on December 1. "This would be very important for our reputation."[10] By

December 15, he told Canning the sculptures were "superior in design and execution to anything found at Khorsabad."[11]

But his work began to get bogged down. He complained in letters about the hard ground making spades useless and the need to increase the number of workmen. Canning, understandably, was concerned over the final expense. Still, he wrote Layard, "My own curiosity is not only on tiptoes, but on stilts."[12] But he made no promises on the firman and told Layard to be patient.

In the meantime, Layard had "come to an understanding" with Daoud, and it sounds like work quietly went on, and a few small bribes had worked wonders. "I continued to employ a few men to open trenches by way of experiment and was not long in discovering other sculptures." He found "gigantic figures, uninjured by fire"—a crouching lion, a pair of huge winged bulls, bas-reliefs of a couple of winged lions, and a nine-foot-tall human figure carrying a branch with three flowers. But he was careful not to expose these works completely in case word got back to the pasha.

He saved his excitement for letters to Canning and to his mother at home, whom he wrote on December 1 that he hoped "some day you will see the fruits of my labour in the British Museum or some other public place in England. You can scarcely form an idea of the perfection of the art, even in those remote days; the warriors and horses are really beautifully executed." As for the structure itself he'd uncovered, "the whole building seems to have been pillaged and burnt and nothing besides the slabs remains, except a few copper nails."[13]

With Christmas approaching, he decided to take some time off and arranged for the work at the mound to be carefully disguised and protected, with a hired man keeping an eye on things for him in Selamiyah. But when he arrived in Mosul on December 18, he was in for a surprise. Regime change. The conduct of Mohammed Keritli Oglu had finally disgusted Istanbul so much that he had been replaced. All of Mosul was celebrating. The town's inhabitants were especially pleased over his replacement as temporary governor, a Major-General Ismail Pasha, who had progressive views in the military and enjoyed a reputation for his tolerance of Christians. As for the one-eyed tyrant who had persecuted his subjects, he was tossed into a leaky, cold cell where he allegedly ranted, "Yesterday, all those dogs were kissing my feet. Today, everyone and everything falls upon me, even the rain!"

★   ★   ★

Layard decided to wait out the transitional period and spend Christmas in Baghdad. It was a shrewd choice. Henry Rawlinson was happy to have him as his personal guest at the consulate, where the two men could eagerly discuss antiquities, languages, and ancient civilizations.

Britain's man in Baghdad lived in luxury, and his official residence was a massive building that once belonged to the East India Company. It sat on the left bank of the Tigris with moorings for paddle steamers, while the compound offered a visitor a wide array of galleries and offices, intricately painted rooms in the Near Eastern style, baths, and fountains. An army of servants handled everything from kitchen care to pipe filling to stable grooming duties.[14] There were also exotic animals who had the run of the place: a pet mongoose, a domesticated black panther, and a Mesopotamian lioness, one of a smaller breed that was eventually hunted to extinction.

Layard was impressed as well with his new friend's library and wrote home to his mother, "The results of our deliberations lead me to hope that before two or three years have expired, we shall be able to get at the mysterious contents of the Assyrian cuneiform inscriptions and then Nimrud will furnish us a rich historical collection."[15]

Layard and Rawlinson, however, were fundamentally different in their characters and their attitudes. For an article in the *Journal of the Royal Asiatic Society*, Rawlinson—the polyglot who knew Persian and Hindi—once pontificated that the "discovery of an historical inscription appears to me to be of far more importance than the mere laying bare of sculpted slabs, which however interesting the design, neither furnishes us with new ideas nor convey any great historical truth."[16] Layard, of course, measured his success by finding slabs. His host was probably—hopefully—more tactful while the younger man was his houseguest, but their differing perspectives brought them into sharp conflict years later. For now, Layard could relax in splendor, conditions so much better than the rude hut he was used to.

When he returned to Mosul on New Year's Day 1846,

Henry Rawlinson at the age of forty, after a portrait by Thomas Phillips used to illustrate Rawlinson's memoir.

it was clear things would be different from now on. Ismail Pasha had no objections at all to the excavation work continuing. In fact, the new interim governor assigned a guard detail to help Layard's efforts and give him protection. An investigation was started into the ousted tyrant's ruthless taxes, and villagers began tilling the neglected farmland while Arab tribes pitched their tents once more on the banks of the Tigris.

Layard moved to another rough hut outside the village of Nimrud, one with barely any furniture and where his servants built him a crude kitchen. His grooms slept in the stalls with the horses. Hormuzd Rassam, brother of Christian Rassam, the British vice-consul at Mosul, came to live with Layard and took over managing and paying the domestic staff; it's probably from this period that their lifelong friendship really developed. Layard had a couple of greyhounds that could catch hares for a good meal, and he occasionally went hunting wild boar with a spear.

But now he had a new problem. Ever the fanatical meddler, the kadi now spread rumors that the Englishman was carting away treasure. The inscriptions supposedly proved that the infidel "Franks" once held this region, and these would be used to stake a claim and start an invasion to take back the country, slaughtering the Muslim faithful. Layard knew he couldn't afford to ignore them: "These stories, however absurd they may appear, rapidly gained ground in the town."

Hormuzd Rassam, circa 1854, photographed by Philip Delamotte.

They were enough of a problem that Ismail Pasha summoned Layard to Mosul, and while he assured Layard that he thought they were ridiculous, he had to tread carefully when it came to religious matters; he made a personal request that Layard suspend his excavations for a while. Work, however, didn't entirely stop. Layard trimmed down his labor force to escape notice, but the men soldiered on, digging trenches and finding more slabs of bas-reliefs.

Layard decided to go visit the camp of Sheikh Abd-ur-rahman, in charge of the Arab bandits who had recently tried to rob him. Given that these tribes-men regularly pitched their tents close to Nimrud, it would be a smart idea to get on their good side. So he brought gifts of a silk gown and a supply of coffee and sugar. The sheikh himself was "one of the handsomest Arabs" Layard had ever seen; a tall, well-built man of about forty with a fiercely intelligent face and an unusually clean-shaven one at that, for which Layard was to discover there was a reason.

As camels knelt on the grass outside and the Englishman relaxed on the numerous cushions and carpets, he got a sense of his host's elaborate manners. It took a while to convince Abd-ur-rahman to share a carpet with him. After Layard had his servants present his gifts, he declared that he and the sheikh were "now friends"—then gently chided the man for having tried to rob him.

The sheikh took this well, but he made no apologies. Instead, he began to tell Layard about how Mohammed Keritli Oglu had thrown him into prison and had him tortured. "Look at these hairs," he said, lifting his turban of dark linen. "They have turned white in that time, and I must now shave my beard, a shame amongst Arabs." Free but impoverished, he and his men had been reduced to stealing what they could from travelers. But he promised not to raid Layard's operations anymore.

Mission accomplished, Layard was riding back to the excavation mound on February 20 when he saw two Arabs galloping their horses toward him. "Hasten, O Bey!" shouted one of them. "Hasten to the diggers, for they have found Nimrud himself!" Then the men rode off in the direction of their tents.

When Layard got to the excavation site, he found the workmen standing near a heap of baskets and cloaks. He descended into a new trench, where he could hardly believe what they had found in the earth. There in the trench sat a stone sculpture of a human head.

★   ★   ★

"I was not surprised that the Arabs had been amazed and terrified at this ap-parition," recalled Layard. "It required no stretch of imagination to conjure up the most strange fancies. This gigantic head, blanched with age, thus rising from the bowels of the earth, might well have belonged to one of those fearful beings which are pictured in the traditions of the country, as appearing to mortals slowly ascending from the regions below." When one of his workmen first caught sight of the head, he ran off toward Mosul in a panic.

As Layard's men carted more earth away from the find, there was the sound of approaching hoofbeats. Abd-ur-rahman and half his tribe wanted to see what all the commotion was about, but it took several minutes for the sheikh to brave stepping down into the trench and confirming for himself that the head was stone. "This is not the work of men's hands," he declared. He believed instead that it had come from "infidel giants" cursed by Noah. Layard arranged for a couple of men to guard the stone head during the night while he ordered a sheep slaughtered for a feast in celebration and hired some local musicians to play dances for the gathering people. News of the discovery spread, and by morning, Arabs from the other side of the Tigris and distant villages were coming to see the sight.

Discovery of the gigantic head. Illustration from *Nineveh and Its Remains*.

The kadi also heard, and his reaction was predictable: another protest to the governor. Once again, Ismail Pasha, hoping for the public sensation to die down, asked for the work to stop. Once again, Layard gently acquiesced, went away, and was determined to discreetly carry on as he wanted. The head, as it turned out, belonged not to a bull but to a winged lion, and his men soon found another like it. By the end of March, he and his men had found a second pair of "magnificent winged lions with human heads."[17]

Word came from Botta that the French government had paid him 60,000 francs for his finds at Khorsabad, which gave Layard mixed feelings. Happy for his friend, he felt for the first time in his life that it would be nice to be rich and not simply have prestige from his archaeological discoveries. But he had to look to London for compensation, and he had no idea how much would be offered. When would Canning secure his firman? And what would he do for money? France's latest vice-consul at Mosul, a man named Guillois, had no reservations about telling Layard he intended to renew excavations started by Botta at Kuyunjik; the French were busy trying to secure their own firman in Istanbul. Layard wrote Canning that he would like to dig a few trenches at Kuyunjik before Guillois secured permission. For the time being, he was stuck in limbo.

Canning was doing his part on at least one front. He wrote to Britain's Prime Minister Robert Peel on April 18, "M. Botta's success at Nineveh has induced me to adventure in the same lottery, and my ticket has turned up a prize. On the banks of the Tigris not far from Mosul, there is a gigantic mound called *Nimrud*. My agent has succeeded in opening it here and there, and his labors have been rewarded by the discovery of many interesting sculptures and a world of inscriptions. If the excavation keeps its promise to the end, there is much reason to hope that Montagu House [the original home of the British Museum] will beat the Louvre hollow. Although the operations have hitherto proceeded at my personal expense and without any formal permission from this government, I look forward to the time when you will think it worthwhile to step in and carry off the prize on behalf of the museum."[18]

It's worth noting the language here. Canning doesn't bother to use Layard's name, and it's easy to infer from his phrasing that the entire excavation was his idea. As we'll see, these weren't oversights, and egos would flare up and reveal themselves in nasty ways down the line.

Back in Mosul, the spartan life was taking its toll on Layard, and he admitted as much in a letter to his aunt, Sara Austen. "Fancy me in a mud hut in the centre of a deserted village, for my neighbours have wisely taken to their tents. I have no companions in misfortune and am rapidly losing the little I once knew of the English language."[19] He wondered if he had any future at all, especially once the excavation was over.

Keep in mind, there was no such thing as a *professional* archaeologist—not then. The law chambers off Fleet Street were closed to him. He didn't really know business. And it was only thanks to Canning that he had wedged his foot in the door of diplomacy. If you stand even for a moment in the vast expanse of Kurdistan with its grim mountains and its plains around Mosul, it would be hard for a Victorian Englishman not to ask himself if he'd come to the end of the line.

There was, at least, the work.

Each day, he rose at dawn and had a quick cup of coffee before heading to the mound. He directed his workmen and drew inscriptions until sunset, then returned home for the sad comforts of a bath and a quick dinner, then bed. He desperately needed money and the firman. What he got was punishing heat, scorpions, gnats and sand flies, lizards, and the occasional dust storm that hurled and scattered his belongings yards away. When a storm whipped up, Layard would dive under a stone lion while his hired men crouched in the trenches, "almost suffocated and blinded by the dense cloud of fine dust."

With his dwindling funds, he decided in May it would be smart politics to hold a feast to earn the goodwill of the local Arab tribes as well as the Christian families who hadn't had the chance to see the sculptures. Layard showed everyone he knew how to throw a party. The Rassams were invited; so was the French vice-consul and his wife. White pavilions borrowed from the new permanent governor were set up on a lawn full of flowers by the riverbank. Sheikhs and chieftains arrived with their retinues, some engaging in mock war games, while Kurdish musicians entertained the guests and prompted feverish dancing and foot stomping. Fourteen sheep were roasted and boiled.

The "belle of the ball" was the wife of Guillois, and Sheikh Abd-ur-rahman couldn't take his eyes off her. "*Wallah!*" he whispered to Layard. "She is the sister of the sun! What would you have more beautiful than that? Had I a thousand purses, I would give them all for such a wife. See, her eyes are like the eyes of my mare, her hair is as bitumen, and her complexion resembles the finest Basra dates." Layard recalled that the sheikh was "almost justified in his admiration."

The whole extravagant party lasted three days, and it did the trick in helping Layard's reputation. More good news soon came. Layard had been invited to go gazelle hunting with Abd-ur-rahman, and as he lay sleeping in the sheikh's tent, a messenger woke him up with letters from Mosul. One of them was from Canning, who still hadn't won him a firman but had managed to get a letter from the grand vizier to the governor of Mosul. Layard was granted permission to keep digging and send his discoveries back to Britain. "The sincere friendship which exists firmly between the two governments obliges that such demands be granted."[20]

This loosened the chains but not the purse strings. Layard still needed money, but he was excited enough by the open terms of the letter that he seized on the opportunity to poke around Kuyunjik, much to the annoyance of Guillois. As much as the French official wanted to make trouble, however, he wasn't the one who sparked a crisis—that turned out to be Layard's old nemesis, the kadi. It happened like this:

To carry out his excavations at Kuyunjik, Layard needed to cross the Tigris twice a day, and there was a ferry service in place when the river was swollen by the spring rains. One day, with the sun going down, he and his workmen hired the last rustic vessel before it pushed off. Lately, he carried around a short, hooked stick, the kind the Bedouins used as a riding crop for their camels. A couple of Albanians had literally come close to missing the boat, but Layard gave them passage, and they were suitably grateful. The boat was about to hit the stream when Layard noticed some new arrivals who might be stuck for the night on the shore unless they were included, too. The more, the merrier, so he ordered the boatmen to go back. He must have been a little surprised to see the kadi and his retinue, but with good English manners, he invited them to come along.

The ferry crafts were spacious and deep but usually dirty and crudely built. By habit, Layard sat in the prow with the boatman, who steered. The kadi took a place just below him, and as the current became rough, he shouted out of the blue, "Shall the dogs occupy the high places, while the true believers have to stand below?" And then he muttered a few more insults about Christians. Layard, dumbfounded at the man's abuse and lack of gratitude, lost his temper and gave him a whack in the head with his stick.

He didn't mean to hit the kadi so hard, especially as the man wore a thick turban, but Layard was "surprised to see the blood streaming down his face." Now the situation was like a brawl on a pirate deck: the kadi's men drew their swords and pistols, squaring off with Layard's workmen, while the Albanians, who already liked this Englishman, drew *their* weapons—and they were better armed. As for Layard, he jumped into the center of the main deck, grabbed the kadi by the throat, and threatened to toss him into the river if his attendants didn't back down.

He wasn't out of trouble yet, and he knew it. As soon the ferry reached the opposite bank and Layard let go, the kadi—blood still on his face—rushed through the bazaars and streets of Mosul, shouting that he'd been assaulted by an infidel and that the Prophet and Islam had been insulted.

Layard rode as quickly as he could to brief Ismail Pasha, who had grown to detest the kadi almost as much as everyone else. Given the fanatic's insult, said Ismail Pasha, Layard was entirely justified in punishing him not only for himself but for all Christians who were subjects under the Turkish constitution.

Then the governor summoned the chief of police to make sure Layard was protected, and he offered to put him up for the night in his residence. Layard being Layard, he wouldn't back down and decided to sleep in his own house. The Albanians also "seemed determined to stick to me and to see me safely through the affair." Still, Christian Rassam paid the governor a call to offer a delicate apology for the Englishman's rash behavior.

Soldiers and police kept Layard safe from everything in the streets except ugly looks, but he still received intelligence that a core group of zealots loyal to the kadi were hatching plots and possibly his assassination. His source was impeccable. "I had by a singular chance made the acquaintance of the daughter of the kadi himself, who came frequently to see me, notwithstanding the great risk she ran. As she knew all that was passing in her father's house, she kept me fully informed of what was going on against me."

For a while, there was talk of his staying with Rawlinson in Baghdad until things died down. Rawlinson himself scolded Layard in a letter: "The insult was certainly gross, but no provocation justifies personal violence and viewing the case as I do at present, I am inclined to think Rassam was right in apologizing."[21] Layard, however, wouldn't budge; he had no intention of hiding out in Baghdad. It wasn't bravado this time—he correctly appraised his enemy and knew it looked better to stay put than turn tail. The kadi was so unpopular in Mosul that his rantings never built further momentum.

A complaint about Layard did manage to reach the desk of Stratford Canning in Istanbul . . . who couldn't have cared less. His reaction was to send word through Charles Alison, who passed on a quiet message that amounted to yes, *unofficially* the fool deserved what he got, but Layard ought to be more cautious in the future.

· 7 ·

Devil Worshippers

That same month, Botta's finds from Khorsabad sailed at last on a frigate to work their way to France. Layard had lost his shot to be the first with Assyrian treasures, but he could still make an impression. His men carefully packed up his discoveries in crates to be sent on the river to Rawlinson in Baghdad, but it's a small miracle even this happened. Layard was flat broke over the enterprise; he had to borrow £100 from his mother to help with the freight costs.[1] In July alone, twelve crates were drifting down the Tigris.

But when Rawlinson finally inspected them, he showed an appalling lack of tact, informing Layard in a letter in August that "the battle pieces . . . are curious, but I do not think they rank very highly as art. Ross is altogether disappointed with the specimens and I must confess I think the general style crude & cramped, but still the curiosity of the thing is very great, if not a full compensation."[2] Imagine Layard reading these lines in a remote stretch of country where the sun got up to a blistering 50° Celsius. All that expense, all that effort, and here was his friend and colleague's verdict.

Despite all the boxes of correspondence held by the British Library, we don't know what Layard wrote back, but Rawlinson soon realized he ought to backpedal and assuage the younger man's hurt feelings. "I am sorry you have taken such desperate alarms at my criticisms," he wrote. "I never pretended to depreciate the *value* of the marbles [emphasis in the original]. I merely objected to their style & execution, which in my opinion have nothing whatever to do with value." After some more comments on aesthetics, he assured Layard that the Nimrud slabs were "invaluable" and that their real value was in unlocking historical information. What is particularly telling is that he went on to write, "Heaven forefend that I should do anything to impede the excavations."[3]

Layard must have worried—and expressed his fears—that Rawlinson's initial judgment could force the dig to shut down altogether. Fortunately, it didn't.

To be fair, Rawlinson was no different than the rest of the experts and critics in London in this era. The British government had bought the Elgin Marbles only forty years before, and the art of ancient Greece was widely considered at the time to be the ultimate ideal. The British considered themselves the natural heirs to a culture of democracy, philosophy, architecture, and other studies, and a casual stroll around London took visitors past neoclassical pillars and colonnades in a variety of buildings, from Somerset House to Greenwich Hospital to many other examples.

But Layard's finds would be a revelation. Here was a new kind of art, here were scenes from an empire people had read about in the Bible. He wrote to his aunt, Sara Austen, on July 27 that the discovery and opening of another chamber "is already beginning to make a noise in Europe, and every post brings me letters from people wanting information and offering (scientific) assistance. I only hope that as much interest will be excited in England as on the Continent, and that the government will not be able to back out of the matter."[4] Even at this stage and with his notoriety growing, he feared authorities might abandon him.

The oppressive heat now made any work impossible, and Layard was run down, his health failing. Looking for a cooler climate to pass the time, he decided to journey into the Tiyari mountainous region and visit the area inhabited by Nestorians or Chaldean Christians. Many of the workmen for his dig were, in fact, Chaldean, and so was young Hormuzd Rassam, whom he took along on the journey. Today, we often hear about the Chaldeans because the terrorist group ISIS has targeted them, but in fact, the wholesale culling of their numbers had started after the fall of Saddam Hussein. And persecution of them had been going on long before that, as Layard discovered.

The Kurds, emboldened by the example of Egyptian revolt against the Ottomans (despite its eventual failure), resented the Nestorians and Chaldeans for not helping them with their own uprising. Layard was likely the first visitor to the mountains since a Kurdish emir, Badr Khan Beg (whom Layard refers to in his texts as Beder Khan Bey), led his soldiers in an attack that slaughtered an estimated 10,000 Nestorian faithful in 1843. While the death toll may be uncertain, we know for a fact that a massacre took place. Layard himself explored ruins and burned-out houses. "The slaughter," he wrote to Sara Austen, ". . . must have been immense. In one spot, I saw the bones of about 800 persons—men, women and children (the Nestorians say 2,000) still exposed—heaped up with the tresses of women, ragged garments and old shoes. The villages are deserted, the houses in ruins and fine old trees level with the ground."[5]

Badr Khan Beg also dragged off numerous girls and children who would have been condemned to slavery had Stratford Canning not petitioned the Turkish government to intervene. A commissioner was sent out to appeal to the emir's basic instincts—that is, the man's avarice—and negotiate a hefty ransom plus payments to other Kurdish chiefs to liberate their slaves. Christian Rassam also worked to free others. He even supplied clothing and other provisions for many of them over several months, including the Nestorian Patriarch. But buying off a genocidal rebel was never going to work in the long term, and it wasn't long before Badr Khan Beg was on the warpath again until he was finally defeated and sent off to exile in Crete.

Now that the region was back to relative stability, Layard had the chance to take in the country and the customs of the people. He wrote home that he thoroughly enjoyed himself, and the simplicity of the Nestorian religious practices appealed to him. Though raised with exposure to other cultures and religions, he couldn't shed completely the inherent biases of his Protestant English roots. Even these foreign rites were superior to "the superstitions and ridiculous ceremonies of the Roman Catholic and other sects of the East." Unfortunately, he couldn't find one of their holy books, as the Kurds had destroyed the entire library of the patriarch in the massacre.

Not long after he returned to Mosul, he and Christian Rassam both got an invitation to attend the great feast of the Yezidis. Here is another ancient people whose modern descendants have become victims of the recent turmoil in Iraq. Few people in North America and Western Europe had probably ever heard of them ten years ago, but such has been the scale of the persecution that it's been the introduction to their existence. Ethnically, the Yezidis are Kurds, a defiantly independent people who earned the wrath and poison gas of Saddam Hussein's forces. Most Kurdish people, however, are Sunni Muslim. So Yezidis have been a persecuted minority within an already persecuted people. Thousands have been slaughtered within the past few years, and ISIS forced its male captives to fight in its ranks while keeping female prisoners in sexual enslavement.[6]

Even today, the old slur of "devil worshippers" for their unique religious beliefs has sometimes cropped up in headlines for the sake of ironic, eye-catching effect. A writer for *National Geographic News*, Avi Asher-Schapiro, got to the heart of the religious issue quite succinctly for a brief article in 2014: "While the Yezidis believe in one god, a central figure in their faith is Tawusî Melek, an angel who defies God and serves as an intermediary between man and the divine. To Muslims, the Yezidi account of Tawusî Melek often sounds like the Koranic rendering of Shaytan—the devil—even though Tawusî Melek is a force for good in the Yezidi religion."[7] Tawusî Melek, sometimes rendered as "Melek Taus," is also known as the Peacock

Angel. They apparently have taboos about pouring hot liquids on the ground and have prayers that can involve kissing the neck of a sacred shirt. Fire is considered a divine manifestation.

So Yezidis were being called "devil worshippers" way back when the invitation was sent for the feast. Rassam couldn't go on the trip, and Layard, intensely curious about the people, went alone with the vice-consul's guide and interpreter to learn what he could about these people.

Past Khorsabad, they reached the village of Baadri, where the Yezidi religious chief, Sheikh Nasr, and their political leader, Hussein Bey, greeted him like an honored guest. The next morning, in fact, Layard found himself swept up in a ceremony that was a kind of informal christening for a newborn, though he was assured the proper baptism would take place days later. While Layard wanted to be respectful of their beliefs, he "was naturally anxious to ascertain the amount of responsibility which I might incur, in standing god-father to a devil-worshipping baby." The officials put his mind at rest; all he had to do was select a name, and Layard—probably to ingratiate himself with his hosts—picked Hussein Bey. Everyone was satisfied, there was great applause, and Layard was told that the child's mother was thrilled. Invited to the harem, Layard was brought honey and dried figs and told entertaining stories until he thought he better get back to the *salamlik*, the formal reception room.

He went to visit the Sheikh Adi, the great temple of the Yezidis for their annual festival, and in a letter to Sara Austen, he declared that "I never witnessed a more curious or interesting sight." About 6,000 people had gathered for the event. He watched as black-turbaned priests in coarse, brown garments carried lamps through the ranks of the faithful, who passed their right hands through the flames and then rubbed their right eyebrows. He was offered helpings from the platters of boiled rice and roast meat and heard slow and sweet, dirge-like melodies.

As night fell, torches were carried through the nearby forest, and the effect was "magical . . . Thousands of lights were reflected in the fountains and streams, glimmered amongst the foliage of the trees and danced in the distance." Layard saw nothing that qualified as an indecent gesture or perverse ceremony—quite the contrary. "So far from Sheikh Adi being the scene of the orgies attributed to the Yezidis, the whole valley is held sacred, and no acts, such as the Jewish law has declared to be impure, are permitted within the sacred precincts."

He stayed for three days at the temple and explored the valley and surrounding mountains. With no Muslims or Christians nearby, the Yezidi women went about their business in the mountains unveiled. Once, as Layard rested under the trees, a group of girls satisfied their curiosity, examining his clothes and asking him all sorts of questions. The bolder ones gave him their strings of beads and engraved stones, while the more cautious girls stood off, "weaving wild flowers into their hair." As for the men, Layard noted how they happily chatted near fountains, with priests and sheikhs easily mixing with their ranks.

He wrote Sara Austen that "I never received more kindness than from these poor people, and there was so much good humour and quiet enjoyment everywhere displayed that I feel very much inclined to turn devil worshipper myself."[8]

★   ★   ★

In Mosul, a new permanent governor had recently been installed, an old-school Turkish aristocrat named Tahyar Pasha, whom Layard considered "bland and polished in his manners, courteous to Europeans and well-informed on subjects connected with the literature and history of his country." Tahyar Pasha was planning an expedition into the Sinjar Mountains, partly to get an idea of the state of the country and to deal with the aftermath of his cruel predecessor. Layard asked for and got permission to come along.

On the day of departure, Layard noticed a ridiculously elaborate entourage attached to the pasha. "The attendants of his Excellency were hurrying to and fro, laden with every variety of utensil and instrument; some carrying gigantic telescopes or huge bowls in leather cases; others laboring under bundles of pipe-sticks, or bending under the weight of calico bags crammed with state documents." There was "the lord of the towel, the lord of the washing-basin, the lord of the cloak, the chief of the coffee-makers and the chief of the pipe-bearers, the treasurer and seal-bearer." Though the governor was an older, studious "man of the pen," Layard found him strutting about with his sword and spurs, being followed around by clerks and inkstand bearers.

The procession rode for hours over the countryside, with Layard able to spot ancient mounds that demonstrated all this land once belonged to the Assyrian Empire. They eventually stopped at Tel Afar, where Layard climbed to the top of its citadel and explored its castle, finding a wonderful view of the plains stretching west toward the Euphrates. Few could imagine how this Ottoman fortress would become important again to warfare more than a century later. It was used to house the municipal and police headquarters during the 2003 invasion of Iraq, and tragically, in 2014, ISIS destroyed large parts of its walls with bombs.[9]

The governor's procession moved on to a village called Mirkan, one of the main Yezidi settlements in the mountains. Chiefs from other communities came out to pay their respects, but there was no delegation from Mirkan—its inhabitants had known only the butchery and hate of the governor's predecessors.

Instead, they sent word they would defend their village. Tahyar Pasha sent a small delegation with a reply that he meant no harm, and Layard went with them. When two horsemen arrogantly pulled ahead of the officer in charge, they were shot down on the spot. Then others were wounded, and the detail had to fall back. The pasha got fed up and ordered an all-out attack, but by now, most of the Yezidi had taken up defensive positions in nearby caverns.

Now their village was set ablaze, and even the pasha helped light abandoned houses with a torch. A few old men and women were bullied and paraded about, and Layard appealed to the pasha to order his men to bury the slain, but the troops ignored the governor's order for hours. The next morning, the small army tried to advance on the gorge where the Yezidi were dug in, but the town folk turned out to be skilled guerrilla fighters and ruthless snipers. As far as Layard could tell, a whole day passed without a single Yezidi getting shot. The next morning, the pasha ordered the attack to resume.

"To encourage his men, he advanced himself into the gorge and directed his carpet to be spread on a rock. Here he sat with the greatest apathy, smoking his pipe and carrying on a frivolous conversation with me, although he was the object of the aim of the Yezidis." As they lingered, men a few feet away dropped dead while the sniper fire kicked up the dust in their faces. But they might as well have been in a café—coffee was brought, the pasha's pipe refilled with tobacco. "I have frequently seen similar instances of calm indifference in the midst of danger amongst Turks when such displays were scarcely called for," wrote Layard, "and would be very unwillingly made by a European."

As the stalemate went on, the local kadi reminded the governor that slaying the Yezidi infidels would win the holy warriors a trip to Paradise. Tahyar Pasha asked him in turn, "If I swore an oath to these unbelieving Yezidis and in consequence thereof, believing their lives to be secure, they should surrender, how far am I bound thereby?" It seems the pasha wanted to know how far he should extend protection to what was a widely hated and oppressed sect.

The kadi's logic went like this: the Yezidi were infidels, so they couldn't understand the true nature of God, which meant they couldn't understand the true nature of an oath. That meant it wasn't binding on them, which meant it wasn't binding on the governor, so he was free to break his word and slaughter them. In fact, he should. As soon as the kadi went away, however, the governor condemned the idea of such atrocities to Layard and assured him that the man "was an ass." Even more interestingly, Layard made a point of telling his reader in *Nineveh and Its Remains* that the kadi was typical of only the religious fanatics in the border towns of Kurdistan trying to whip up hatred against Christians. "I need scarcely say that the abominable opinions which they profess are not shared by any respectable Turk or [Muslim]."

In the end, the issue was moot. When the attack was resumed the next morning, the soldiers soon realized there was no return fire. The caves were abandoned; their enemy had fled with expert stealth. Layard, after having a look around at other parts of the district, decided he should go back to Mosul. And there, he discovered four letters from Canning in London written over August and September that would change his life.

★ ★ ★

Canning's efforts to win support for Layard's excavations had paid off—but only so much. "The British Museum undertakes Nimrud in my stead," he wrote Layard. "The Treasury allows £2,000. You are the agent. You will have £500 for yourself, besides £100 for your expenses home. My outlay will be repaid."[10] That meant the Trustees of the British Museum would reimburse Canning £400. They did not think to reimburse Layard for *his* out-of-pocket expenses. They also earmarked only £1,000 for the rest of the costs of the excavation. And they assigned a hard deadline for completion, June 30, 1847, which gave Layard only ten months.

Layard was angry and disappointed. He could point to the French, whose government had the foresight and generosity to allocate £5,000 on Khorsabad. And the Trustees wanted him to resurrect Nineveh on a pitiful £100 a month? He expected to employ more than 100 workmen, and though he paid many of them small wages, the cost still added up to £5 a day; then there was the cost of packing, construction of the rafts to carry all the material downriver, and his own living expenses.

No one at that time considered it a good deal. Canning himself recognized its miserly terms and suggested to Layard not to complain about the details. He knew his protégé well, and he decided to reinforce his warning days later: "I shall be disappointed if you are not satisfied."[11] Layard was definitely *not* satisfied and couldn't resist complaining to the Trustees. From his perspective, he had little to lose. Their accounting simply didn't make sense, making the work impossible to complete. But the money was only one issue. Office politics was another. His friend Charles Alison had been looking out for him and had kept an eye on the correspondence. He warned Layard in early December that "Sir S.C. is very jealous and suspicious as you know, fearful above all things that his part in this concern should be lost in yours; he therefore gives it as his discovery, mentions you as superintending the excavations, and the clerk draws out the instructions as if he were addressing them to a log of wood."[12]

The Trustees would probably have given more respect to a log. Canning was their man, and they made it clear that when the work was over, they considered it "impossible to provide in any way for Mr. Layard's further employment." The very last paragraph of their offer read, "The Trustees wish that every cause of offence should be avoided as well to the authorities as to the population, and particularly that proper respect should be paid to the religious feeling and habitual prejudices of all, whether Mohammedans or Christians. It will be very gratifying to the Trustees to find when the operations on which Mr. Layard is engaged are concluded that his prudence and good feeling have enabled him to leave in Kurdistan an impression entirely favorable to the English character."[13]

And there it was. A clear tip-off that his ugly confrontation with the kadi on the Tigris was still making the rounds and had damaged his reputation.

And it got worse. The museum's secretary was a man named Josiah Forshall, who had lived his life between dusty shelves and had never spent a day in a distant land on an archaeological dig. But Forshall devoted seven numbingly turgid, pedantic pages to lecturing the new agent on how to do his job: "The first object of the Museum is the preservation of monuments of antiquity. Mr. Layard will therefore be extremely careful not to injure any sculptures, inscriptions or other objects." If he found he was in competition with "agents of other European powers" (i.e., the French), he should "maintain a spirit and bearing of honorable liberality." This is a peculiar instruction given that the whole point of the mission was to increase the prestige of the museum. Forshall also thought that while Layard was there, his conduct ought to "teach the natives some respect for the remains of the great works of art executed by the early occupiers of their country . . ."[14]

Layard was furious. He wrote to his uncle, Benjamin Austen, how the museum treated him like a bricklayer. Even Rawlinson, when he eventually got to read the text of Forshall's letter, called it "thoroughly disgusting." If he had been sent a letter like that, he told Layard, he would have been tempted to mail it back without a response. "Those lousy English Commissioners."[15]

His old pal Alison reminded Layard he should keep his eyes on the prize: "This Nimrud thing is only a means to procure something else, and if that something comes out of it, I would be content to see all your stones at the bottom of the Red Sea. In what can the stones themselves and all the reputation connected with such things avail a man who has to make his way in the world?"[16]

The situation was bad enough for Benjamin Austen to visit Canning at his house in Grosvenor Square and try advocating for his nephew. He also had some out-of-the-box thinking to offer. Why not give his discoveries to the French? He thought it would serve the museum right. It was more than doable. Layard could have easily written and published his findings in French, a language he spoke as well as his mother tongue. Botta would have been delighted and likely helped. But such a move would no doubt have killed any possibility of Layard finally securing a Foreign Office career, and it likely would have made him a social pariah in London.

But Layard did have other allies, and his name was beginning to get tossed around more frequently in London. One of the popular magazines of the time was *The Athenaeum*, which offered a progress report on the excavations in early October along with a scathing criticism of the government and museum's parsimony: "It is painful after witnessing [the] munificent patronage of science by the French government to think that up to this moment, nothing whatever has been done to assist Mr. Layard in his researches by our own." It was true, the magazine noted, that Canning had dug into his own pockets, but "you can imagine how mortifying it must be to Mr. Layard to find after a year's indefatigable exertions—crowned too with such brilliant results—that nothing has been done by the British Government to mark its interest in his labors."[17]

Weeks later, his friend, architect George Mair, sang his praises at a meeting of the Royal Institute of Architects in November, passing along his descriptions and drawings of the Parthian ruins in Hatra and reading out a letter from Layard about his findings at Nineveh. The report got an impressive degree of coverage from the press, including, once again, *The Athenaeum*: "Mr. Mair exhibited to the meeting drawings of one of the bas-reliefs representing chariots and warriors, and of one of the winged, human-headed lions—which excited considerable attention and curiosity."[18]

In the end, Layard agreed to work for the museum, though he pushed for better terms. Forget his compensation, at least for now, he would put their funds toward the daunting expenses of the excavation.

It took ages, of course, for exchanges of letters, and when Layard finally heard from the Trustees (in a response from late January), he must have been frustrated all over again. No, he could not do his work pro bono, he had to accept their offer of £500, and no, he could not dip into it to cover his expenses; those had to be drawn from the other fund. Their one concession was that his travel costs and the costs for the shipping would now be reimbursed separately—but he had to supply them with a detailed budget for the transport of the large lion and bull sculptures *first*. And while he was at it, they expected him to make regular reports with thorough accounting.

In addition to the physical miracle of bringing Nineveh back to life in London, they expected a financial miracle in doing it.

★   ★   ★

As November began, the excavations took on a new character, with Layard focusing on Nimrud.

He arranged to have a mud-brick house built for himself, and Henry Ross later described the slapdash manner of the construction. "It was run up in a hurry, the bricks were not properly dried, and it rained before the roof was done." The inside was lined with "sprouting barley" which kept growing and "hung down the walls in fantastic festoons."[19] A similar set of houses were built for his Nestorian workers overlooking the first pair of winged lions to be discovered as well as a guesthouse. About forty tents for workers were pitched on the mound, while forty more went up in the village near his house, all the men armed to defend the site. He also recruited his own head of security—a standard-bearer, or *bairakdar*, from the irregular troops in Mosul. The man's name was Muhammed Agha, and Layard wrote that he had seen "convincing proofs" of the man's courage on his trip to Sinjar.

Young Hormuzd Rassam served as accountant and paymaster. "He soon obtained an extraordinary influence amongst the Arabs, and his fame spread through the desert." Layard cunningly (and somewhat ruthlessly) mixed up the ethnicity of his workers, scattering men who belonged to tribes that were hostile to each other so he "could easily learn if there were plots brewing and could detect those who might attempt to appropriate any relics discovered during the excavations." But the boss wasn't above picking up a shovel himself, and he supervised the work closely. He wanted to make sure no zealous worker ruined a sculpture with a careless swing of his pick. The museum also didn't care enough about the dig to send an artist, so Layard filled that role and made crude casts of sculptures and inscriptions with "brown paper simply damped and impressed . . . with a hard brush."

The verdict of *The Oxford Companion to Archaeology*—even though it considers Layard one of "the immortals" of the field in its infancy—is that "his excavation methods were brutal by modern standard."[20] As many others have pointed out, he was treasure hunting more than conducting field research. He was on the tightest of budgets and schedules, and neither allowed him to fully explore the palaces and their chambers. Instead, he dug along walls, using trenches, looking haphazardly for sculptures and bas-reliefs, and he didn't bother to cart away the earth inside the chambers. "Thus, few of the chambers were fully explored," he admitted, "and many small objects of great interest may have been left undiscovered." In this, he was right. In 1949, the British School of Archaeology returned to the site and found additional impressive ivories.

It must have been frustrating to stand sweating in the heat, staring at a buried palace and knowing he simply didn't have the time or the means. In *Nineveh and Its Remains*, he wrote, "I felt myself compelled, much against my inclination, to abandon the excavations in this part of the mound after uncovering portions of two chambers."

Despite the restrictions and setbacks, though, Layard was happy with his progress. "Every day produced some new discovery." His Arab workmen became almost as emotionally invested as their boss. The workers spent many meals with a simple jug of water being passed around as the only beverage and tall stories begun that would be continued the next day in the style of *The Arabian Nights*. "The Arabs are naturally hospitable and generous," he noted. They shared what they had, and Layard was invited frequently to join them. In turn, he endeavored, "as far as it was within my power, to create a good feeling amongst all and to obtain their willing cooperation in my work." He had great instincts for how to boost morale. If a peddler from Mosul came by with a donkey carrying dates and raisins, Layard bought up the stock to distribute among the men.

"In the evening, I receive the Arabs and others of the neighborhood, hear complaints and dispense justice," he wrote his Aunt Sara on July 27. The Arabs preferred having him adjudicate because Layard didn't take bribes or charge fees. His judgments were never appealed "and are generally executed with great promptitude and alacrity." Like *My Fair Lady*'s Henry Higgins, he saw women as "the great fomenters of dissensions and the principal source of violence and wrong. Cases of abduction occur very frequently, and it is a melancholy fact that scarcely a day passes without a Helen [of Troy] and Paris case." Knowing he couldn't impose his own values, he tried to judge according to theirs but "raised the value of a respectable female to twenty sheep" to deter more quarrels.

But he didn't ignore the incredibly hard life of the women. "They were obliged to look after the children, to make the bread, to fetch water and to cut wood, which they brought home from afar on their heads." The women carried babies and small toddlers on their backs even while they performed heavy tasks, such as loading pack animals or raising tents. "The men sat indolently by, smoking their pipes or listening to the gossip of some stray Arab of the desert."

He managed to enact a few reforms on their behalf. He relieved them of the arduous task of carrying water from the river; horses and donkeys could carry the full goatskins. He punished men who beat their wives. In time, the women brought him any complaints about their husbands. But they also understood that one day the Englishman would go home. "But what shall we do when you leave us?" they asked him. "Which God forbid you should ever do." It says a lot about how accepted Layard was in the small community.

Meanwhile, the work went on. It was in the center of the mound where Layard made one of the greatest discoveries in archaeology. Working on the logic that the pair of winged bulls he'd found earlier flanked the entrance to a building, he dug around the sculptures, expecting to find the remains of walls. No luck. Instead, Layard came back from an errand in Mosul to learn that his workmen had discovered a black obelisk—six feet, six inches long—lying on its side in a trench, perfectly preserved.

It had long cuneiform inscriptions, plus five relief scenes on each of its four sides, "and the figures were as sharp and well defined as if they had been carved but a few days before." They depict five different kings offering tribute and prostrating before a powerful Assyrian ruler, identified eventually as Shalmaneser III. Brought before the king was a menagerie of exotic animals—an elephant, rhino, Bactrian camel, ibex, baboons, and monkeys. Layard theorized that the obelisk might have been built and decorated to commemorate the conquest of India or another Near Eastern kingdom. (Today, it's thought to have been erected around 825 BCE.) But its special significance comes from one of the men bowing on his knees in front of Shalmaneser. This is generally thought to be Jehu, a king of Israel who switched alliances from the Phoenicians to the Assyrians—which would make the monolith one of the earliest depictions of a figure from the Old Testament.

It would take some time to decipher the obelisk, but after it was shipped to Baghdad, Rawlinson was ecstatic and recognized the monolith's importance. "It is, I conceive, the most noble trophy in the world and would alone have been well worth the whole expense of excavating Nimrud."[21]

Layard kept digging away. "The whole entrance was buried in charcoal and had evidently been destroyed by fire." In the debris of the mysterious blaze, he found a pair of winged sphinxes. One of them "had been nearly reduced to lime," but Layard hoped to rescue the other one. "I endeavored to secure it with rods of iron and wooden planks, but the alabaster was too much decomposed to resist exposure to the atmosphere. I had scarcely time to make a careful drawing before the whole fell to pieces; the fragments were too small . . . [for] future restoration." Fate compensated him with more modest finds—rummaging through the charcoal, he picked up a small head of alabaster and then a smaller replica of a winged sphinx.

It took five months to send another shipment, mainly because it was so difficult to find mats, felts, rope, and other packing materials. When Layard did, he learned that his workmen in Mosul—who were afraid to cross the dam in the dark—had left their goods on a raft tied to the shore only to be robbed by a group of bandits. "I appealed to the Turkish authorities, but in vain," Layard recalled. "The Arabs of the desert, they said, were beyond their reach." Layard didn't like the idea of his mats furnishing robbers' tents; if he let this matter slide, it might easily happen again. He decided to do a little amateur sleuthing and soon learned who was responsible. With his *cawass*, his guide, and his tough veteran of the irregulars, Muhammed Agha, he rode out at dawn into the desert to hunt down the tribe. They turned out to have more men than expected, but Layard, ever impetuous, marched into the sheikh's tent and sat down.

He couldn't come out and slander the sheikh as a thief. Instead, he made the usual courtesies, acknowledged the custom of "what's mine is yours, what's yours, etc." in the desert, but pointed out the tribe hardly needed the materials they had swiped from the raft. The sheikh tried a bluff; oh, no, he didn't have such things, go ahead and look. It was a darkly comical moment since Layard and his men spotted one of his newly purchased ropes supporting a tent pole. Fine, Layard told him in so many words, the governor of Mosul could sort things out, and Muhammed Agha promptly slapped handcuffs on the sheikh and dragged him outside. His men were dumbfounded and rushed out of the tent. They had the numbers and were better armed, but most of them were too shocked to take any action.

"Now, my sons," said Layard with swashbuckling aplomb, taking his time as he mounted his horse, "I have found a part of that which I wanted. You must search for the rest."

The bairakdar had his pistol cocked and ready, already trotting his horse away with the sheikh uncomfortably behind him. One of the tribesman tried to grab the bridle of Layard's horse, but the cawass gave him a snap of his rhinoceros-hide whip across the back. And then they were off. The sheikh, who had been preying on villages near and far, was scared witless of ending up in front of the governor, and along the way, Layard began spinning tales of what the man could expect from a stay in the Mosul prison.

By the time the group reached Nimrud, the sheikh made a full confession and sent word back to his tribe. The next day, Layard found a donkey in his courtyard, loaded with the stolen items, along with a lamb and a baby goat as a peace offering. Layard's dig would have no more trouble from the sheikh—or from any of the other marauding tribes in the region.

★   ★   ★

Layard celebrated the Feast of the Nativity with Christian Rassam and his family in Mosul, but over Christmas, he kept a steady pace of writing notes, filling in the tedious accounting ledgers, and writing up a report to London on his progress. On New Year's Day 1847, he was hard again at the excavations in Nimrud. And in his very first week, he found eight new chambers with intriguing new reliefs of hunting and mythological scenes. By early February, even Canning wrote from London that his protégé should adopt a less grueling pace for himself.

It was during these weeks that he also discovered "ivory ornaments of considerable beauty and interest." Many of them were in fragments that were adhesively stuck to the soil in such a stubborn fashion that Layard spent hours, lying on the ground, pecking away at them with his penknife. The ivory sometimes separated itself in flakes, and if the earth that gripped a piece came away wrong, it could reduce a precious shard to powder. "Scattered about were fragments of winged sphinxes, the head of a lion of singular beauty, but which unfortunately fell to pieces, human heads, hands, legs and feet, bulls, flowers and scroll-work. In all these specimens, the spirit of the design and the delicacy of the workmanship are equally to be admired."

Layard gathered what he could, taking his multiple jigsaw puzzles back to his quarters, where he and Henry Ross tried to fit them together. Ross recounted in his memoir how they struggled with the "strange bits of what seemed to be brittle, whitish stone or porcelain. In vain, they were turned and twisted, till one night the light fell at an angle on a splinter I had in my hand, and I recognized the waving texture of ivory. These pieces, no doubt, formed part of a throne, some of them had portraits in enamel and gold of a king, others were in the shape of rosettes."[22]

They were examples of what have come to be known as the Nimrud Ivories. After they were shipped off to London, restoration workers at the British Museum used a process—quite ingenious at the time—of replacing the decayed, original animal gluten of the fragments with a gelatinous compound. What they brought back to life are indeed exquisite works of art.

Back in London, Canning still insisted to the Austens that he would recommend Layard to Palmerston for diplomatic service in the Middle East. But as Charles Alison had warned before, he was also jealous of his protégé, especially peevish after an article in *The Bombay Times* discussed Layard but didn't bother to mention him. Maybe this is what prompted Forshall to poke his nose in again because he chose to lecture Benjamin Austen about his nephew's apparent lack of loyalty to the great man.

That prompted Austen to give him both barrels: Layard wasn't Canning's servant or the museum's, and if they didn't like the way he did the job or his conduct, good luck finding someone else to take over. Layard was tired himself of how Canning inflated his role. "I contemplated the excavations whenever it might be in my power to undertake them, even before Botta made his discoveries," he wrote his uncle. "And altho' I was enabled by the liberality of Sir S.C. to carry out the plan, yet it can scarcely be said that he made the discovery and only employed me to look after the diggers."[23]

News of the impressive discoveries, however, eased some of the friction with the Trustees. In a letter for January 22, Forshall congratulated Layard on a job "well done" so far and informed that whether he wanted it or not, £500 had been deposited into his personal account with Coutts. Layard felt enough of a boost to reassure his mother, "You need not be vexed about my affairs with people at home. I think I shall be able to do as much as I wish and fully as much, if not more than the Trustees . . . can reasonably expect." He had decided now that "on the whole, I think I ought to be content with what I have got and endeavour to finish my work as soon as possible."[24]

★ ★ ★

The Trustees of the British Museum had never dreamed of carting a *lamassu*, one of the winged bulls, or the lions all the way to London. It would be a Herculean feat, and there was already the precedent of failure when Botta had tried to move winged bulls from Khorsabad. Botta had abandoned one sculpture on its arduous journey to reach the Tigris, and he had decided to cut another bull in two for easier shipment, vandalizing it to keep it. The great stone pieces sat idle in Baghdad, awaiting transport, as Layard contemplated moving his own finds. The museum executives told him he should cover up his sculptures with earth from the excavation, and maybe they could be moved later at some distant yet vaguely more convenient time. Layard was "loath, however, to leave all these fine specimens of Assyrian sculptures behind me."

And what could be more impressive, secure his reputation better, than to have the colossus of a winged bull, matched with the gigantic lion, brought to London? "Some, who may hereafter tread on the spot when the grass again grows over the ruins of the Assyrian palaces, may indeed suspect that I have been relating a vision." No, he didn't imagine these wonders or hear a fanciful tale around an Arab tent in front of a fire—they were real—and he would have the proof for all to see.

If you can, go visit the British Museum or the Louvre or the Metropolitan Museum in New York City and stare at an example of these marvels: sometimes thirty tons in weight and standing more than thirteen feet high. Just to move them to Baghdad would be an amazing feat. Forshall, mindful of Botta, wrote to Layard that the Trustees were reluctant to have the sculptures cut into pieces. But Layard didn't want to damage his finds either.

Rawlinson sent him hawsers, jackscrews, blocks, and tackle, but the job still came down to a massive effort of physical labor. His men removed earth and debris from around the sculptures and then wrapped them in felts and mats to protect them from the ropes chipping and rubbing them and in case of a fall. Now the moment was at hand. On March 18, Layard stood on a high pitch so he could survey the work and direct the 300 laborers. There was even a crowd of curious onlookers and musicians to celebrate the moment. Wooden beams supported the first bull against a wall of earth, while rollers—made of polar trunks and greased—were laid on the ground parallel to the sculpture. The bull would be lowered onto these.

"The bull descended gradually," Layard recalled, "the Chaldeans propping it up with the beams. It was a moment of great anxiety. The drums and shrill pipes of the Kurdish musicians increased the din and confusion caused by the war-cry of the Arabs, who were half-frantic with excitement. They had thrown off nearly all their garments; their long hair floated in the wind, and they indulged in the wildest postures and gesticulations as they clung to the ropes. The women had congregated on the sides of the trenches, and by their incessant screams . . . added to the enthusiasm of the men."

Then there was trouble. As the bull got closer to the rollers, the beams couldn't be used anymore. The dry cables snapped when the sculpture was about four feet from the rollers, and men fell backward as the bull landed with a massive thud, sending up a huge cloud of dust. Silence. . . .

Layard was horrified, rushing down to the trenches, prepared to see his treasure split into pieces. Instead, "I saw it lying precisely where I had wished to place it, and unbroken!" Soon his workmen formed a great circle with the women, dancing with joy. The musicians played for all they were worth. Layard knew he couldn't stop them all even if he wanted to; he would allow "the men to wear themselves out."

Looking on, Sheikh Abd-ur-rahman couldn't see the point of it all. "In the name of the Most High, tell me O Bey," he asked Layard, "what are you going to do with those stones? So many thousands of purses spent upon such things! Can it be, as you say, that your people learn wisdom from them, or is it as his reverence, the Kadi declares, that they are to go to the palace of your queen, who with the rest of the unbelievers, worship these idols? As for wisdom, these figures will not teach you to make any better knives or scissors or chintzes, and it is in the making of those things that the English show their wisdom."

The next day, the bull was rolled on to a large iron cart, specially built in Mosul, which would take the sculpture down to the river. At first, oxen were supposed to pull it, but they were stubbornly not up to the job, so men took their place. Things were going well until two of the cart's wheels sunk into the earth. The workers tried in vain to free it, but at sunset, Layard let them call it quits and posted an armed guard to see that none of the ropes and mats were stolen by bandits.

It was a wise precaution. No sooner was he getting into bed for the night when there was a ruckus outside, with the village of Nimrud turning up over an exchange of gunfire. Bedouin raiders had indeed tried to take what they could, but Layard's men fought them off. The one casualty was the winged bull—a musket ball had ripped through the mats and felts and left a mark on its side. It can still be found today on the bull as it sits majestically in the British Museum.

The following day, his workmen used thick planks to dislodge the cart, and the lamassu was on its way again to the Tigris. By the middle of April, Layard was ready to have one of the winged lions removed and carted the same way. Even the rafts to carry these gigantic sculptures downriver had to be specially constructed, each with 600 inflated goat and sheep skins. But now Layard had new problems, and they weren't mechanical—they had to do with labor relations. His raft builders doubted their constructions could handle the loads, and they begged for more payment. Layard stuck to his guns; a contract was a contract. He also had confidence in the builders.

Then his workmen went on strike for more pay. A recent drought had driven away many of the tribesmen, and those still on the payroll figured they now had the upper hand. They guessed wrong. Layard sent a messenger to Abd-ur-rahman, and by the time the sheikh's men were on-site and finishing the journey of the bull and the lion, the strikers pleaded for their old jobs back—and failed.

On April 20, there was a slight rise in the Tigris, and Layard knew this was an excellent time to get the bull and the lion on their way. The high bank of the river was landscaped into a slope, and men grunted and pulled on ropes as the bull was slid along greased beams of poplar wood onto its raft. Then the same exertions had to be spent to move the lion onto its own raft. By nightfall,

The winged bull comes to London. Its arrival at the British Museum. The Illustrated London News, *February 28, 1852.*

the sculptures secured along with a collection of bas-reliefs going along for the ride, the stone giants were ready to float down the ancient river to Basra.

On April 22, as Layard watched the rafts disappear behind a riverbank, he was awed himself at what he had set in motion. The sculptures had been buried for centuries "beneath a soil trodden by Persians under Cyrus, by Greeks under Alexander and by Arabs under the first successors of their Prophet." Now they would adorn a museum in Bloomsbury. "Who can venture to foretell," he wondered, "how their strange career will end?"

★ ★ ★

As his contractual deadline loomed, Layard realized he should wrap things up by May. Almost as an afterthought, he allotted some time to poke about Kuyunjik, where, on the southwest corner of the mound, his men discovered a grand palace with winged bulls flanking the entrance.

Layard also wanted to explore Kalah Sergat, which he knew was infested with bandits, but he figured it was worth the risk. He sent one of his foremen ahead, while he followed a few days later with armed men, the bairakdar, and young Hormuzd Rassam. Ten miles to the north of Kalah Sergat, they reached the camp of a friendly sheikh between the Tigris and a range of low hills. The sheikh introduced Layard to his wives and his sister, "whose beauty I had often heard extolled . . . and who was not altogether undeserving of her reputation." When they finally started for the ruins, Layard couldn't help but notice the plentiful game: hares, wolves, foxes, jackals, and wild boar. This was also lion country. When Layard visited the site about a year before, he had heard the roar of a lion but hadn't seen one. The sheikh's men "beat the bushes" for one and for other animals, but they couldn't capture any.

Layard had better luck with his excavation. His workmen dug for an hour, uncovering a headless and handless sculpture of black basalt, and he guessed correctly that it was a king (it was, in fact, Assyria's Shalmaneser II). The men found tombs and reliefs, but the efforts were ultimately foiled by the limited time and resources. Layard knew this spot had to be "one of the most ancient cities of Assyria," but he could only speculate—there weren't enough days available to patiently unearth another spectacular find or confirm his suspicions. Was this place once Calah, one of the primitive cities of Assyria mentioned in the Bible? Maybe it was Ur. It certainly wasn't Ur because he was literally miles off, and it would be more than half a century before it was found.

No, without realizing it at the time and ever knowing for the rest of his life, Layard stood on the site of the capital of the Assyrian Empire, Ashur.

He spent only two days at Kalah Sergat. On his first night, "a violent storm broke over us," Layard wrote in *Nineveh and Its Remains*. "The wind rose to a hurricane—the rain descended in torrents—the thunder rolled in one long peal—and the vivid streams of lightning, almost incessant, showed the surrounding landscape. When the storm had abated, I walked to a short distance from the tents to gaze upon the scene. The huge fire we had kindled threw a lurid glare over the trees around our encampment. The great mound could be distinguished through the gloom, rising like a distant mountain against the dark sky. From all sides came the melancholy wail of the jackals—thousands of these animals having issued from their subterranean dwellings in the ruins as soon as the last gleam of twilight was fading in the western horizon. The owl, perched on the old masonry, occasionally sent forth its mournful note. The shrill laugh of the Arabs would sometimes rise above the cry of the jackal. Then all earthly noises were buried in the deep roll of the distant thunder. It was desolation such as those alone who witnessed such scenes can know."

That evening, Layard and his team slept near the tents of a reputed *sayyid*, a descendant of the Prophet Muhammad. The man was known for curing the diseased with a touch of his hand, but Layard never found a patient to give a testimonial. He wrote later, "There is a charm in this wandering existence, whether of the Kurd or the Arab, which cannot be described. I have had some experience in it and look back with pleasure to the days I have spent in the desert, notwithstanding the occasional inconveniences of such a life, not the least of them being a strong tendency on the part of all nomads to profess a kind of communist philosophy, supposed in Europe to be the result of modern wisdom, but which appears to have been known from the earliest times in the East." According to Layard, the nomad "believes that the town corrupts the wanderer; and he remembers that until the sheikh of the desert visited the citizens and was feasted in the palaces of their governors, oppression and vices most odious to the Arab were unknown in his tribe."

A cynic would call this romanticism over the noble savage, but that would not be entirely fair. True, he had grown up in England as the industrial revolution leapt forward with the momentum of its powerful steam engines, grinding lathes, and noisy mills. But he saw the Arab and the Kurd plainly, their cultures, the faults of individuals, as well as virtues. More than a century later, Wilfred Thesiger, the explorer who wrote so movingly about the Empty Quarter of Arabia, would express a similar sentiment: "Even as a boy, I recognized that motor transport and aeroplanes must increasingly shrink the world and irrevocably destroy its fascinating diversity. My forebodings have been amply fulfilled. Package tours now invade the privacy of the remotest villages; the transistor, blaring pop music, has usurped the place of the tribal bard. While I was in the desert with the Rashid [people], they would light a fire by striking a dagger blade against a piece of flint; now they hear the world's news on their radio or watch it on their television set."[25]

The modern world hadn't yet touched the wanderers Layard met in his travels, but it was gaining on them.

★ ★ ★

Bandit raiding parties were now sighted on an almost daily basis, and Layard had to keep patrols around his house. While they had the numbers to hold off most attacks, a chronic problem was petty thieves in the night swiping items large and small—a donkey, a copper pot, or the odd grain sack. A particularly bold group killed several of the villagers and drove off many of their sheep and cattle. Layard knew it was time to formally end the excavations. By the middle of June, the work was over. The trenches were filled in, the ruins and palaces covered up again and hidden to protect them from the elements—as well as bandits and the fanatical who considered these treasures to be blasphemous.

Layard decided to throw himself one hell of a going-away party. In a small village to the west of Kuyunjik, platters of food were served, and the dancing went on through the night with constant shouts. Members of both sexes attended, and Layard recalled that the "quiet Christian ladies of Mosul, who had scarcely before this occasion ventured beyond the walls of the town, gazed with wonder and delight on the scene; lamenting, no doubt, that the domestic arrangements of their husbands did not permit more frequent indulgence in such gayeties." Layard gave out presents to the principal workmen and was touched by their expressions of warm feeling and the hopes that he would return one day. As he rode out slowly with his young friend Hormuzd Rassam to start his journey to Istanbul, several of the wives and daughters of his workmen clung to his horse and shed tears as they kissed his hand.

On the day before Layard had left Mosul, his first shipment of bas-reliefs from Nimrud were proudly put on display at the British Museum. They were an immediate hit with the public. After eight years of being away, the Victorian Slacker who had galloped away to the Near East with few prospects and little ambition was coming home in triumph.

· 8 ·

Nineveh and Its Remains

Layard arrived in Istanbul on July 31. He learned that Canning was off in England while Henry Wellesley, a career diplomat, minded the embassy (he would later take over when Canning retired). Layard was eager to reach London so that he could publish his findings, along with the thick collection of drawings of sculptures and his numerous copies of the cuneiform. But whether he was technically on staff or not, he felt obliged to get Canning's permission to go. His boss didn't answer his letters, and Layard's best guess was that Canning probably wanted him to stay put so he could rely on his expertise over the Turkey–Persia dispute.

Then fate lent a hand. Layard took a trip with friends to Nicomedia, where no one had a clue that malaria was endemic to the region. Most of the group got sick, Layard one of the worst of all, so that the embassy doctor urged him "to leave the country without delay and return to England, or he would not answer for my life." Wellesley signed off on a health certificate, and Layard spent seven days in quarantine and recovery on a steamship for Malta. By the time the ship reached Naples, he felt strong enough to go sightseeing.

He traveled to Rome and Florence, slightly amazed at the "craziness" going on across the land. Though it would be more than another twenty years before the Kingdom of Italy came into existence, the momentum for unification was under way, moving in fits and starts and bloody upheavals. These were the years when Garibaldi and Cavour rose in stature. "Great changes have taken and are taking place," he wrote his Aunt Sara that December. Always a keen observer of social and political behavior, he noted there were "extravagant hopes—particularly among the lawyers and *hommes de lettres*. Nothing short of a general confederation of the Italian states appears to be their aim."

In Paris, he reunited with Paul-Émile Botta, who generously introduced him to important people at the French Institute and gave him a chance to discuss his findings at Nineveh. Layard, though not quite over his latest fever bout, was shrewd enough to treat his presentation like a rehearsal for wowing the scholarly and important in London. The French were indeed impressed and talked about making him a "corresponding member" of the organization. He also got the chance to peek in on their hall of Nineveh exhibits—and was probably both relieved and disappointed. Despite the French having larger examples of Assyrian bulls, the exhibit contained "scarcely anything worth notice." He was getting impatient to have his work published.

As with Italy, Layard picked up in France on the stirrings of political change and revolution in the air. Walking after dinner with Botta and the academics through the Palais Royale, he was told how there was growing discontent among the populace, and these men were convinced that a crisis would break out and "end in the fall of the reigning dynasty and lead through anarchy and bloodshed to a republic." They were right. Months later, with the country paralyzed by strikes and violent demonstrations, Louis Napoleon Bonaparte was swept into the presidency on a wave of populism . . . only to betray the revolution three years later and establish the Second Empire. Napoleon III's power grab and his crackdown drove Karl Marx to London and Victor Hugo to Guernsey, where he took inspiration from barricade skirmishes and student uprisings for *Les Misérables*.

Layard, however, wouldn't be sticking around to witness the trouble in France. He was back across the English Channel in England four days before Christmas 1847. Like any prodigal, he must have felt ambivalence over how little London had changed in some places and had drastically changed in others.

When he had left in the summer of 1839, there was bitter public wrangling going on over the design and placement of Nelson's Column in Trafalgar Square. Nobody seemed to like it, neither the fact that the column would interfere with the view down Whitehall nor the idea of Nelson wearing a hat nor that he sat on a column, and on it tediously went. But in 1843, when the seventeen-foot-high statue of the naval hero was plunked down at Charing Cross, about to gaze forever high above the square, 100,000 Londoners came to look at him.[1] Layard would have missed this. He must have noticed the relatively new fountains in the square, but the famous lions that tourists still bravely climb on weren't there yet.

Only a week before Layard came home, Emily Bronte published *Wuthering Heights* under a pseudonym. Two months to the day of his arrival, Karl Marx and Friedrich Engels published *The Communist Manifesto* in London. Meanwhile, a group of devout Christians in the city had already formed the world's first Vegetarian Society. Across the Atlantic, American troops had recently won the war against Mexico. In Copenhagen in early November, an art collector and philanthropist named Jacobsen had brewed a new beer dubbed Carlsberg.

Layard was the toast of the town. He went to parties and met the rich and influential. There was good news on the career front, too. Canning had put in a good word for him with Lord Palmerston, now the foreign secretary, and as 1847 came to an end, the word became official—Layard would have a job with the legation in Istanbul, helping to delineate the Turkish–Persian border. Still feeling rather weak, he arranged to get a leave of absence on health grounds. He wouldn't be needed on the frontier for some time anyway.

Meanwhile, the Trustees of the British Museum, seizing the moment, asked the government for £4,000 to underwrite the cost of publishing his findings. But a museum official warned Layard that asking was one thing, receiving was another. He still felt he had enough support now with the Trustees to lobby for a massive and ambitious set of excavations that would cover all of Assyria and take at least three years. Of course, it would be expensive: about £5,000 for the first year alone. It was necessary, he reasoned, because this was a race against time. The value of antiquities had dawned on the Ottoman authorities, and a museum for them was planned in Istanbul; excavations were under way. Unfortunately, according to reports he'd received from Rawlinson, Christian Rassam, and Henry Ross, the Turks were conscripting villagers against their will for the digs and not paying them. To avoid being used as slave labor, the villagers tried to destroy any remains they encountered.

No surprise, with the Tories' Robert Peel as prime minister, the current government wasn't interested in funding the publication of Layard's findings, and it certainly didn't want to fork out thousands on digging in the dirt in the Near East. "The state of the finances and the events occurring on the Continent," he wrote Ross, referring to the revolution going on in France, "have driven Nineveh and all other antiquities out of people's heads." Recurring bouts of malarial fever, along with a problem with his liver, forced him to get an extension of his sick leave for another six months.

His health had a severe effect on his mood, along with the natural letdown of ordinary life in England. In the East, he had led workers in excavations and been looked to as a mediator in communities; in London, he could be easily dismissed as another middle-class upstart. At the end of February, he complained to Rawlinson in a letter, "One cannot but regret the system." An acquaintance had just landed a job that paid £1,000 a year, "I believe because he has a pretty sister." Despondent, he confessed this intriguing notion: "One can't begin life once again—if I could, I should certainly go to the United States."[2]

He decided to spend much of 1848 recuperating and working—when he felt strong enough—on the book about his discoveries. There are writers who have always wanted to write and those who stumble into publishing, never expecting anything from it. Layard was the second type. He had written articles, but he needed persuading to tackle a book. Both his Aunt Sara and Rawlinson encouraged him. So did his old drinking buddy and colleague, Alison, who also thought it was a great idea: "Write a whopper with lots of plates; fish up old legends and anecdotes, and if you can by any means humbug people into the belief that you have established any points in the Bible, you are a made man."[3]

Layard's social life also took a front seat now, and he built up a friendship with his cousin, Lady Charlotte Guest, staying with her and her husband at Canford Manor in Dorsetshire or at their home in Wales. Charlotte had married money—a lot of it. John Guest ran an impressively large ironworks out in Dowlais, near Cardiff, that employed more than 7,000 men. At the time, a noble young lady didn't "marry into trade," as the British liked to put it back then, but Charlotte didn't let anyone tell her what to do. As for John Guest, nothing helped better to get you into society than sitting on a tall stack of cash . . . which rested in turn on a tall stack of railroad steel. John Guest soon became Sir John and got a seat in Parliament. When the two married in 1833, Charlotte was twenty-one while he was forty-nine. By the time Layard met the couple, Charlotte was in her active mid-thirties and her husband in his sixties and becoming fragile.

Charlotte never settled for being a trophy wife. She knew Latin, Greek, Arabic, and Persian and learned Welsh so well that she made a landmark translation of the literary classic *The Mabinogion*, which later inspired Tennyson. She organized and ran six schools in Dowlais while helping her husband run his business—*and* while taking care of their family. It's no wonder that Layard and such a gifted woman should feel a deep intellectual bond. She took great interest in his drawings and descriptions of the archaeological treasures. When Charlotte played piano, Layard accompanied her on flute. Most historians and biographers are convinced that despite the rumors at the time, there was nothing going on sexually between them.

During these months, he ran into Disraeli again and made friends with another guest, Henry Austin Bruce, later Lord Aberdare and a home secretary under Gladstone. At thirty-one, Layard was at the height of his charisma and his attractiveness. "His face was singularly attractive and impressive," noted Aberdare, "his figure suggested strength and power of endurance rather than exceptional activity."[4] Layard would often beg off from joining the other guests at hunting and spend a happy afternoon with Charlotte's ten children, playing charades and entertaining them with stories from *The Arabian Nights* and his own adventures. One of the children was a sweet little girl, five-year-old Enid, who closely resembled her mother and would come back into Layard's life in a surprising way years later.

His long stays in Dorsetshire and Wales clearly did him some good. From Canford Manor in early March, he wrote to Henry Ross, minding the store back in Mosul: "These comfortable places and the pleasures of English country life spoil one for the adventures and privations of the East. I find a great improvement in the upper classes; much more information, liberality of opinion and kindness towards those beneath them. I think that on the whole, things in England are much better than could be expected."[5] This was quite a change in attitude from his class-conscious grumbles to Rawlinson, but then the view is always better from the private box than the cheap seats; Layard's opinions would mature, given time.

As he worked on his book, he had two champions separately lobbying for its publication, Sara Austen and Charlotte Guest. His Aunt Sara wrote the publisher, John Murray, and Charlotte was willing to help finance publishing the illustrations. In July, he got another nice boost to his morale. For his impressive discoveries and scholarly contributions, Oxford awarded him a doctor of civil law degree. Having never been able to afford university, he was touched by the honor. Instead of Jesus College and All Souls, his campus had been a mound of dirt and a shabby village, but the autodidact had made good.

Henry Ross had taken over the excavations at Nimrud and Kuyunjik, "where the excavations are regular catacombs, and in spite of the perforated skylights, I had to examine some of the slabs by candlelight."[6] Layard wrote to ask about his female friends back in Mosul; Ross reported that he hadn't seen them, but as a staunch bachelor, he avoided women in general: "Not another woman shall put her foot within my door; for I know that fatality attends everything I have to do with women." By mid-July, he had finished up the work and had left Mosul because he had to get back to his business. He advised Layard on August 13, "If you have not seen *The Bombay Monthly Times* for May get it, and you will find that at the Bombay branch of the Royal Asiatic Society, they have made the wonderful discovery that the remains found by *Major Rawlinson* at Nimrud are of the time of Darius Hystaspes! And that the figures on the black marble obelisk were probably copied from the Egyptian! So much for learned societies [emphasis in the original]."[7] Layard must have scratched his head over this odd report, but it had more significance than either he or Ross knew.

Meanwhile, Layard's career hit another pothole. He had assumed—almost everyone in his circle had assumed—that when he finally started his job with the border commission, he would have equal status with his old acquaintance, Colonel Fenwick Williams. It soon turned out that he was expected to serve *under* Williams despite his knowledge of the region. Canning shared his indignation: "I do not like the idea of your going on this trumpery frontier work," which could entangle him "in endless squabbles about tribal pretensions." He ought to quit, Canning told him, and Layard did just that, asking in a formal letter to Palmerston that he instead be given a job at the embassy in Istanbul. The Foreign Office let him know that in quitting the border commission, he had just given up a salary of £250. And what would he be paid as an embassy attaché? Not a shilling.

There was more bad news. In October, more than fifty cases from Nimrud arrived from the HMS *Jumma* at Chatham. Then came the anxious moment when Layard and officials at the British Museum opened them; they were shocked to discover objects were out of order, pieces were removed from their original packaging and carelessly packed up again, and several valuable items were missing. The story in *The Bombay Monthly Times* offered a clue. It turned out that when the shipment had arrived in Mumbai, some British expats had casually helped themselves. It was an embarrassment for the East India Company, which made sure future shipments were closely guarded.[8]

Thinking he had few prospects in England, Layard decided to settle for the job at the Istanbul legation, and he didn't even wait for John Murray to bring out his book. In a short note in mid-November to his old friend Cecilia Berkeley, he wrote, "I am ordered off, and I must go—but I return with nothing, just an unpaid attaché without a sixpence. I do not know how it is all to end."[9] By the end of December, he was in Istanbul and waving goodbye to Williams, who was setting out for the long work on the Turkish–Persian frontier. Layard would stay behind in the embassy, handling dispatches and meeting Ottoman officials. Without knowing it, he was on the eve of international success. Early in the new year, bookshops were shelving his two-volume set, *Nineveh and Its Remains*.

★   ★   ★

Layard's book was a sensation in 1849. It sold almost 8,000 copies that year, which may seem a modest figure to us, but that was a best seller for its time. *The Quarterly Review* devoted forty-six pages to it. Its reviewer admitted he was impatient to tuck into a scholarly account of the findings and instead was "carried away" by the story. Layard was "not merely an industrious and persevering discoverer in this new field of antiquities, but an eastern traveller distinguished . . . beyond almost all others by the freshness, vigor and simplicity of his narrative." These words ran in the same issue that reviewed *Vanity Fair* and *Jane Eyre*. With perfect timing, a new shipment of sculptures arrived and was displayed at the British Museum, helping book sales and drawing Queen Victoria's husband, Prince Albert, to go down to take a look.

Layard wrote his uncle that he blushed when he read the verdict of *The Times* of London on February 9, 1849. The paper called it "the most extraordinary work of the present age" and went on to say, "We question whether a more enlightened and enterprising traveller than Mr. Layard is to be met within the annals of modern history."[10] The author had genuine reason to blush—it turns out that Murray had tipped off Sara Austen that a more critical piece ("monstrous" was how he put it) was due to be printed but that she had the chance to replace it with an article of her own if she could offer new and exclusive information. If her praise was an insider's public relations job, the bouquets from other reviewers were not. There was genuine admiration and awe for what he had done, and in late May, the Royal Geographic Society awarded him its Founder's Gold Medal.

But it wasn't book sales or museum exhibits that finally gave Layard a lift in his career—it was cholera. True, letters had been flying around country estates and Whitehall over him, nudging Palmerston to keep the young man in mind, but it took several deaths among the British legation staff before Layard was finally granted a paid position with Canning's staff (exactly what he had lost from quitting the border commission: £250). Better still, the government finally saw the light and took the archaeological work seriously. A Royal Navy ship sailed for Basra just for the mission of collecting the winged bull and lion. And the government at last granted its support and blessing for the museum to undertake a fresh excavation in Assyria.

★ ★ ★

This second expedition would prove ultimately less successful, less rewarding, and it nearly cost Layard his life.

In the beginning, he and his circle had high hopes. The Austens had heard through their contacts that £20,000 might be spent on the two- to three-year venture. The project would have its own artist, Frederick Charles Cooper, who was young but highly talented, and a medical officer, Dr. Humphry Sandwith. Hormuzd Rassam, who was enjoying his studies at Magdalen College in Oxford, was enlisted to come along—reluctantly. He told Layard that he would rather be a chimney sweeper in England than a pasha in Turkey.

Then came a shock: the museum expected Layard to run the whole enterprise for the first eight months on £1,500. It was ridiculous and all too familiar. Layard did the math, working out the deductions for travel and living expenses, and the sum left for the excavations was pitiful. He promptly complained, and the principal librarian at the museum, Sir Henry Ellis, resorted to a bit of blackmail. The Trustees, he argued, had so many projects to consider that if Layard didn't take the deal soon, the available funds would go elsewhere.

It was a cynical bluff, and yet it worked . . . because Layard came up with a new source of funding, his own pockets. *Nineveh and Its Remains* was such a block-buster that he made £1,500 a year in royalties for years. When Layard wrote about the beginning of this expedition for a new book, he tartly observed, "Arrangements were hastily and of course inadequately made in England."

In Istanbul, with Cooper, Sandwith, and young Rassam in tow, Layard rehired his bairakdar and a cawass and retained a couple of servants. Along for the journey was a contingent of Yezidi nobles, who traveled to the capital for Layard's help with the Ottoman government. The Turkish authorities didn't really care who they conscripted, but serving in the armed forces violated certain practices of the Yezidi faith. The Yezidi religion forbade its adherents to bathe with Muslims, as they would have to do if forced into the army ranks, and they couldn't eat the rations provided. Layard noted that the practice still went on of Yezidi children being sold into slavery. Thanks to his intervention and lobbying, Canning took their cause to the Sublime Porte, and the Yezidis were granted a limited firman that released them from military service and partially respected their religious freedom.

Layard was one of the first to write about the Yezidis sympathetically, and it's worth noting in our era when this minority has faced steady persecution and slaughter that he was arguably the first westerner to compellingly champion their human rights.

The group took a steamship and headed out on August 28 for what is now Trabzon, nestled on the Black Sea. Layard chose the route for its "novelty" of geography and to see how the politics were working out in a region brought only recently under Ottoman rule. From Trabzon, their caravan worked its way through Armenia and Kurdistan to Mesopotamia. At the Kurdish village of Funduk, infamous for its savage tribes and their hatred of Christians, Layard chose to be prudent and lead his travel party through the streets after sundown. Hormuzd Rassam, with an impulse of mischief, had got the young artist Cooper scared out of his wits with tales, both real and imaginary, of the lurid murders and raids by the residents of Funduk. Then Layard suddenly heard voices, and he spotted a group of Kurds rushing toward his group. No one could tell what was going on, but Cooper was so terrified by now that he readied his pistols. Then a Kurd seized Layard's bridle—and told him the local chief wouldn't let his group pass without partaking of his hospitality.

In the Assyrian plains, they sweltered under "that heavy heat, which seems to paralyze all Nature, causing the very air itself to vibrate." Close to exhaustion and making a badly needed stop at a Yezidi village, Layard was informed that Bedouin raiders had been targeting the region, and he was urged to move on before the raiders overtook the area.

Back on the road again, it looked like the caravan was in big trouble when a large group of horsemen appeared on high ground to the east. "We could scarcely expect Arabs from that quarter; however, all our party made ready for an attack." Layard and one of the Yezidis' high priests decided to ride out to look things over, while the others in the caravan could only wait in anxious suspense. In the stillness of the plain, they trotted their mounts forward. Then two riders from the mysterious group on the hill advanced slowly, hesitantly. . . .

The priest by Layard's side suddenly recognized a black turban, "dashed forward with a shout of joy, and in a moment, we were surrounded and in the embrace of friends." Layard's old allies and some of the Yezidi elders had ridden almost forty miles in the night to meet up with them and provide an escort—if necessary all the way to Mosul. "Their delight at seeing us knew no bounds, nor was I less touched by a display of gratitude and good feeling, equally unexpected and sincere."

When they reached the village of Tel Kef, there were more happy re-unions with Layard's old workers and superintendents and even the next day with his greyhounds and his horse, Merjan, "the noble animal looking as beautiful, as fresh and as sleek as when I last saw him." Layard felt as if he'd "but returned from a summer's ride; two years had passed away like a dream." He made a quick visit to Kuyunjik and poked around in the underground passages excavated so far, where he could see the extensive damage of an ancient fire in the palace. But he didn't linger, as there were more reunions and social calls to enjoy, including attendance at the Yezidis' annual festival, a great honor, clearly one bestowed in gratitude over his efforts to protect them from persecution.

By late October, he had inspected Mosul and toured the area with Hormuzd Rassam on horseback. When they rode to the mound of Nimrud, they noticed some travelers, and Layard was surprised to find "in an excavated chamber, wrapped in his travelling cloak, was Rawlinson, deep in sleep, wearied by a long and harassing night's ride." Layard thought there was much to talk over. But Rawlinson, laid up by fever, spent two days mostly in bed. On his third day, Rawlinson could only manage a "hasty survey" of ruins at Kuyunjik. The whole visit was marred by a grotesque accident. As Rawlinson recounted later in his journal, Christian Rassam's wife had insisted he take her horse, but the animal killed her cawass by "kicking the poor devil's testicles into a jelly. It was certainly no fault of mine, but the poor wretch's look of extreme agony as he rolled on the ground has haunted me ever since."[11] Rawlinson left the next day for Istanbul before heading back to London.

Always more interested in the abstract riddle of the texts than the physical inscriptions themselves, Rawlinson was a poor audience for Layard's tour, whether fit or ill. The friendship between the two was always delicate, and it was about to suffer more cracks.

★   ★   ★

At Kuyunjik, Layard noticed a set of bas-reliefs that showed how the ancient Assyrians transported their massive sculptures to their positions—using ropes to drag sleds on rollers. He marveled at how even with the passage of centuries, he had "used almost the same means" to bring his treasures down to the Tigris. He also found a facade with the remains of ten gigantic bulls and six colossal human figures. Though the entire facade couldn't be excavated, Layard learned enough to help architect James Fergusson bring the palace vividly to life in stunning works of art.

On several of the great bulls were 152 lines of inscriptions—and the seeds of vindication. Layard had suggested in *Nineveh and Its Remains* that the palace had been built by Sennacherib, but as scholar Mogens Trolle Larsen points out, this was "a pure guess."[12] In August 1851, Rawlinson—checking Layard's copies of the inscriptions—confirmed it *was* Sennacherib. It's telling that in his book on the expedition, Layard—while giving Rawlinson his due—felt the need to remind readers that he first floated his guess "in a series of letters published in *The Malta Times* as far back as 1843." It seemed the rivalry between artifact work and text decoding would go on for a while longer.

As for artifacts, the British Museum wanted the two lions from the great hall in Nimrud's northwest palace, which years ago Layard had covered with earth for protection. Now his workmen needed to build these stone beasts their very own road from the palace for their transport, and even this monotonous digging revealed carved ivory fragments.

Meanwhile, a new chamber had been opened in the northwest palace, and inside, there were enough relics to keep the experts busy for decades: copper and bronze dishes, cauldrons and lions' and bulls' feet made of bronze; exquisite cups and plates, some decorated with silver and gold. One fascinating detail is that Layard found a rock-crystal lens, which some ancient craftsman had obviously used as a magnifying glass. He found swords, daggers and shields, and the decayed remains of a wooden throne—it had a foot stool with feet carved into lion paws and pinecones.

Late in the year, the excavation got a new pair of volunteers. A young English couple, the Rollands, were traveling through the region on their way to meet Colonel Fenwick Williams. Stewart Rolland had served with the British army's 69th Regiment, and he was an enthusiastic equestrian, delighted to buy horses for dirt cheap. His wife, Charlotte, was intelligent, charming, and attractive. The Rollands were fascinated by the work and were soon pitching in, Charlotte taking care of delicate objects and cataloging and packing them, while Stewart Rolland was put in charge of some workmen and allowed "to dig where I pleased." Layard opened his modest home for the couple to share, "which was little more than a mud hut." But he put in glass windows and some sofas and tried to make it as comfortable for his guests as possible.

"Layard is the most delightful companion I have ever met," Rolland wrote to an uncle. "He is exactly the same age as myself. . . . I never in my life was so well or so happy as I am at present. My wife, too, thoroughly enjoys the wild life."[13] Rolland was sympathetic to his new friend's lack of funds and resources and awed by the challenges Layard faced, knowing the work "is literally groping in the dark, and all sorts of buried treasure may lie within his reach while from the very small amount of funds placed at his disposal, he is unable to make anything like a proper search."[14] At one point, Rolland spent eight hours scratching ornamental cups and bowls out of the hard clay from the newly opened palace chamber, while Charlotte worked through the evening, packing them up.

As the work went on in the dirt of Mesopotamia, Henry Rawlinson enjoyed his turn in the spotlight off in London. He gave two lectures on his new findings at the Royal Asiatic Society, the first on January 19, 1850, and the second one a month later with Prince Albert chairing the session. Layard had naturally deferred to him over chronology and put the date of Nineveh at 2500 BCE in his book. But only five months after *Nineveh and Its Remains* sat in stores, Rawlinson had revised his estimates, and now he told audiences that Nimrud wasn't Nineveh, it was Calah from the Bible and its heyday was between 1300 and 1200 BCE.

Layard, however, was the one who had committed himself first to print, and it was his reputation that could suffer as the recognized expert adjusted his opinion. Canning, always feeling that he never got his due, seized on the discrepancies over estimates and reacted with schadenfreude. He wrote Layard from Istanbul, "I know not how to console you for the loss of those fifteen centuries of which Major Rawlinson is determined to curtail you."[15]

Rawlinson, never sensing he had caused a problem, was amiable, even cheerful, in his correspondence to Layard. "People talk of you more than I ever suspect, at any rate wherever I go. I hardly hear of anything else but Nineveh and Babylon." When he dined with the Austens, "of course, the whole conversation was about you."[16] A sulking Layard wrote his aunt that Rawlinson "quietly sets me up to knock me down again." While conceding his brilliance at cuneiform, "I have no doubt that he will ere long change most of his readings. He is much too eager at snatching at a theory, propounding a paradox and poohpoohing at once anyone who does not agree with him."[17]

By the last week of January, the palace lions could be dragged to the river for shipment, but they had to wait for the river to rise for their transport. In *Nineveh and Babylon*, Layard wrote movingly of his ambivalence over prying them from their resting place: "We rode one calm cloudless night to the mound, to look on them for the last time before they were taken from their old resting-places. The moon was at her full, and as we drew nigh to the edge of the deep wall of earth rising around them, her soft light was creeping over the stern features of the human heads, and driving before it the dark shadows which still clothed the lion forms. One by one the limbs of the gigantic sphinxes emerged from the gloom, until the monsters were unveiled before us.

"I shall never forget that night, or the emotions which those venerable figures caused within me. A few hours more, and they were to stand no longer where they had stood unscathed amidst the wreck of man and his works for ages. It seemed almost sacrilege to tear them from their old haunts to make them a mere wonder-stock to the busy crowd of a new world. They were better suited to the desolation around them; for they had guarded the palace in its glory, and it was for them to watch over it in its ruin."

Along for the brief inspection was Sheikh Abd-ur-Rahman, and Layard noted the man had no such misgivings. He dismissed the "folly of the Franks," remarked on how the night was cold, and then turned his horse around to return to his tents.

★   ★   ★

What complicated the excavations most were people. Cooper, the artist, was forever homesick and, having married not long before joining the expedition, kept pining for his wife; he drew a portrait of her from memory and pulled it out often to look at it. Sandwith, the doctor, was bored with cuneiform and winged bulls and, with so few medical duties, didn't make himself useful at all. Instead, he wiled away the hours hunting and lost one of Layard's favorite guns on one of his shooting trips.

On top of this, Layard had to put up with an old nemesis, a Reverend Percy Badger, who was the brother-in-law of Christian Rassam and staying in the Rassam home. Badger was the kind of hypocritical busybody—preaching the milk of human kindness while plotting in anger—that populates Somerset Maugham short stories. He was familiar with the Near East and had once even suggested to Canning his own excavation project at Nimrud. Nothing came of it, and he must have been furious with envy when Layard's digs earned him glory. Worse, Layard had criticized missionaries like Badger, arguing their interference had often led to Nestorians being routinely massacred. Badger was in Mosul to write a book on Nestorians and their religious practices, and he intended to argue in it that *he* had discovered the true site of Nineveh.

No one bought that idea, and in *The Nestorians and Their Rituals*, Badger appears almost desperate to find mistakes in Layard's scholarship and show him up. His book was published before Layard's account of his second expedition, and Layard seemed to take the view that you don't fire a cannon at a mosquito. He dismissed Badger's criticisms in footnotes, never granting him a cameo in the proper text itself. Time has made its own judgment, and Badger has been consigned to obscurity while Layard's *Discoveries among the Ruins of Nineveh and Babylon* is still in print.

Badger—and his wife—likely played a role in vicious gossip and attitudes toward Charlotte Rolland. Layard certainly thought so and wrote to his friend Ross, "Mrs. Rassam has behaved very unkindly to her—all the fault of those cursed Badgers who are a regular pest."[18] Layard's friendship with Stewart Rolland, however, had soured by then. Layard wrote his aunt that Charlotte's "position in society was inferior to his. Instead of endeavoring to raise her, he appears to do everything in his power to keep her down." He judged Rolland as "one of the most selfish, ill-bred, unfeeling and conceited men I ever met."[19] Dr. Sandwith had begun to think Rolland was mentally disturbed, prone to violent tantrums. Things had deteriorated so badly that Layard provided Charlotte with her own room in his tiny house, but this must have only exacerbated the tensions.

In mid-April, the whole group traveled to the region near the Khabur River, where they could inspect ruins and Layard would make notes for a discreet political report to Canning. When he needed to visit a sheikh's camp, Charlotte came along, riding behind him on a fast-moving camel. "We crossed a perfect carpet of flowers, and I never saw anything more beautiful than the desert today." Whether it was this outing or something else, Stewart Rolland eventually snapped.

On the journey back to Mosul, he barely spoke to Layard except to make insulting remarks, and when they reached Kuyunjik, he suddenly dragged Charlotte into one of the large communal tents. Layard was suddenly "alarmed by her screams," and one of his servants ran up at the same time to yell "that Mr. Rolland had thrown his wife to the ground and was attempting to murder her."[20]

Layard rushed over to find the jealous husband beating his wife "most brutally." He had his men grab the half-mad, sputtering Rolland and hold him fast. Rolland was "calling for his arms—because I had dared interfere between him and his wife."[21] When he was finally released, he attacked Layard and had to be restrained again. "When he recovered from his mad fit, he apologized, etc, but I refused to accept any apology or reparation unless he consented to return to England immediately."[22] After the group returned to Mosul, the embarrassed Rollands soon left.

We can only speculate whether a genuine physical attraction sparked between Layard and Charlotte and if either one acted on it, but there are clues in one of his letters to Henry Ross: "I shall feel her loss much, as she is the only person who has given me the slightest assistance—copying inscriptions, notes, M.S. and taking bearings." These aren't the words a man uses for a lover. At the same time, Layard trusted Ross with a sealed letter to pass on to Charlotte, expecting "she will probably write a few *private* lines to let me know how they have got on, which she will entrust to you—pray take them and forward them to me [emphasis in the original]."[23]

Layard wondered months later how Charlotte Rolland got on, writing Ross that "her letter greatly relieved my mind in many respects, and I hope she will reach England safely and receive that protection which she so much requires from her parents." The whole melodrama left him bitterly disappointed in his old friends Christian and Matilda Rassam and still loathing the Badgers. "I am disgusted with the whole circus & shall probably never put my foot into the [Rassam] house again."[24]

★   ★   ★

Then more disaster. While Layard and the others were away at Khabur, storms had made the Tigris flood the plain, and the palace lions were swept away from their resting spots by the riverbank. When they were eventually retrieved, one of them cracked in two, and some ignorant vandal had broken its nose, causing minor damage. Then on the leg of the journey to Basra, the swollen river dragged away the raft carrying the broken lion and several cases packed with valuable reliefs. It was feared lost until a resourceful British steamship captain rescued both the cases and the lion in a couple of trips. The lion was eventually restored back at the British Museum.

Back in Layard's camp, everyone was suffering bouts of malaria. Luckily, Hormuzd Rassam and Layard didn't experience attacks at the same time and picked up the slack for each other. Even in the scorching month of July, Layard rose every morning at six and worked until midnight or one in the morning, drawing, copying inscriptions, and packing sculptures. Sandwith and Cooper, the laziest of the crew, not surprisingly turned out to be the worst patients and, with the punishing heat, were dispatched off to the mountains.

In the autumn, Layard haggled in correspondence with museum officials over the latest expenses (they were upset with the Khabur expedition), and he was annoyed that he would have to fork out £100 to £150 to pay Dr. Sandwith . . . who had spent most of his time killing wild animals instead of healing humans. It was true, however, that the doctor and the artist were seriously ill and not improving; he decided to send them home, and by mid-August, he could rely only on the ever-loyal and resourceful Hormuzd.

After organizing another shipment of sculptures to London, Layard, Hormuzd Rassam, and thirty of the Jebour workers boarded a kelek down the Tigris for Baghdad. The whole region was now in a state of political anarchy, and there was rampant looting of caravans. Bedouin robbers had already attacked one of Layard's rafts on the Tigris, and he was astonished at how the raid had turned into a bloody skirmish. "The men I had hired to accompany it defended themselves well," he wrote proudly to Canning, "and after killing twenty-five of the assailants and wounding a considerable number, compelled the remainder to retreat."[25]

Layard got a sheikh from the Shammar tribe to journey along with his group and provide protection. While the sheikh smoked his pipe and offered old war stories, one of his sons rode a mare along the banks, keeping an eye out for trouble. They made a brief stop at Tikrit, the birthplace of Saladin, the founder of Islam's Ayyubid dynasty who fought against the Crusades. In our time, the town has the more dubious distinction of being the birthplace of Saddam Hussein and would serve as a bloody battleground for both the Iraq War and the conflict with ISIS. In Layard's era, however, it was a sleepy little burg, and while Bedouins were camped on the riverbanks, he wrote that "under the protection of our sheikh, we met with no hindrance."

On October 25, the kelek drifted through date palm groves as it approached Baghdad, and as it floated around a bank, "two gilded domes and four stately minarets, all glittering in the rays of an eastern sun," rose above a "dense bed of palms." It was the beautiful Al-Kadhimiya mosque. Layard was fond of Baghdad, but he hadn't visited in a decade, and for all its mixture of "Turks, Arabs, Persians, Indians," its long, vaulted bazaars and its "painted palaces and unsightly hovels," he found the city worse for wear. "Dams, watercourses and any other public work has been allowed to go to ruin," he wrote Canning in early November. "The result has been that during several months of the year, Baghdad stands, like an island, in the midst of a vast, pestilent marsh. From the effects of the malaria, according to the government returns which are undoubtedly far beneath the mark, 11,000 persons died last year in the city alone!"[26] No one could venture beyond the city gates without getting preyed on by bandits.

Rawlinson was still away in England, and bouts of fever and bandit marauders in the countryside kept Layard in Baghdad until early December. Meanwhile, he kept his Jebour workmen busy excavating some mounds not far from the gates of the city. It was important that Layard have the right permissions to go digging around in the south, and so he finally went to pay his respects to Abde Pasha, the governor of the province. The governor thought if he could dam a large canal, it would drain the marshes west of Babylon where bandits and rebels preferred to hide. Layard paid a call on his army camp, and the two hit it off, with the governor entertaining him with displays of falconry. Layard didn't have permission from the vizier in Istanbul, but the governor and several influential sheikhs had given him impressive enough letters that he decided to go ahead with his excavation.

The excavations, however, were a major disappointment. Bricks without sculptures and no ornamentation as he had found at Nimrud. He warned Canning that if he kept working, the effort would hardly justify the expense. Layard moved on to try the ruins of one of the ancient cities of Sumeria in what is now modern-day Nuffar. At the time, they were a few miles from small islands in the center of vast marshes formed by the Euphrates River. Here, Layard saw a fascinating and ancient way of life that had been in danger of extinction for decades, the culture of the Ma'dan of Iraq.

Wearing keffiyeh and long shirts, the Arabs here traveled around on their traditional canoe-like boats called *tiradas*, steering with long bamboo poles. People herded water buffalo and cultivated wheat and barley. Their *mudhifs*, traditional guesthouses, were (and still are, where examples can be found) spectacular feats of architecture, with pillars and archways built out of bundled reeds. When Layard was taken around in one of their narrow wicker boats, he saw the traffic in the "lanes" and was reminded of scenes in the bas-reliefs from Kuyunjik of Assyrian wars in marshes; he doubted that little in the swamps had changed.

Inevitably, it would. The explorer Wilfred Thesiger lived among the Ma'dan over several years in the 1950s. He produced the travel classic *The Marsh Arabs* and predicted how these special wetlands would be drained for the sake of industry in the wake of the Middle East oil boom.[27] Saddam Hussein's regime and war threatened the marshes further, but efforts have been made more recently for restoration. Layard spent time with the Marsh Arabs long before even a whisper of modernity could touch their gigantic, tall reeds. He gained their trust and respect by checking his almanac and predicting a partial eclipse of the moon.

At Nuffar, Layard found examples of pottery and decorated coffins, but each time a sarcophagus was opened, the remains of the buried dead crumbled to dust. He hoped to move on to another site, but there was too much political unrest going on. Not used to the marsh climate, he suffered another bout of malaria made worse by an attack of pleurisy. On top of all that, the rains pounded down with monsoon torrents, lifting the marsh waters and flooding into the Arab tents. The villagers began to pack to go elsewhere. Layard was so weak that he could barely move from his bed, and he came close to dying.

Out of panic, he self-medicated with a "blistering fluid" that was supposed to be for an injured horse. Whatever it was, it helped. Hormuzd Rassam recovered enough from his own sickness to join him, and Layard returned his group to Baghdad before it got caught up in the anarchy of the widespread revolt.

He hadn't been well for two weeks, and yet he rode with his small caravan for an incredible fourteen hours. The next day before dawn, he could barely mount his horse, but they set out again. As the sun rose, he spotted the ruins of Ctesiphon, the ancient capital of the Parthians, across the Tigris River, and Layard saw the "remarkable effect" of a mirage. "As the quivering sun rose in unclouded splendor, the palace was transformed into a vast arcade of enormous arches resting upon columns and masses of masonry. . . . In a few minutes, this strange edifice began to melt away into air, and I saw a magnified though perfect image of the palace, but upon it was its exact counterpart upside down." Layard had seen mirages before but never one "more striking or more beautiful."

Once the riding party reached Baghdad, a doctor soon put Layard to bed. His Jebour workmen had to make their own way on foot, and while looking for water, bandits stole everything they had, leaving the men naked in the desert. Luckily, they received some clothes and food later from compassionate residents of a small village.

★   ★   ★

The work went on at Kuyunjik. By the spring, Layard was bitter again over the familiar lack of support from the British Museum. Enough was enough, and he decided to quit and go home to London. "I feel that it is full time that I should turn my attention seriously to my profession," he wrote to Canning. If his boss "knew how very inadequately I have been supported throughout and how many difficulties I have had to contend with, I do not think you would concur [with the Trustees]."

He even found fault with the artist sent out to eventually replace Cooper. Layard noted that Thomas Bell, though competent, was "a mere boy, very willing and industrious, but not the person any enlightened government would dream of sending out on such an expedition." All these conditions amounted to a lost opportunity, and "I feel heartily ashamed when I compare my published drawings with those of the French. With the subjects, we had enough to have produced a ten times' finer work than our neighbours."[28]

Near the end of April, Layard packed drawings and small items he could take in his own baggage, and he left the whole expedition in the hands of young Thomas Bell in Mosul. Years of his life had been spent under the harsh sun and in trenches and dirt, collecting the "evidences of ancient greatness and civilisations" and revealing them "in the midst of modern ignorance and decay." Now it was all over, and even he knew he would probably never return here. On April 28, he "bid a last farewell to my faithful Arab friends, and with a heavy heart, turned from the ruins of ancient Nineveh."

But in passing through Alexandretta in May on his journey home, he was in for a shock. Christian Rassam had sent a letter telling him that Bell was dead. The artist ignored the warnings of locals and went for a swim in the Gomel River, an offshoot of the Tigris, where he promptly drowned. A shaken Layard blamed the Trustees for assigning such a young man in the first place. By June, he was on a ship from Beirut, bound for home.

When Thomas Bell lost his life, a unique opportunity was also lost. He had been trained in using an early kind of camera, one that worked with what used to be called "calotype" or "talbotype" photography (after its inventor, Fox Talbot). We could have had still shots of one of the earliest excavations of Assyria.

Henry Layard in Bakhtiari dress. Portrait made in 1843 in Istanbul and used as the frontispiece of the first volume of his *Early Adventures*.

Layard in Albanian dress. Portrait by Henry Phillips used as the frontispiece for the first volume of his _Autobiography_.

The Siq at Petra. *Photo courtesy of the author.*

The stunning Treasury at Petra.

Layard being lowered down to examine an Assyrian rock sculpture at Bavian. *Monuments of Nineveh.*

Ancient Nimrud, as envisioned by James Fergusson.

The hall of an Assyrian palace, as envisioned by Fergusson. *Monuments of Nineveh.*

Relief showing a scene of after a royal bull hunt. *Photo used with permission of the British Museum.*

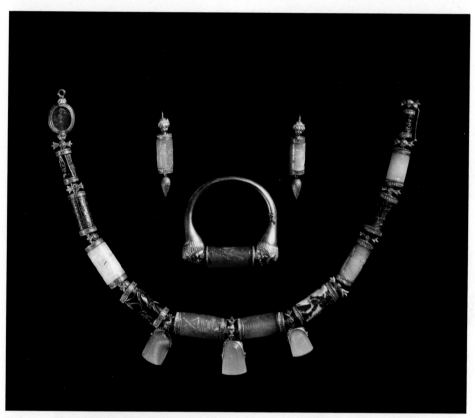

Lady Layard's necklace made with treasures found by Layard in his excavations. *Photo used with permission of the British Museum.*

Winged sculptures flank an entrance to part of the British Museum's stunning Assyrian collection. *Photo used with permission of the British Museum.*

A winged bull (*lamassu*) at the Metropolitan Museum of Art in New York City.

Enid Layard, wearing her Assyrian jewelry, painted in 1870 by the Spanish artist Vicente Palmaroli González.

The exterior of the Hagia Sofia modern day. *Photo courtesy of the author.*

The interior of the Hagia Sofia in our modern age. *ThingsToDoEverywhere.com.*

Galata Bridge, Istanbul, circa 1890, what the city still looked like more or less around the time Layard left for good. A postcard colorized in the era with the Photochrom process. *Photo courtesy of the U.S. Library of Congress.*

The Great Sage of Archaeology: Henry Layard at age seventy-three, portrait that hung in the British embassy at Ankara.

The Grand Canal, circa 1890, in Venice, the city where Layard spent his happy retirement. A postcard colorized in the era with the Photochrom process. *Photo courtesy of the U.S. Library of Congress.*

Ludgate Hill, looking towards St. Paul's Cathedral in 1896, two years after Layard's death. *Author's personal collection.*

The mountains of what today is the autonomous region of Kurdistan in modern Iraq. *Photo courtesy of the author.*

Peshmerga officers and soldiers at the Kurdish Front in 2015. *Photo courtesy of the author.*

• 9 •

Forward the Light Brigade

$\mathscr{J}$anet Duff Gordon—who would grow up to be an accomplished historian and biographer—recalled in a memoir how as a nine-year-old girl, she sat in the garden of her family house in Esher, Surrey, when a guest introduced her to Layard. "Here is the man who dug up those big beasts you saw in the British Museum, and he is called Mr. Bull." Henry Layard, she wrote, "accepted his nickname with a good grace, and for years, all his youthful and many old admirers and friends (and they were numerous) never called him anything else."[1] She would become one of those good friends and write him often, with Layard even signing his reply letters to her, "Mr. Bull."

When she was in her teens, Layard brought to dinner his friend Henry Ross, and young Janet was spellbound as Ross described how he was once pigsticking in distant Mesopotamia, and his horse caught its foot in a hole and rolled over him; he might have been gored to death had Layard not galloped up and distracted the boar.[2] At eighteen, Janet married Ross.

Layard was the toast of London when he returned in 1851. John Murray had already put out a new edition of *Nineveh and Its Remains*, and Layard's more academic work *Inscriptions in the Cuneiform Character from Assyrian Monuments* had also been published. But flattery and fame made him uncomfortable, and he soon tired of London's beautiful people. He remained unsettled for much of the year.

"My plans are still so uncertain that I cannot give you the slightest idea of them," he wrote Ross in late November. "I shall certainly not leave England again if I can help it, but I may be forced to do so, as at present at any rate, I have no means of making ends meet without some employment. I shall make a desperate effort not to return to the East, not even to Istanbul, which does not agree with me in any way—the climate always disagrees with me,

129

and I can find neither books nor society. I should like to get into Parliament in England and think that, if once there, I could push my way. My book is still far behind, and there is no chance of its being ready before spring."[3] This was his *Nineveh and Babylon,* and it would be more than another year before it was in print.

His relations with the Trustees of the British Museum were strained, and he had no desire to do more excavations for them. Fortunately, he impressed enough of the right people for a job where his talents could be used. It took a while, but by early January 1852, he was offered the post of secretary for the British legation in Paris at a salary of £500. The offer, he thought, was "very flattering," and it "may be, in many ways, the means of bringing me into notice and enabling me to be of use."[4] But then Lord Granville, serving as foreign secretary in the fragile coalition government, made an even better offer: undersecretary of the Foreign Office. From unpaid attaché in distant Istanbul to a lofty position in Whitehall? This was a coup!

On his second day of work, Layard wrote his friend the Countess of Aboyne, "I am in a desperate state of mind about finding lodgings and establishing myself respectably. I have every hope to be able to carry out many of the ideas we have so often talked over together, and my first object must be to get a decent establishment where I can collect people about me. There is, unfortunately, little time for this, but perhaps one morning a week may be spared. The book is the difficulty which must be got over before all others, and I must devote an hour or two daily to it. Unfortunately, it is almost a duty to go into society, and I suspect I shall have very few evenings to myself."[5]

He would have more time than he thought. The fragile conservative coalition in power broke apart, and Layard was out of a job after only eleven days at his desk. Though Granville suggested he stay on until his successor could arrive from India, Layard felt pressure from his Liberal allies, particularly the influential politician John Russell, who sent word that he should resign early. Layard did, and the decision turned out to be a mistake; when he needed Russell to find him another appointment, the Great Man was conveniently unavailable.

Layard now threw himself into politics. The Liberals offered him several choices for an election battlefield, but he settled on Aylesbury, the town where his parents used to live. It would not be a cakewalk—Aylesbury was a Tory stronghold. But he had celebrity on his side and was promoted as "a man of powerful mind, of indomitable courage and lofty principles." He wrote to his friend the Countess of Aboyne, "I am up at 6 a.m. and at work from then till a late hour at night. But the country is beautiful, and the hard work and pure air [are] all for my good."[6] Politicians, then as now, could play dirty, and his education began with the campaign. When arrangements were made for him to give a lecture in the town hall, three visiting justices—all staunch Tories—vetoed use of the venue. A local schoolroom had to be found at the last minute.

In the end, he won the seat by a healthy majority. "I never saw such a scene of triumph as our chairing procession," he wrote Aboyne. "Every window full of well-dressed ladies, showering down bouquets of flowers, sending cakes and wine, waving flags, etc., etc. The procession must have extended half a mile. Women brought their babies and carried them before us. It was a complete triumph and most gratifying."[7] Granville wrote Layard to congratulate him on his win and passed along some political wisdom he'd been given himself when he first entered the Commons: "Never, till your reputation is established, speak on any subject but those that you both know and are supposed by others to know and never, however tempting the occasion may be, condescend to personalities." It was good, solid advice. Pity that Layard wouldn't always follow it.

He didn't make any mark in the Commons his first year, but then backbenchers seldom do. Before the turn of the twentieth century, being a member of Parliament in Britain amounted to a gentleman's leisurely pursuit. There was no salary; you were expected to make your income elsewhere. Layard had banked on his political career helping to carry him through the Foreign Office. Now his prospects were shrinking. John Russell offered him the position of consul general in Egypt. He was perfect for it, and it paid £1,700 a year. Layard still didn't want to leave England.

If he had to travel, let it be for short periods, and he reluctantly agreed to join Canning on a unique mission to Istanbul during Parliament's April recess. The Russians were saber rattling again, causing a lot of mischief in Jerusalem at the holy sites—backing Greek Orthodox officials against France and the Roman Catholic Church. Canning's task was to help settle things down, with Layard acting as his right-hand man. But the former protégé chafed over working again under his old mentor. He was no longer a callow young adventurer but a mature MP in his thirties, while the years hadn't mellowed the bad-tempered Canning at all. Little was accomplished on the mission, and by May, Layard headed home to London.

There was the small comfort that John Murray had brought out his latest book, and it sold well. This time, it was a single volume titled *Discoveries among the Ruins of Nineveh and Babylon*. Like Layard's first opus, Victorian de rigueur required a long-winded subtitle: "with travels in Armenia, Kurdistan and the Desert, Being the result of a Second Expedition undertaken for the Trustees of the British Museum." If that wasn't enough Assyria for readers, more discriminating fans could buy a second series of *The Monuments of Nineveh*, which had prints of the bas-reliefs. To add to his celebrity, Layard was made an honorary citizen of London.

In 1853, Layard also began a stimulating and lasting friendship with another best-selling author: Charles Dickens. They shared certain similar views on religion, and they were often in tune over politics. Through the years, the creator of Scrooge and Tiny Tim wrote to his friend about his plans for the holiday season, often urging him to visit: "Pray come to us in time for dinner on Christmas."[8]

★   ★   ★

The dispute over holy sites in Jerusalem held greater significance than anyone could have anticipated, for these were the months that led to the Crimean War.

Britain, France, and Russia were playing a dangerous game of *Risk* on the board of Europe. Napoleon III wanted to keep his Catholic supporters happy while humiliating the Russians. Arguably far more dangerous were the ambitions of Tsar Nicholas I, who kept warning anyone who would listen that the Ottoman Empire was about to collapse—and then kept saying it was about to collapse for more than twenty years.

But in late 1852, Nicholas had written a detailed memorandum on how he'd like to see it broken up: Russia would get parts of what is today modern Romania; Serbia and Bulgaria would become independent; Austria would get the Adriatic coast; Britain would collect spots like Cyprus and Rhodes, and oh, yes, Egypt for good measure; France would be mollified with Crete, and Greece would be expanded; and Istanbul would be run as an international city.[9] It was a grandiose vision that evicted the centuries-old Ottoman squatter from Europe, and on the surface, looked intended to satisfy the other powers, but it really served the long-term expansionist aims of Russia.

Nicholas needed Great Britain on his side, and the current prime minister, Lord Aberdeen, had always been more sympathetic to Russia than to France. Still, Nicholas badly miscalculated that Aberdeen would let him have his way. Thinking he could get things done in one big push, Nicholas sent a special envoy to Istanbul in February 1853, and it was this situation that had prompted Aberdeen to use Canning.

The tsar's man wasn't a diplomat at all; he was Prince Alexander Menshikov, an admiral who helped his country's forces beat back the French in 1812 and who had fought in the Russo-Turkish War of 1828–1829. At the siege of Varna, when he was put in charge of prying the Bulgarian city away from the Ottomans, a cannon shell exploded and emasculated him. Now sixty-five, Menshikov was the perfect choice for the tsar's purpose, which was to deliberately provoke and intimidate the Sublime Porte. He had a big ego, and his sarcasm made him "a little dreaded by St. Petersburg society."[10] On arriving in Istanbul, he offended the entire diplomatic corps by showing up in civilian clothes instead of his proper uniform. Then he curtly refused to talk to the Turkish foreign minister and called for him to be sacked. It's easy to see how shaky the Ottoman Empire was given that the Turks *did* sack their official and let Menshikov's aide interview his replacement before the man took office.

But Menshikov had more bullying to do. His demands would put the Ottoman holdings in Europe directly in Russia's control. The Russian army was poised on the frontier and the Black Sea Fleet was ready to sail in and take Istanbul if the Porte said no; the situation was so grim that Grand Vizier Mehmet Ali confidentially asked British and French envoys to mobilize their own fleets in the Aegean. The British held back, but Napoleon III—wanting to appear strong—sent ships as far as the waters around Salamis Island.

This made Whitehall look bad, and Canning stiffened the grand vizier's backbone, urging him to appear open-minded on the holy sites but to keep turning down Menshikov's more inflammatory demands. Britain would come to Turkey's defense. The Russians must have sensed that the mercurial Canning—who still had plenty of clout in Istanbul—was working behind the scenes, and Menshikov broke off diplomatic relations with the Porte in late May and left for Odessa.

On June 13, Layard asked in the House of Commons whether the Royal Navy had been given orders to sail to Besika Bay or a point near the Dardanelles. John Russell, speaking for the government, admitted that the British admiral at Malta had indeed proceeded to Besika Bay and that the ambassador had been given contingency orders in case hostilities broke out. By July 1, Layard asked in the House if the Russians had blocked the entrance to the principal channel of the Danube, but Russell was forced to admit the Foreign Office simply didn't know. To get his way, Tsar Nicholas sent troops to occupy Moldavia and Wallachia, the Danubian principalities of the Ottoman Empire that now form part of today's Romania. Layard saw this invasion for what it was, a "calculated" attempt to extort more, and he said so.

The whole affair was politically embarrassing for Aberdeen, who coaxed *The Times* into printing an article that scolded the young backbencher for talking about issues that should be left to confidential negotiations. Layard, however, was one of the most informed men on the region. As time dragged on, the situation only got worse and vindicated his opinions. On August 16, Layard made the first major speech of his parliamentary career.

He felt nervous as he started but found his rhythm and pressed on. He attacked Menshikov's tactics and bullying as "examples of duplicity, falsehood, injustice, and insolence unequalled in diplomacy." He noted that Russia's "great object has been to crush the spirit of political and religious independence which has manifested itself of late years among the Christian subjects of the Porte, and she will spare no effort to effect that end." To those who were intellectually lazy or callous enough to think that Russia humiliating the Turks hardly mattered in the grand scheme of things, he reminded them that the Turks were the "dominant" tribe, with Syrians, Arabs, Jews, Armenians, Kurds, and other ethnic groups held together only by the Ottoman regime. Was Britain prepared then to take them over or leave them to their fate with Russia?[11]

His impression, as he confided in a letter to an acquaintance, Lady Huntly, was that the members "received what I said exceedingly well and were evidently with me. I was well cheered throughout by a very large House for this time of the session." He impressed others, too. On hand to cover the discussion was Karl Marx, correspondent for *The New York Tribune*. For his dispatch published in early September, Marx wrote that Layard "made by far the best and most powerful speech—bold, concise, substantial, filled with facts, and proving the illustrious scholar to be as intimately acquainted with Nicolas as Sardanapalus, and with the actual intrigues of the Orient as with the mysterious traditions of its past."[12]

But his speech also contained a couple of unnecessary barbs at Aberdeen's expense—treading into personalities when Granville had warned him not to. In speaking out, Layard knew he had made a final break with the government. "The split between myself and the Ministers is now complete, and I suppose all chance of employment out of the question. I do not mind. I have done what I believe to be my duty, and I trust I shall always be able to refer back to what has occurred with conscientious satisfaction." But not at the moment. The idea of war and the failure of those on Aberdeen's side to act drove him to distraction, and he took the September recess in Parliament to visit Italy and lose himself in the paintings of great masters.

The issue, however, would not go away, and as much as it might confuse ordinary Britons at first—the Muslim Ottoman Empire cast as underdog versus the traditional Christian ally of Russia—sympathy grew for Turkey. Dr. Humphry Sandwith had managed to become the correspondent for *The Times* in Istanbul, but its powerful editor, John Delane, sent him a chastising letter over his sympathy for the Turks. Sandwith preferred to quit, and *The Times* was soon in the minority. Papers such as *The Standard* pointed out that loss of trade with Turkey threatened British commerce more than any deficit from Russia, while others, like *The Daily News*, *The Morning Chronicle*, and *The Morning Herald* pinned their arguments to the honor and safety of Europe.[13]

Edward Bulwer-Lytton, who would become one of Layard's friends and give us prose such as "It was a dark and stormy night," also recognized the threat from the tsar: "Surely, if there ever was a war waged on behalf of posterity, it is the war which would check the ambitions of Russia."[14]

The Turks had been divided among themselves as well, with Muslim clerics and other religious leaders insisting the sultan either declare war on Russia or step down. The military had been reluctant; its officers knew what they would be up against, and their hopes rested on Britain and France coming to their aid, but their allies dithered. It took months for their resolve to harden, and as Layard's profile grew, Henry Grey, the latest Earl Grey, played apologist for Aberdeen's fence-sitting and took the young MP to task in the House of Lords on February 14. He pointed out that anyone could dip into Layard's latest book and find passages with examples where Ottoman subjects trying to improve their lot "were checked by the utter corruption, extreme tyranny, and total want of faith with which they are treated by the Turkish authorities."[15]

Three days later, Layard fired back in the Commons. He acknowledged that "barbarous acts of oppression" had been committed in Turkey but argued that it was more advanced than Russia. He wouldn't stand in the House "to defend a religion [Islam] which is repugnant to my feelings and common sense, and which I believe to be false." This was disingenuous, as Layard often found Christianity offended his common sense, but he kept those thoughts private. He reminded his fellow MPs that Grey had suggested Britain should allow Russia to exact what terms it liked and maybe take over the Ottoman Empire. Layard found this "a most dangerous doctrine. Where are you to stop Russia? Is she to go on taking the whole world?"[16]

His speech earned him significant respect, including from old family friend Disraeli, now Leader of the Opposition. "How Layard is coming out!" Henry Ross wrote his sister on March 16. "He is improving as an orator, and his words are true. It is my conviction that he will be high place some day, borne along by that popular wave whose swelling I have marked for years, and which will finally overwhelm the landmarks of aristocracy."[17]

Ross was a good and loyal friend, but his young wife likely understood better how Layard could be his own worst enemy: "The impulsiveness which made him so lovable in private stood in his way in public life. Generous and high-couraged to a fault, he would rush into the fray and occasionally make assertions he could not prove without giving the name of his informant and getting him into trouble—a thing he would rather have died than do. A sentence in one of his letters to me as a young girl, 'I am always getting into hot water,' was only too true."[18]

Finally, Britain and France threw in their lot with the Turks and declared war on Russia on March 28. Days later, Layard expressed his delight at the news in the Commons but then let loose an attack on Aberdeen and his circle. Tom Taylor, the editor of *Punch* magazine, had warned him in a letter that he shouldn't personalize his criticism: "I *know* you are not acting for personal motives. . . . I *know* you feel strongly on this question and that your course is dictated by motives worthy of respect. But! But!"[19]

Layard didn't heed his advice. He insinuated that each time Aberdeen was in a position of power, the tsar had come calling, looking to get his way. He singled out *The Times* for trying to build pro-Russian sentiment by getting hold of documents leaked by the prime minister's powerful allies. He was on firmer ground in the House when he pointed out that Britain was going to war woefully unprepared; everyone respected his knowledge of the frontiers involved.

"You do not know what Turkey is, or what are the resources of the country for the maintenance of an army. The troops may become infected with the worst of fevers, and you do not know how many of those men who are now going to that country will return, unless you make some preparations more worthy of the occasion than you appear to have done."[20]

As the bitter divide over the war went on, Layard always performed better when he relied on his experience in the Middle East. One time, a prominent backbencher foolishly tried to take him on, asking if a Christian in Turkey could be a kadi or a magistrate. Layard shot back that he might as well ask whether a Muslim could become Archbishop of Canterbury, and under the reforms of the Tanzimat, Christian Greeks, Armenians, or even Jews could hold office "with a liberality not even known in this country."[21]

When the Commons recessed in August, Layard decided to see the Crimea for himself with Delane of *The Times* and Alexander Kinglake, who's remembered mostly today as one of the pioneers of travel literature for his book *Eothen* about the Middle East. Kinglake later wrote the first comprehensive history of the Crimean War. For his part, Delane found the two authors "capital travelling companions, and I seem to have heard more good stories [lately] than in the last twelve months."[22] While Delane skewered Layard in the pages of *The Times*, they were good friends on a personal basis.

From Istanbul on September 5, Delane wrote to a friend that he expected no fighting. "Such is the discouragement of the army, and so bad the tone of its commanders, French and English, that I am half inclined to rejoice that nothing is to be entrusted to them." There were peers given commands who "complain that they are to be sacrificed to please the English press and the English people; that it is of no use attacking; that they are sure to be defeated; that it is too late this year; that they are sick of the whole thing, etc."[23]

Kinglake and Delane traveled on the *Britannia*, the flagship of Admiral James Dundas, the commander in chief of the Mediterranean fleet, while Layard had been invited by Admiral Edmund Lyons to join him on the *Agamemnon*. Lyons's vessel was the Royal Navy's first screw-propelled steamship, which was still equipped with square-rig sails. Both Delane and Layard would hear of general complaints over the incompetence of Dundas, even that the admiral allegedly neglected to take on adequate supplies of coal.

Before the *Agamemnon* reached its harbor in the Crimea, Layard wrote home, "It is difficult to conceive anything more beautiful than the sight before the cabin window as I write. Twenty-three magnificent ships in line of battle, enclosing to the southward several hundred transports. . . . I intend to see as much as I can of the land operations. It is as well to have some experience of these matters when one talks about them in the House of Commons, and I wish some of my friends were here."[24]

★ ★ ★

The Crimean War is no longer taught in schools, but it bequeathed to us powerful icons and imagery. This is the war with "The Lady with the Lamp," Florence Nightingale, sainted in posterity but in real life a prickly customer. It had Mary Seacole, a cheerful and determined lady from Jamaica, pouring lemonade and serving sponge cake for soldiers at her "British Hotel" in Balaclava. It had one of the first superstars of journalism, William Russell, flitting from battle to battle, revealing the pointlessness of the campaigns as effectively as any correspondent in Vietnam. While Napoleon's rise and fall had been captured in vivid splashes across canvas, Britons saw the stark reality of the Crimea frozen in photographs, with the famous cannonballs on a road in a shot by Roger Fenton. The war once mattered, and with Vladimir Putin's modern grab of the Crimea, we can appreciate some very old dynamics and the magnetic pull of history.

Britain's military leaders were a geriatrics' club for aristocrats who had bought their positions and were often related to each other. Lord Raglan, the commander in chief, had lost an arm at Waterloo and was sixty-five. The army's chief engineer, John Burgoyne, was seventy-two. The Earl of Cardigan, at sixty, commanded the 11th Hussars (and had paid £40,000 for the privilege to do so). Lord Lucan, his brother-in-law (whom he detested), had also bought his command and had no combat experience at all except to evict starving Irish from villages during the Great Famine; they dubbed him "The Exterminator."[25]

Layard, the middle-class upstart, knew of the highborn and dim, and before he left with Kinglake and Delane, he had put forward a remarkable idea in the House of Commons. "Why does not the government allow some great firm to contract for carrying on the war?" He noted that if a great railway needed to be built in a foreign land, a contractor could forget cronyism and instead "seek out those who by their abilities, experience, and knowledge,

Men of the 4th Dragoon Guards with a woman, a shot taken by the famous photographer Roger Fenton in 1855. *Courtesy Roger Fenton Crimean War Photograph Collection, U.S. Library of Congress.*

were best calculated to carry the undertaking to a successful, speedy, and economical conclusion. It is upon the same principle that the public wish appointments to be made, and until appointments are made upon this principle we shall ever have to complain of failures and fatal errors."[26]

He had no idea how prophetic these words would be in this conflict.

The disorganized Allies had first hoped to capture Sevastopol by surprise but chose to land their forces forty-five kilometers away at Kalamita Bay in mid-September. British soldiers were late to the offensive, their numbers stricken with cholera. On the Alma Heights, the Russians waited for the challenge, led by Alexander Menshikov. When the advance on Sevastopol finally started on September 19, there was a minor humiliation for the Light Brigade when it had to be ordered to withdraw from the slopes south of the Alma

River or get obliterated by Cossacks and infantry forces. A British private wrote home, "Serve them bloody right, silly peacock bastards."[27]

Layard watched the battle unfold from the maintop of the *Agamemnon*. While the view was spectacular, it's surprising he could parse so many fine details, but he was in the company of officers who surely could explain the deployments and action. His diary entry for September 20 is reasonably accurate: "The enemy's cavalry formed to protect the rear, and as we were without cavalry, we could not pursue. Had we possessed sufficient cavalry, the retreat would have been a rout, and nearly all the guns would have fallen into our hands." This was true. The Allies had left important supplies like tents and other items aboard the ships, which were providing cover fire and medical support. To sever the umbilical cord to the fleet would have spelled disaster.

Nevertheless, the Allies prevailed. As the ship's artillery fired on the retreating Russians, Layard and a group of naval officers went ashore. He wrote in his diary, "We found a large number of slain Russians and French on the heights and many wounded—very dreadful scene." Layard had been in the thick of skirmishes before, but here was "a continuous heap of the dead" torn apart by cannon fire and Enfield rifles. "Only those who have seen a field of battle can know what such a scene is—and can understand the feelings which it excites. The amount of suffering is so great, the mutilations are so awful, and death is seen under so many forms that there is too much for sympathy and almost complete indifference succeeds to the first feeling of consternation. . . . You aid a wounded man without scarcely remembering the intensity of his sufferings."[28]

The next day, he went ashore again and was appalled by the carnage. Dead and wounded lay scattered in every direction, the ground littered with the helmets, rifles, and packs that Russian soldiers had abandoned as they fled. He considered the lack of medical facilities and personnel disgraceful. When the army's Fourth Division took over an old Russian encampment, its men soon came down with cholera. "The unfortunate sick were brought down in bullock carts, packed one above the other like so many sacks."

In Paris, London, and parts of the British Empire, the Battle of Alma was enthusiastically hailed as a victory. Ordinary French and British citizens badly needed a win to justify all the expense and the trouble filling their newspaper pages. Newborn girls were named "Alma"—and so were streets and pubs. Paris has the Pont de l'Alma over the Seine, and Belfast has its Alma Street. The Canadian Maritime provinces have two small communities named Alma, one in New Brunswick and one in Nova Scotia.

Back in Crimea, the Russians might have been humiliated by Alma, but the broader picture was not so simple. The French persuaded the British to hold off from trying to take Sevastopol in one risky gambit, and now it promised to be a long siege. Two days after the battle, when the Russians realized their ships couldn't match the enemy, they stripped their guns from the vessels, took down their flags, and sank the ships smack in the mouth of the harbor. It was a bold and incredibly ruthless tactic, and it worked. The British generals and naval commanders were forced to move on to Balaclava . . . where disaster waited for them.

In the interval, Layard had an unexpected reunion. Men of the Third Division were sick with cholera and shivering in their camps, badly undersupplied without tents and other essential gear as the first chills of winter blew across the Crimean terrain, and among them was his brother, Arthur. Like Layard, Arthur was fluent in French and Italian, and his famous older brother arranged to have him reassigned to serve as liaison with soldiers from the other allied armies.

Conditions for the rest of the soldiers didn't improve. By the time Layard was in Balaclava, he wrote to his fellow MP Henry Bruce that "all the commissariat and medical arrangements are bad. The men are exposed to great unnecessary suffering, and the ravages of the cholera have been doubled by the want of common precautions. Up to this day, the men have not had their tents, and the officers only received them two or three days ago. You would be surprised at the state of things. . . . There are a number of red-waistcoated gentlemen with their hands in their pockets, idling about—men of undoubted gallantry, but without a spark of enthusiasm or energy—all voting the thing a great bore and longing for Pall Mall."

He thought he knew where to place the blame for the debacle of the war. "The fault lies at home. Dundas will probably be made a peer, and Lyons not noticed. A guardsman gets the command of a division, and the man who is competent is overlooked. Being at headquarters, I have an admirable opportunity of seeing everything."

That included a view of the disastrous Charge of the Light Brigade on October 25, 1854.

★   ★   ★

According to Layard, "who gave this frantic order, no one seems to know—as usual, there seems to have been no command."[29] The fighting men themselves were courageous, but he considered Lucan and the Earl of Cadogan, who led the Light Brigade, both incompetent. The blame really should begin with Raglan, who often lapsed into calling the French "the enemy." Whole books have been written on the Charge, but the essential facts boil down to these.

At Balaclava, Raglan had an enviable view from his perch high in the western valley, and it made him reckless. He issued a vague and tactically ludicrous order to Lucan to retake the Causeway Heights and recapture the artillery guns that had fallen into Russian hands. The order suggested Lucan's riders would get backup from the infantry, but Lucan couldn't see the infantry from his position, so he lingered for forty-five minutes. Back on his hill, Raglan lost his patience. He sent a second order: "Lord Raglan wishes the cavalry to advance rapidly to the front, follow the enemy, and try to prevent the enemy carrying away the guns. Troop horse artillery may accompany. French cavalry is on your left. Immediate."

Even on its face, this is unclear. *Which* guns? Besides the captured British guns, there were Russian guns in the north valley and still more at another spot. A Captain Louis Nolan, generally considered to be an arrogant, reckless fool, delivered the order to Lucan and overstepped himself by claiming that "the cavalry should attack immediately."

Lucan was naturally confused. "Attack, sir! Attack what? What guns, sir?"

Nolan threw his head back and gestured toward the left front corner of the valley. "There, my lord, is your enemy; there are your guns."

In 2016, a letter was discovered that was written by a Lieutenant Frederick Maxse, who served on Raglan's staff. Nolan "was always very indignant at the little they had done in this campaign & bitter against Lord L," wrote Maxse, who went on to claim, "All the cavalry lay this disastrous charge on his soldiers & say that he left no option to Lord L to whom they say his tone was almost taunting on delivering the message . . ."[30]

It's been argued that Nolan pushed for an attack when Raglan supposedly only intended a "mere show of force." But this makes little sense. No simple display would recapture the guns. And if Raglan merely wanted a show, he wouldn't be increasingly exasperated.[31] Far more damning when it comes to Nolan's motives is the probability, just as Lucan claimed later, that Nolan didn't motion to the British guns on Causeway Heights but to the Russian ones in the north valley. Captain Godfrey Morgan, in charge of the 17th Lancers, said to a fellow officer, "We are in range of them now from that battery on our left."

The Charge of the Light Brigade didn't start as a charge at all. More than 600 men rode their mounts in a trot straight toward Russian rifles and artillery. A shell burst in the air about 100 yards in front of the horses. Then the reckless Nolan impatiently raised his sword and spurred his mount into a gallop, rushing past Cardigan in command, only to be killed by an enemy shell. Lieutenant Maxse passed his body and wrote later, "If he was to blame, he has paid the penalty."[32] But so did others. As cannonballs rained down and the field was blanketed by heavy smoke, soldiers were cut to pieces.

Captain Godfrey Morgan of the 17th Lancers felt he rode "straight on to the muzzle of one of the guns, and I distinctly saw the gunner apply his fuse. I shut my eyes then, for I thought that settled the question as far as I was concerned. But the shot just missed me and struck the man on my right full in the chest."[33] Another man saw a sergeant's head "clean carried off by a round shot, yet for about thirty yards further, the headless body kept in the saddle, the lance at the charge, firmly gripped under the right arm."[34]

Yet in all the confusion, those who survived in the first line managed to charge the defending Cossacks, who fired on their own men at point-blank range to break free. Then amazingly, survivors of the charge regrouped as best they could, only to retreat across the north valley while still under enemy fire. One hundred and thirteen men were killed in the charge, with more than 130 others wounded and forty-five captured. Miraculously, the British did better than the Russians, who lost 180 men.

In the aftermath, the highest officers all blamed each other. William Russell, the famous correspondent for *The Times,* summed up the debacle by reporting, "Our Light Brigade was annihilated by their own rashness, and by the brutality of a ferocious enemy."

Back in London, Alfred, Lord Tennyson read Russell's reportage and scribbled down the lines of his most famous poem in a matter of minutes. "The Charge of the Light Brigade" was published in *The Examiner* on December 9, only six weeks after the event that inspired it. A few of the middle lines still echo in the popular imagination:

> "Forward the Light Brigade!"
> Was there a man dismayed?
> Not though the soldiers knew
> Some one had blundered:
> Their's not to make reply
> Their's not to reason why
> Their's but to do and die:
> Into the valley of Death
> Rode the Six Hundred.

As a firsthand witness, Layard didn't wax poetic: "It was a frightful sight to see the poor fellows led into almost inevitable destruction for no earthly object, and reflects great discredit upon our military authorities."[35]

★   ★   ★

The grim standoff at Sevastopol dragged on, and Layard grew increasingly frustrated. "After three weeks' almost complete inactivity during which the

Russians were allowed to raise numerous works without any interruption whatsoever, we opened our batteries," he wrote John Murray from the front lines. "This is the seventh day of operations against the place, and as yet, the results are but small." He considered the siege so deficient in men and materials that it was terribly crippled. "The men are so few in number that they have little more than five hours rest at the time under the most terrific fire that was ever known."[36]

The batteries were so far from the Russian front lines that they could do little serious damage anyway. "The French powder magazine was blown up on the day we opened, more than 100 men were killed or wounded, and their works were so much injured that for two whole days, they ceased their fire and left us to bear the brunt of the battle."[37] The plan was for the French to destroy a couple of Russian batteries at the mouth of the harbor and then for the Allies to capture it and work their way to the other end. But the Russians were dug in.

"There is a terrible want of men and leaders, and if this war continues, as it appears likely it will do, the government must give up jobs for the public good and have younger and more efficient men to be at the head of operations of every kind. I think that I may prove of some little use in getting this done on my return home, notwithstanding the personal odium which I shall, of course, incur."[38]

Layard carefully appraised the prominent senior officers under fire and considered the feelings of their men as well as the Allies. "I fear that as long as Dundas remains here, nothing will be done. The French are furious against him and say that he deserted them and left them to bear all the fire. Of Lyons, they speak in terms of unbounded admiration. Our cavalry is altogether inefficient, owing to the manner in which it is commanded by Lord Lucan—who is generally known in camp as 'Lord Look-on.'"

Layard's own sympathies were with the captains and subalterns who were "terribly overworked and [had] to remain under a most terrible fire. I cannot describe to you the uneasiness one feels as the hour approaches for their miserable mess of salt and pork. . . . I spent one afternoon in the trenches—quite enough for an amateur. I can do no good there, and it is no pleasant sight to see one's fellow creatures smashed into a heap of old rags. Some of the mutilations are frightful."[39]

At the Battle of Inkerman in early November, the Allies carried the day, but there was practically nothing gained, and there were thousands of casualties. The Russians already made a routine practice of bayoneting the wounded on the field, and the Allies would formally accuse them of mutilating the hurt and dying. Layard attended the funeral of three generals he had known personally.

The soldiers were already cold and miserable, and the worst of winter hadn't even started. The humiliating retreat of Bonaparte's army from Russia was still within living memory for the fathers of these troops and older officers, yet Raglan seemed determined to go through with the siege of Sebastopol. Layard expected high casualties; he would be proved right. Eventually, the Allies would take the city, but at a high cost. With nothing left to accomplish, he went home.

As someone who had seen the war up close and was an expert on the East, he was once again a man to pay attention to; when he stood up in the Commons on December 12, he spent several minutes basically saying, "I told you so," but eventually got to the meat of his argument, cataloging the mismanagement of the war.

"The Commander-in-chief's dispatches are but too frequently the records of the imaginary deeds and virtues of generals, aides-de-camp, and officers of the staff. The more humble individual who does the real work, who has the greater share of the danger, who endures all the privations, and is exposed to all the sufferings, is but too generally forgotten or overlooked." The veteran officers of the Peninsular War from thirty years ago "must no longer be the qualification for high and responsible posts in the Crimea. Men of seventy years of age may have been most gallant and able officers, but Nature, at that age, will no longer support the fatigues, privations, and hardships which those who are charged with arduous duties in war must of necessity go through. . . . We want younger and more active men." And he finished with this tart insult directed at the civil service: "If any private establishment were to attempt to carry on business as Ministers have attempted to carry on this war, it would be bankrupt in a week."[40]

In late January 1855, a Radical MP put forward a motion calling for a select committee to investigate the horrific conditions of the army and the government's mismanagement of the war. But it turned into a vote of no confidence in Aberdeen's administration. Queen Victoria was now forced to ask Palmerston, a man she deeply disliked, to form a new government. Where would Layard fit into the new puzzle? Palmerston offered him undersecretary for war. He could have achieved brilliant things there, and many knew it. One of his friends and admirers, Arthur Otway, wrote decades later that had he got the job, "in all probability, many of the disasters and miscarriages which occurred (during the war in South Africa), owing greatly to the inefficiency and want of organization in that office, would have been averted."[41]

But Layard had offended too many people. The Queen told Palmerston bluntly that she didn't like the appointment. He didn't help himself by setting conditions for his acceptance, demanding that certain colleagues he respected also get positions. Worse, he criticized the new government in the House over the war even while negotiations were under way to give him a job. Inevitably, Palmerston withdrew his offer of the War Office but had a consolation prize: undersecretary for the colonies. Friends urged Layard to accept, but he didn't feel he could take a position for which he wasn't really qualified.

He was frustrated and miserable, and he got into squabbles that carried over into the Commons—where he couldn't win. He exchanged some nasty letters with a peer over the old boy network behind the promotions of army officers. During those weeks, he was coping with a relapse of malaria. But his critics pounced on small errors he made and were merciless in the House, shouting insults and baiting him.

Maybe Layard's fortunes lay outside party lines. A new movement was gathering momentum. The name for it was painfully dull, as if coined by a bureaucrat—administrative reform—but it was really about overthrowing the old boy network and enfranchising ordinary people. We can recognize it as similar to the protests we have in our own day against capitalism and big business, and then as now, those in power argued this was setting "class against class." But it had crowded meetings across England, and, significantly, it earned press attention and raised money.

Layard was one of its front men, and he was caught up in its fever. "There is a spirit rising in the country," he wrote a friend in February, "which will be more formidable than our good, easy aristocratic families, who look upon Ministers as their perquisites, can now comprehend. I only hope it may be changed in time. Circumstances may lead me into leading the great movement which is now in progress. I have no wish to, but if I am forced into it, nothing will turn me aside from my end, and an immense struggle will be the result, in which I do not think I shall fail. Before many months are over, things will change."

• *10* •

"We Never Get the Indian Story"

By April, Layard had old friends such as Charles Alison and newer ones like Dickens writing to offer moral support and urging him to stand his ground. He also had the backing of influential newspapers and magazines thanks in part to Dickens's powerful influence. The novelist wrote him on April 3, "You will find yourself the subject of [*Punch's*] next large cut and of some lines in an earnest spirit." And thanks to his putting a word in, a contact "will do what is right in *The Illustrated London News* and *The Weekly Chronicle*, papers that go into the hands of large numbers of people."[1]

Days later, he wrote again to express his shared sympathies with Layard for the working class, who didn't have the vote, and how there was a possibility of an uprising. The smoldering discontent, thought Dickens, was much like the mood in France before the Revolution "and is in danger of being turned by any one of a thousand accidents—a bad harvest . . . a defeat abroad . . . with such a devil of a conflagration as has never been beheld since."[2]

Meanwhile, the attacks on Layard in the Commons went on, and he seemed to bounce from scrappy enthusiasm to moments of self-doubt and minor despair. There is a telling letter he sent on May 14, 1855, in reply to Arthur Hamilton-Gordon, Aberdeen's youngest son, who had served as assistant private secretary when his father was prime minister. "I am led to hope that notwithstanding some kind of presentiment to the contrary, I may be of little note in my generation. It is, no doubt, a very mortifying thing to one who has given up every prospect in life as I have for politics to find some of the best years of my life thrown away. In this country, it is difficult for a man who has not a great fortune or a great party at his back, a great popularity, to secure a place in public life. I always felt during the struggles I had in Parliament that I should have to pay the penalty of trying to be independent, and I have, therefore, no reason to complain."[3]

147

"Palmerston's Nightmare." Punch, *May 19, 1855.*

But less than a week later, Dickens wrote that he found Layard looking more cheerful, "a young man with the spirit of England at his back, and
its heartiest voice cheering him on, is bound to look his best." The famous
novelist coaxed him out to dinner with the editor of *Punch,* Mark Lemon,
and one of the magazine's illustrators. Dickens hoped the artist would use the
opportunity "of making the Nineveh Bull a little more like."[4]

By June, Layard was even impressing *The New York Times,* which saw
signs of a "profound political revolution." It reminded Americans that the
English people "do not like noise and bluster," but in a "deep, quiet way, a
revolution may be working which shall leave the English nobility where the
French was after the revolution of '98." The paper gushed over the man of the
hour. "Mr. Layard, as we understand, feels deeply for the oppressed nations
of Europe. . . . We believe no man in England has, for the next ten years, so
brilliant a prospect. The *Times* upholds him; the great, uprising middle class
back him; the aristocracy, the place-hunters, the jobbers and the toadies hate
and oppose him."[5]

On June 13, there was another meeting over administrative reform at
London's Drury Lane Theatre. Using the latest census, Layard got to the heart
of the issue: there were 4.5 million men in England over twenty years old, but
less than a million had the right to vote (the notion of women's voting rights
was ignored). But then he veered into a personal attack on Palmerston, whom

he accused of making jokes over the suffering of the soldiers in the war. Once again, his inflammatory comments came back to bite him in the Commons.

Two days later, he put forward a motion that asked the House to condemn party and family influence over public appointments—in effect to support administrative reform. It could have eventually brought down the government, but Palmerston still had strong support. Edward Bulwer-Lytton moved to tack on an amendment that the "House recommends . . . the necessity of a careful revision of our various official establishments" and introduce tests of merit. It was a face-saving move that worked for almost everyone—except Layard—and it passed. That was politics. But a furious Palmerston was deeply offended by Layard's slurs and called them "the Drury Lane Theatricals." He wanted to tell Layard to his face "that there is not a word of truth in the assertions which he then made. I never jested at the sufferings of the soldiers. I never made light of their unfortunate condition."[6]

There was yet another meeting for administrative reform close to the end of the month, again at Drury Lane, and this time, Dickens was a speaker. He defended Layard for stating "what the whole country knows perfectly well to be true" and quipped that while a Spanish bull rushes a scarlet matador cape, here, it was the scarlet cape that rushed the Nineveh bull. This meeting might have been the last big hurrah for the movement. For all the worries over revolution expressed in front of warm fireplaces at White's or the Travellers Club, England was *not* France. The rich and powerful wouldn't feel the ground really shift under their feet until the cultural and technological upheaval after World War II.

By being a firebrand, Layard couldn't take the reform proposals from the streets into the Commons chamber. He was no consensus builder, not when it came to ideas for which he felt passion and personal investment.

★ ★ ★

On August 7, Layard's brother, Arthur, died a pointless death in the Crimean War—but not in battle. Arthur came down with dysentery while aboard a ship in harbor, and he was buried near Balaclava. An army chaplain wrote with the sad news to Layard in Italy, where he was studying frescoes to serve his battered nerves.[7]

The war itself sputtered to its close. The Allies finally drove the Russians from Sevastopol, but it cost them dearly. When the British sailed into the Dardanelles, the Russians talked armistice but still encroached on Istanbul—until Her Majesty's ships made their presence felt at San Stefano, a nearby village. More than 20,000 British soldiers had lost their lives, most of them from disease and illness, not combat.

Layard had moved on from the war and the disillusionment over political reform. He busied himself with a new project that would consume his time for months and would have lasting implications into our own day. He was helping to create a bank.

Layard while a member of Parliament, date unknown but possibly 1860s. *Author's personal collection.*

His move into high finance was nothing short of astonishing. Here he was, an amateur archaeologist without a proper education and still only a backbencher member of Parliament— a man *loathed* by many in the upper classes—and he could get powerful private bankers to listen to him. A man whose closest brush with big numbers had been adding up the wages of day laborers in Mesopotamia. But the Turks were supposed to be allies now, and that prompted London businessmen to think "emerging market." Layard knew all the important people in the Ottoman Empire and served as chairman. Canning also got behind the venture, as did the chairman and deputy chairman of the Union Bank of Australia.

The group modeled their charter for the Ottoman Bank after the Bank of Egypt and started with comparatively modest capital: £500,000. Layard preferred to keep out the French, who wanted to make their own splash in Turkey's financial market, but he ended up negotiating with the country's bankers anyway to bring them into the fold. At a diplomatic conference in Paris, he obtained formal permission for the venture from the Turks. It helped that Layard kept up a steady stream of correspondence with the Ottoman authorities, picking holes in the schemes of competitors and lobbying for his group's project. He was one of a core group of visionaries who saw the modern evolution of European finance as broadening its horizons into the Near East.[8]

With offices in Istanbul's Galata district, it would evolve into the Imperial Ottoman Bank, serving as public treasurer and becoming a mainstay of the Turkish banking landscape for more than a century. There's even a museum dedicated to the bank at its old headquarters on beautiful Voyvoda Street.

★ ★ ★

In the election of 1857, Palmerston and his Liberals won a healthy majority. Layard lost his seat in Aylesbury, but this didn't mean he would fade away. The ink had barely dried on the election news when the Indian Mutiny spilled onto the front pages.

Ask the average person in the West today what caused the rebellion, and you'll probably get a vague answer that it was the result of anger boiling over British colonialism—which is reasonably close to the mark though still vague. In fact, much of India was controlled at the time by a ruthless private corporation that had its own private army. As William Dalrymple has chronicled in his landmark book *The Anarchy*, the East India Company ran roughshod over vast provinces of the subcontinent for close to 100 years, installing princes, plundering resources, and gobbling up territory as it pleased. What lit the match for the fire was a case of appalling insensitivity worthy of our own age's culture wars.

The bar was high given how local populations were treated with horrible contempt. A British sergeant recalled in his memoirs how a fellow soldier threw his boot at a servant who brought coffee into the barracks in a clay pot on his head; it shattered, and the hot liquid ran all over his body.[9] It never occurred to most of the "sahibs," particularly the younger officers, to learn the languages of the men in their units. The sepoys—the Indian foot soldiers, most of whom were either Hindu or Muslim—were compensated with a pitiful seven rupees a month, which was far above the wages of ordinary civilians but barely a third of the pay for their white counterparts.[10] For that seven rupees, a white son of England could call them "nigger" and subject them to tantrums of coarse abuse. Add to all this, there was ethnic rivalry between Sikhs recently added to the ranks and the other religious groups, and the British irritated the sepoys further with exasperating policies on everything from the mail to headgear.

The way a rifle was loaded tipped the balance. At the time, to load the paper cartridge into a soldier's Enfield, you bit the cartridge end to free the powder so the charge would ignite. To help load the muzzle, the cartridge was greased. That was fine if you were on a battlefield in the Crimea; who cared? But the new grease tallow was made with beef fat—sacrilegious to Hindus—and pig fat—deeply offensive to Muslims. The adjutant general of the Bengal army realized the problem, but no one back home paid attention.

After most of a cavalry unit in Meerut refused to use the cartridges on a parade ground, they were sentenced to ten years' hard labor in prison. Before being taken away, they were stripped of their uniforms and put into ankle shackles. The humiliation as well as the cruel punishment sparked a wave of riots, but some sepoys warned British officers of trouble and got them and their families to safety. In Delhi the next day, mutineers from Meerut arrived and with angry civilians went on a killing spree of Europeans. People were shot and hacked to pieces. The fact that the rioters didn't spare women and children incensed the public back in England. Uprisings and the clash between rebels and British forces would go on for more than a year.

Layard's brother, Frederick, was serving as a captain in the Indian army in Berhampore, Bengal. "A fearful crisis has come upon us which will lead to great changes in the country and its constitution," he wrote in June. "We are but a handful at the mercy of armed and trained mercenaries."[11] Back in Britain, the press screamed for blood. On August 25, *The Times* of London published a lurid tale that claimed rebels in Bangalore "took forty-eight females—most of them girls from ten to fourteen, delicately nurtured ladies—violated them and kept them for the base purposes of the heads of the insurrection for a whole week." After that, they were supposedly stripped nude and passed to local miscreants in Delhi. Writing for *The New York Daily Tribune*, Karl Marx doubted this story, guessing it was dreamed up by a "cowardly parson" in Bangalore, "distant from the scene of the action."[12]

Layard had always been interested in India and, unlike others who felt outrage, had the experience to know the violence bubbled up from a stew of bitter grievances. If today people still need reminding that Africa has more than fifty countries, that not all Muslims are the same, imagine for a moment how Layard needed to show patience with his fellow Englishmen's lack of cultural awareness, indeed their frequent *pride* over ignorance. "I want to see India as an Indian, not as a European," he wrote the Countess of Aboyne. "It is always the fable of 'The Lion and his Man.' We never get the Indian story."[13] He decided to get it for himself.

He thought he could roam around as he did in his youth. "I shall travel as I used to in the Near East if I can. Buy a pony, throw a pair of bags over the saddle and go straight on trusting providence and my own good management."[14] This was almost comical naïveté, and he should have known better. When he reached Mumbai in November, the prominent English locals made sure he was put up in a luxurious bungalow with servants, and each time he ventured out, he had a detail of sepoy guards. He found Mumbai fascinating. "I had rather expected a kind of Brighton," he wrote to his Aunt Sara on December 13, but instead he fancied it a mix of Istanbul and Beijing with a touch of Hampstead. "It is indeed difficult to conceive a city containing more objects of interest: the curious mixture of races from all parts of Asia, the various forms of idolatry at every turn, the singular architecture, and the variety of tropical vegetation form a picture which no description I have ever read has given me the least notion of."[15]

Layard hoped to see the north, but roads were closed, and there was still unrest going on. "Outbreaks may occur in any part of the country when least expected," he wrote home, "but the really formidable part of the rebellion is now put down." He settled on going to Hyderabad in the south, but traveling in India proved to be slow and expensive. He hired a palanquin with twelve bearers, who managed to carry him only twenty-four miles a day, while servants followed in a bullock cart and on ponies. On his way to Aurangabad, officials insisted on foisting an "enormous escort" on him, including the loan of a pony and an elephant, so that "with my own suite and that of my cavalry, who have their own servants, camels and other encumbrances, I am altogether at the head of a considerable caravan."[16]

Yet he didn't allow the luxury or the distractions of an entourage to keep him from learning what he wanted to know. In Mumbai, he made "many native friends," and a young Brahmin scholar named Bahnoo Daji came along on the trip south as interpreter. It was impossible to study Indian issues, he wrote his aunt in mid-January, without being on the spot and talking to the people under British rule. "The sooner people in England open their eyes to the truth and no longer believe with the government and the *Times* that this is a mere military mutiny, the better; the more chance there will be of our taking measures . . . for the future."[17]

Toughened up by past experiences, he made progress but wished he could go faster. India was just too big to cover. Still, at a slow pace, he was glad to notice details of culture and nature he might have ordinarily missed. In the heat of the day, he rested and pored through books on India, and in the later afternoons, he explored villages and spoke to headmen in charge. He got the chance to visit the Buddhist cave monuments of Ajanta, but, though he found some beauty in them, overall, he considered them inferior to sculpture work by the Assyrians and the Greeks. Unfortunately, there is a break in the narrative of his travels and adventures because some of his letters have been lost. On his way to Delhi, his caravan had a narrow escape from falling into the hands of Nana Sahib, a flamboyant Indian aristocrat turned rebel leader. But beyond this tantalizing scrap of information, nothing else is known.

Meanwhile, officials throughout India responded to his letters and offered useful intelligence about how things worked here; he learned the most, of course, from Indians themselves. By February 1, 1858, Layard had solidified his opinion. "We have done nothing to form any other bond of sympathy or to create mutual interests," he wrote his aunt. "The people we govern are treated like a distinct race, inferior to us—more, indeed, as if they were of a lower order of creatures . . . in too many instances with brutality [and] with that sort of kindness which would be shown to a pet animal. They are excluded from all share of government, they can never rise to anything beyond the most inferior posts."

He noticed, too, that British overseers tried "to force upon them our old worn-out judicial system" while "meddling with customs which are of no real importance and yet are clung to with extraordinary tenacity by the people. We are breaking faith in the most scandalous manner with native princes, and annexing their territories."[18]

He easily saw through the propaganda that the Indians were better off under the British than their indigenous rulers, and he found the lack of investment in public works, such as irrigation, "perfectly incredible." Much of the blame he put on the East India Company, a slumlord over vast domains. But the rebellion was the final push London needed to take India away from the company and put it under direct rule. Layard considered this an improvement, but the government could do better . . .

After six months, he was ready to come home, and he had a lot to say. In May, he gave a speech at St. James's Hall in Piccadilly. It wasn't one party or government that was responsible for what was happening in India, he argued, but a whole system. He told his audience how Lord Dalhousie as the governor-general of India had made a landgrab with 15 million inhabitants. (If he casually mentioned Dalhousie's name, Indians held up their hands and said, "For God's sake, don't speak of him!") It was bad enough that the authorities ignored treaties and demanded land titles that the Indians couldn't possibly produce. The police in India were using torture to extort evidence. He had met numerous men in India who insisted "that the practice of torture had increased within the last twenty years."[19]

He played down recent reports that Europeans had been mutilated in attacks, pointing out that investigations by English authorities hadn't found any evidence. "On the other hand, there had been numerous cases of fearful revenge" by the army. He had heard himself the story of an Englishman—who claimed in front of a large group of people—that watched for two days how a wounded rebel sepoy who couldn't escape was eaten alive by crows and eagles, feasting on his eyes and vital organs.

Layard earned cheers throughout the speech, and he wrapped it up with a call for drastic change from Parliament and Whitehall. "India must be governed in India—not in Canon Row or Downing Street." Any governing council there should open to "an Indian element." Native representation was already being tried on "a small scale" and as an "experiment" in Ceylon. "That experiment you must try in India. If you do and if you lose India, it will be no dishonor and no disgrace to you that future history should say that you made the people of India civilized, prosperous and happy, and if it can be effected by our example, let me add, Christian." There was thunderous applause and cheers over his final words, ones that were close to a century ahead of their time.[20]

His speech caused an international sensation and was reported in newspapers as far away as Brooklyn and New Zealand. But the English papers in India and more conservative ones at home went on the attack. "I hear that the Indian Press is hostile to me," he wrote to the Countess of Aboyne. "The tone they took towards the natives and towards Lord Canning, who endeavored to check the cry for blood and extermination, was of the most disgraceful."[21]

None of this should have come as a surprise, and Layard's politics made life difficult for Frederick, who leaned toward his views but had to keep friends and make his career in a close-knit community. Perhaps the best testimony to the force of Layard's arguments is the great number of letters from grateful Indians who had discovered an Englishman who cared about their personal rights and freedoms.

★ ★ ★

Henry Layard was always a polarizing figure. Those who became his friends, dazzled by his intelligence, energy, and liberal compassion, often stayed fiercely loyal. Charles Dickens wrote to Layard on December 4, 1860, "There is not a man in England who is more earnestly your friend and admirer than I am. The conviction that you know it, helps me out through this note. You are a man of so much mark to me, that I even regret your going into the House of Commons—for which assembly I have but a scant respect."[22]

Those who took a dislike to him were equal in their enthusiasm. Along the way in his political career, his enemies had nicknamed him "Mr. Lie-Hard." A minor travel writer and novelist, Emily Eden (great-great-great-aunt of Anthony Eden), once quipped that she could forgive Layard for discovering Nineveh but not Nineveh for discovering Layard.

When John Russell was made an earl in the summer of 1861 and bumped up to the House of Lords, Palmerston understood that the best mind to look after foreign affairs sat on Layard's shoulders. Queen Victoria did not. Mr. Bull had too many radical ideas and kept attacking the upper classes. Appointing Layard undersecretary of state for foreign affairs, she wrote to Palmerston on July 22, was "not conducive to the public good." This began a humorous and quintessentially English back-and-forth until Palmerston finally had enough and thanked her for her "gracious and condescending acquiescence."[23]

The Queen was not amused. Palmerston's sarcasm so infuriated Victoria that a complaint was sent to Lord Granville, leader of the House of Lords.[24] But there was nothing Granville could really do. Layard now had a second chance to make an impact on Britain's foreign affairs.

One month after his appointment, Benjamin Austen died, and Layard was surprised to discover his uncle left him only £500. Fortunately, he was in a secure enough position now that he could afford for the sake of ethics and appearances to quit his chairmanship of the Ottoman Bank. His critics in the Commons often still insinuated he was out to help his old bank associates or that he was too much of a Turcophile.

He now had huge responsibility at the Foreign Office, and his superior, Russell, was content to leave many affairs up to him. "I shall never get through this mass of papers," he wrote his undersecretary. "I leave it entirely to your discretion."[25] Layard tried to rise to the imposing challenge, but he sometimes flirted with indiscretion. When he chaired a lecture given by the Baptist preacher Charles Spurgeon, discussion drifted to the American Civil War. Layard pointed out "it must never be forgotten that we had left the institution of slavery to them as an inheritance." That same year, the British had annexed Lagos as another colony, and with unusual imperialist faith, he believed its objective "was not to aggrandize ourselves, but to put an end to the slave trade on that coast." *The New York Times*, perhaps with its tongue in its cheek, observed, "We trust the result will vindicate his assertion as to the motives of the English in acquiring Lagos."[26]

It was a delicate balance, and Layard knew it. At a speech before his constituents, he argued, "I am not here to discuss whether North or South be right. We have said we will not interfere." The government, he told the sympathetic crowd, had to view the southern states as belligerents, which wasn't the same thing as recognizing them as a nation. "How could we be prepared to treat 12,000,000 people as pirates?" But at the same time, "we proclaim the principle of non-intervention, we are resolved to make the rights of Englishmen respected throughout the world, and to resent outrages committed on the persons of English subjects."[27]

This was telling. He recognized how the emerging Confederacy could easily end up a British migraine. It was one he would feel as well, stuck with the unenviable task of answering in the Commons for diplomatic dustups with the Union and Confederacy in spots from Morocco and Mexico to Brazil and Egypt. In June 1862, he sent a note to Parliament. "In accordance with the practice of this country in similar cases, the propriety of recognizing these states as an independent nation is worthy of the serious and immediate consideration of Her Majesty's ministers."[28] Parliament, he warned, had to deal with the issue one way or another. He also kept his eye on the traps that could drag Britain into the conflict. One of them sprung in November in what came to be known as the *Trent* Affair.

The USS *San Jacinto* interfered with a mail ship, the *Trent*, capturing two Confederate diplomats who were on their way to Britain and France to lobby for diplomatic recognition. From Whitehall's perspective, this would not do—having the Americans board Her Majesty's ships like pirates and carry off whomever they pleased. Sabers started to rattle, but two men kept their heads. One was Layard, and the other was America's J. L. Motley, who had distinguished himself in writing a long essay for the Union's side for *The Times*, earning himself a diplomatic posting in Austria. The two presumably met when Motley visited London on his way to Vienna, and they hit it off.

As the *Trent* Affair intensified, Motley wrote Layard from Vienna in January. "God knows that I share your wish that so dire calamity as war between our two countries may yet be averted. From the very bottom of my heart, I pray for peace with England." Grumbling over war between the two nations was exaggerated. "There *is no party* in America which desires war with England," he assured Layard, promising he had never heard one American even mention the idea "except to laugh it to scorn." Motley asked, "Can any Englishman conscientiously believe that we wish to make the slaveholders a present of the whole enormous strength of England and enlist your fleets and armies in their support?"[29]

No doubt, Motley reported his exchanges with Layard (just as he regularly reported conversations with Russell) to U.S. Secretary of State William Seward, who was mostly indifferent to foreign opinion over the war. Seward wanted it to be viewed abroad as a "minor insurrection," and he wanted Britain to mind its own business.[30] Britain preferred to do just that—though its shipbuilders rolled out the *Alabama* for the Confederacy. On the night of July 29, 1862, Layard sent Russell a memorandum, warning him that the ship had left Liverpool that morning. He sent briefing papers with law officers to get an opinion "with an instruction that they were of urgent importance." The law officers thought "we should stop her." Russell, despite being considered by many to have sympathies for the South, drafted a dispatch which would order colonial authorities to hold the *Alabama* in any British port. But the Cabinet opposed the plan.[31]

The British government would pay dearly for ignoring Layard's diligent advice and Russell's initiative; the *Alabama* wreaked havoc on Union merchant ships for two years, straining Anglo-American relations almost to the breaking point. And after the war, international arbitration decreed that Britain should pay the United States $15.5 million.

★   ★   ★

In 1868, William Gladstone became prime minister for the first time and a figure inexorably linked to Layard's life and the progress of his career.

There has been a fair amount of hagiographical nonsense written about Gladstone, but then politicians can achieve the status of "great statesman" by simply hanging around. Historian A. N. Wilson is probably closer to the mark in pointing out he was bookish but not intellectual, his worldview shaped mostly by long visits to his massive estate in Hawarden, Wales, or the country houses of friends.[32] The brilliant populist once described himself as an *inequalitarian*. His maiden speech in Parliament supported slavery, and even after becoming a champion of the Liberals, he thought the U.S. Confederacy was a good idea.

A master manipulator, he nevertheless was a pedantic Christian zealot whose long-winded letters drove Queen Victoria to distraction. Known for luring London prostitutes to his home for tea and subjecting them to tedious and condescending lectures on sin, he noted privately in 1854 that out of ninety streetwalkers he spoke to, only one ever gave up the life. When his diaries were published about a century later, it turned out he got more out of these talks than they did—after the women left, he would beat himself with a whip.[33]

Gladstone and Layard, so different in their outlooks and backgrounds yet sharing the same party, didn't need much to loathe each other. Just before the start of the Crimean War, Gladstone annoyed his own allies by criticizing the Turks in a speech at Manchester that he bluntly claimed was intended to repair Layard's fanaticism. But by 1868, Layard had enough political capital that he was expected to have an appointment. Gladstone made him commissioner of works and buildings, and Layard was now a member of Britain's Privy Council.

One of the more amusing aspects of his job and a nice snapshot of the times is a petition that landed on his desk from no less than Chancellor of the Exchequer Robert Lowe, who belonged to the Honorable Society of Bicycle Riders. "They have nowhere to ride," complained Lowe, because of the regular traffic of horses, horse-drawn cabs, and pedestrians. He wanted "by way of experiment" to let the cyclists go on the road in Hyde Park from Hyde Park Corner to the end of Rotten Row, "say till 10 in the morning."[34]

Layard was now in his fifties, and several of his friends had already settled down. Perhaps it was time he should, too. For years, his circle had wondered about his close friendship with Charlotte Guest. But after her husband's death, Charlotte waited a respectful couple of years and then married a man fourteen years her junior and the tutor of her teenage son. Layard went one better.

In early March 1869, he married Charlotte's daughter, Enid.

He was fifty-two, Enid twenty-five. This being the Victorian era, the gap in years was less an eyebrow raiser than in our day. Both Rawlinson and Henry Ross had picked up brides more than half their ages. What's possibly more disturbing to our modern sensibilities is the fact that Layard showed romantic interest in the mother and then, years later, her daughter. He played with Enid when she was a little girl, telling stories to her and her brothers and sisters. But Enid had grown up to become a slim and attractive young woman, one who found this seasoned adventurer and politician a catch.

So far, Enid's life had been a quiet one of church visits, playing cricket, and helping with the family's small press operation (its publishing output included some poems of Tennyson). Layard took her places she could hardly have imagined. And he wouldn't settle for an ordinary engagement ring for his fiancée. No, he went around to the S. J. Phillips antique jewelry shop—which had opened its doors that year and is still operating today—and had a bracelet made for her out of the seal of the Assyrian king Ersahaddon. Later, he had a necklace made for her out of cylinder seals.

The wedding took place in St. George's Anglican Church in Mayfair's Hanover Square, and the couple honeymooned in Dorking. In appearances, they might have looked an odd couple. Young Enid was taller than Layard, who had long shed the Byronic prettiness of his youth and was now a burly, bearded, slightly pear-shaped figure. And yet the newlyweds were a good match, and although never having children, they were happy together for the rest of their marriage.

Layard never did lose that streak of lightning that prompted him to impulsively launch a crusade or jump to the defense of a friend. Enid was the gentler soul, with an edge of pragmatism. Layard's writing, even in his diary and letters, can paint pictures for the mind and invites you to follow a compelling narrative. Enid's style is dry to the point of arid, and her diary entries have the understated recital of a police report. Here's an excerpt from a random entry of 1878: "Went to morning church. After lunch, walk in the garden with Henry and Sir A. Kemball. Went to evening church."[35]

The man who had dug up the palaces of Nineveh now had high hopes to change the landscape of London. As commissioner of works, he was in charge of rebuilding the Embankment along the Thames between Charing Cross Station and the Houses of Parliament. In his grand vision, a whole collection of public buildings would make their home on the river, among them the Admiralty, the War Office, the National Gallery, the Museum of Natural History, and a new law courts building. This probably would have been beautiful—if the powers that be had shared his view and signed off on the money. Napoleon III had only to give the order, and Baron Haussman reshaped Paris. But Layard had to contend with bureaucrats and business executives. Both forces balked at his plans as far too ambitious and expensive. And then—only ten months into his job—he was taken out of it altogether.

An official at the Treasury and a friend of Gladstone, Acton Ayrton, had been irritatingly obstructionist over Layard's plans for the Embankment. Ayrton didn't get along either with Robert Lowe, the chancellor of the exchequer. To keep them from each other's throats, Gladstone decided to give

Layard's job to Ayrton and send Layard off to be Britain's representative to Madrid. Layard had been vacationing with Enid in Naples that October while his prime minister shuffled his chess pieces around. While he was glad at first for the new appointment, he was cross with Gladstone when he learned from friends what was really going on.

The Times expressed what must have been widespread befuddlement over the shuffle. With Layard, it grumbled, "We were encouraged to think this much-neglected city would be in capable hands" given that "from the time of Nineveh, no city of similar importance has been so ugly and has boasted so few fine buildings as London."[36] Its one concession was that it thought the lions in Trafalgar Square might one day be worth placing besides the winged bulls. "Madrid is probably the European capital of which Mr. Layard knows the least," though *The Times* expected him to do well enough.

As for Ayrton, the paper greeted his appointment with "a little alarm." It was right to think so. Always cheap, he would turn out to be a disaster as commissioner of works anyway. On his watch, he promoted the idea that scientific work performed at Kew Gardens should be done elsewhere, reducing the space to just a public park; this sparked the ire of Charles Darwin and the geologist Charles Lyell, and the scheme soon died (Ayrton was subsequently moved to a new job).

The Times had hoped that Layard "will someday return to undertake the reconstruction of the 'modern Babylon.'" It's fascinating to consider what he might have accomplished had he been given the chance. But Layard was going back to diplomacy.

Mr. Bull in the Land of Matadors

The Layards arrived in Madrid in December and were forced to stay in a hotel because the British legation was virtually uninhabitable. Bugs crawled within the wallpaper and infested the woodwork, and the single toilet was kept in a box in a dining room cupboard. The legation's stables were a disgusting mess, with horses standing in their own filth. Enid Layard took charge of the cleaning and renovations. The wood that was lousy with insects was burned, and after a few weeks, the couple could occupy the first floor, surrounded by the tapestries and Kurdish carpets hauled all the way from London. Enid was not only wife but skillful aide—copying dispatches, minding the household staff, and entertaining the steady parade of guests, for the embassy was a regular center of social outings for the diplomatic community.

Layard relied heavily on her because his work was cut out for him. Spain was deeply divided between liberal and reactionary forces, and the country had spent the past couple of decades rocked by uprisings, suppressions of revolts, and eventually what was called "the Glorious Revolution." A coalition of liberals and conservatives had managed to drive Queen Isabella II into permanent exile in Paris. Yet Spain's parliament, the Cortes, wasn't ready to replace Isabella with a republic, so it made one of its seasoned military men, Marshal Francisco Serrano, regent while it shopped around for a new individual to sit on the Spanish throne (ironically, Serrano was one of Isabella's former lovers). Another general and revolutionary, Juan Prim, was appointed prime minister. And these were only two of the key personalities involved that didn't get along.

The junta's search for a king led Spain to the brink of war, and Layard would be caught in the middle . . .

As he and Enid settled in, he had little idea of the intrigues brewing across Europe. Spain was a nation that baffled him in some ways. He was the middle-class boy who made good, who could sit around campfires with Arab and Kurdish chieftains. But the Spanish aristocracy kept to themselves. Their pampered lifestyle and parochial view of the world offended his liberal sensibilities. Those on the left, however, often had a streak of dogmatic extremism that was just as unpalatable.

Layard learned to appreciate the great painter Velasquez, but he was amused by how Spanish masters weren't allowed to depict the Virgin Mary's naked feet, "and the infant Jesus is usually swaddled up to the chin with the utmost care. Except in the 'supreme' moment of being skinned or boiled, a martyr cannot be seen without his clothes."[1] The Roman Catholic Church had an almost suffocating influence on the culture and the people, and while never a devout Christian, Layard had a lapsed Protestant's innate bias against Catholicism. He also privately thought bullfighting was cruel but was expected to go and exchange ringside pleasantries with foreign visitors and local VIPs. For Enid, the spectacle of blood and sand was too much. It soon became clear that life in Spain would never be easy. When Layard developed painful stomach troubles, the culprit turned out to be lead poisoning in the drinking water.

He dealt with challenges that originated not only in the Cortes but in the halls of power more than a thousand miles away in Berlin, and he didn't learn of all the machinations going on until later. These were the years when Prussia's Otto von Bismarck was determined to forge a unified Germany in his grand vision. Bismarck, famous in photographs for his walrus moustache and his spiked helmet, knew how to manipulate people, and when that didn't work, he resorted to outright bullying. In 1862, he famously told fellow legislators that Prussia's boundaries wouldn't be resolved by speeches and democracy but by "blood and iron." He meant it. By 1871, he was the first imperial chancellor of the German Empire.

Why he matters here is that his fingerprints are all over the conflict to secure a monarch to rule Spain. While it may seem ridiculous to us today, Spain's prime minister, Juan Prim, and other Spanish statesmen felt strongly this late into the nineteenth century that the fate of the nation depended on casting the right actor in the role, even if it was a member of a royal household from somewhere else. At one point, Prim had on his short list a teenage duke who was the nephew of Italy's King Victor Emmanuel—a mere boy studying at Harrow.

This is where Bismarck enters the frame. His end goal was to isolate the French, and he fully expected a war between his beloved Prussia and France in the future. If he could win Spain as an ally, so much the better. He had told the German Foreign Office back in 1868, "It is in our interest if the Spanish question remains open . . . and a solution agreeable to Napoleon is unlikely to be useful to us."[2] So Bismarck pressured Prince Karl Anton of Hohenzollern into offering his son, Leopold, as a candidate.

This naturally infuriated France, which complained. Then the Leopold option was taken off the table, but thanks to Bismarck's machinations, it was put back on again. The French foreign minister, the Duc de Gramont, openly threatened war. Juan Prim had no desire to see his country dragged into battle, but he was livid over France's complaints over who Spain chose to put on its throne. Layard went to visit Prim at his private apartment in the Ministry of War and found the prime minister at the boiling point. Prim yelled and railed in such a fury that his wife—changing in their bedroom—ran in to find out what was going on.

Like any other diplomat, Layard couldn't be seen meddling in a nation's internal affairs, but Britain had clout. Rather than suggest a "right" choice, he had to steer Prim away from the wrong one. When Prim had calmed down enough, Layard reminded him that Prince Leopold hadn't been officially put forward as a selection yet to the Cortes (never mind that the news had already leaked, and the entire Cortes knew). The deal wasn't done, so Leopold could still be coaxed to pull out of contention. It took a while, but Layard managed to get Prim to send off a telegram to Leopold's father, Prince Karl, explaining the whole mess. Four days later, on July 13, Prim let Layard know in a private note that Karl had taken his son out of the running.

Layard sent a cable to London, letting his government know all was well again. For once, the British government sent him unqualified praise and treated him like a hero. He had kept Spain and France from going to war. It was wonderful. Unfortunately, there would *still* be a war—only with a different pairing of nations. Bismarck made sure of it.

On the same day Layard got his note from Prim, Prussia's King Wilhelm I was taking his morning stroll in Bad Ems, a resort spa east of Koblenz. There, he ran into the French ambassador, who decided this was the best place and time to ask for a guarantee that no Hohenzollern prince ever be suggested again to rule over Spain. Wilhelm let him know he would guarantee no such thing. Bismarck later released a report on this conversation to the press—with some creative editing. This became known as the Ems Dispatch, and a few minutes spent passive-aggressively arguing near a spa was followed by openly aggressive newspapers raging over insults, crowds shouting for blood . . . and then cannon fire.

The Franco-Prussian War, or the War of 1870 as it's called in France, was a seminal event that fueled the passions leading up to World War I. Prussia knew how to mobilize early, made short work of the French forces, and after the smoke cleared, it promptly claimed Alsace-Lorraine, which left thousands of French bitterly waiting for their day of revenge. Meanwhile, Belgium had grown so frightened of invasion by either Germany or France that it over-hauled its military. Sickly and foolish Napoleon III had made the disastrous choice of joining his armies at the front, and he was captured by the Germans.

French radicals decided that if he was going to be absent, he might as well *stay* absent, and so out of this brief conflict, France got its Third Republic. It also got its Paris Commune, with French radicals fighting in the siege of Paris not only with Germans but with the National Guard. It was bloody, chaotic, ultimately futile, and yet the Commune is romanticized to this day.

Months later, Layard and Enid visited Paris on holiday and saw for themselves the devastation from the siege and the German occupation. Many of the great structures of the City of Light—the Louvre, the Hôtel de Ville, the Palais Royal—were blackened by fire damage. Layard thought it "was like a dead city, and the tinkling of the small bells attached to the harness of the horses was the only noise which broke the awful silence." Paris recovered eventually, but the war and the Commune reverberated down through the generations.

And where, it's reasonable to ask, was Spain during the war? The country caught between the superpowers and the excuse for the war in the first place?

Thanks to Layard, it rolled on with its bitterly divisive internal politics and stayed out of the bigger picture. Had he failed to persuade Juan Prim, it's quite conceivable that Spain would have gone to war with France. Yes, it would have had a strong ally in Germany, but its lack of industrial power, coupled with its squabbling internal factions, would have ensured that Spain got the worst of any fight. What could have been a much wider theater of conflict—one that might have dragged in other nations—was kept mercifully to two belligerents. A good portion of credit for that goes to Mr. Bull.

★   ★   ★

Nevertheless, the War of 1870 galvanized radicals in Spain at both ends of the spectrum. Left-wing Spaniards saw what was happening in France and wondered why they needed a king when their neighbor had ditched theirs. Those on the right, the Carlists, remained intent on preserving traditional values. Caught in the middle was Juan Prim, who returned to the household of Italy's Victor Emmanuel and, instead of settling for a nephew, decided the king's second son, Prince Amadeo, the Duke of Aosta, would work out. There would never be a choice that pleased everyone, and two days after Christmas as Prim left the Cortes, six men attacked him, one of them firing a blunderbuss—a crude, early form of shotgun. Prim took six musket balls to his shoulder and elbow, and though his face was bloody and he was horribly wounded, he managed to get home to his wife. He died three days later.

After Spain's "Amadeo the First" took up his new job, Carlists rebelled in the Basque and Catalan provinces, part of the army went on strike, and the nation was groaning under a massive national debt. Layard's sources in Italy confided to him that Victor Emmanuel wanted his son to quit, and Amadeo had also thought of abdicating. The president of the Cortes came to see Layard, getting down on his knees and sobbing, begging the Englishman to go talk the monarch out of it (Layard found this spectacle disgusting since the man was one of those who had bitterly opposed installing Amadeo). Then Marshal Francisco Serrano, Spain's previous fill-in regent, paid a call; he certainly didn't want to be regent again. Couldn't Layard talk to the king?

Well, no, he couldn't. Amadeo had had enough; he wanted out. He abdicated on February 11, 1873, declaring the Spanish people ungovernable. For the time being, they were. Despite the "first" Spanish Republic being declared and a small group of generals assuming control, the situation was fluid. By late April, a new coup d'état was tried and failed, with eleven Monarchist battalions fleeing to a bull ring, where Republican forces disarmed them.[3] To the sound of intermittent gunfire, revolutionaries camped and met regularly in the square near the British legation, which, if some radicals got their way, would be burned down.

Layard had faced mobs before, and he wrote his aunt that "the worst of these revolutions is that they give one such a deal of work and writing."[4] The so-called *descamisados*—"shirtless ones"—behaved themselves in the square, but around the rest of the city, they targeted liberals and moderates for assassination. Many of their potential victims sought sanctuary in the British legation; a politician named Albareda found his way in after literally ducking under the skirt of a female friend in a horse carriage.

Meanwhile, another extraordinary situation developed. One of the members of the ruling junta was the gentle and courtly Emilio Castelar, a man who thought Spain could be reorganized along the model of the United States (with a few constitutional touches borrowed from Switzerland). Castelar sent a note to Layard, asking if he could take in Francisco Serrano—another target of radicals—because his *regime couldn't control the mob*. Layard sent back word he would, though he must have known this put his wife and the entire legation staff in jeopardy. At one o'clock in the morning, Castelar himself appeared on the British minister's doorstep with the civil governor of Madrid, Nicolas Estevanez—and with Serrano, wearing a wig for a disguise. Castelar then fetched another politician named Becorra to stay at the legation.

For a handful of days, three prominent politicians—all with sharply different political views—were cooped up together, and they turned their asylum into a salon. Layard had to tell Albareda to keep his booming voice down in case the nearby mob in the square overheard him. Becorra later left without thanking his hosts. But the most pressing dilemma was how to get Serrano to a safer locale. Serrano, his name associated with the latest coup attempt, had been declared an enemy of Spain—by one of the men who had delivered him to Layard, the civil governor Estevanez.

Inevitably, word circulated that Serrano might be in the British embassy. Republican guards now stood outside in case their target decided to leave. Then on April 30, Castelar informed Layard that some Republicans intended to storm the legation, and his government didn't have enough control to prevent it, even though it wanted to keep good relations with Britain. Amazingly, he suggested England's representative smuggle out the marshal themselves! He expected Layard to take away a high-profile Spanish national from what was supposed to be an inviolable diplomatic residence . . . *and* whisk him off to Santander, where he could leave the country by ship (simply putting Serrano on a train north was considered too dangerous, as the Carlists had control of the railroad).

Layard enlisted Enid to help, and the couple also relied on their English maid, a Miss Hill. Serrano—dressed in one of Layard's suits, wearing a fake beard, and sporting a dye job—was snuck into the train station. Enid led him through the gate on one side, Miss Hill on the other. The jig was nearly up when the mob invaded the train at Avilla, but Layard blocked their way into their carriage at one entrance, while Enid, imposingly tall, warded them off at the opposite end. Serrano snoozed through much of the danger. In Santander, he was escorted after nightfall to a Belgian steamer, where he would be taken to St. Jean de Luz in France—but the group wasn't out of danger yet. A Civil Guard patrol rushed up just as the ship was about to embark.

Enid's nerves finally broke. Sensing it was all over, she turned to her maid and said, "Come away, my legs shake, and I cannot stay here to see him taken at the last moment."

She should have had more faith, especially in her husband. Layard, true to his nature, stood on the gangplank and stared down the guards, informing them that he was a diplomat and if they wanted to board the vessel, they'd have to do it by force. Then in a brilliant move, he didn't give them the chance. He shouted for the captain to head out, and as the little steamer chugged its way from the quay, he jumped onto shore, leaving the guards to impotently watch it sail away.

The news of the Layards' complicity in Serrano's escape soon circulated through Madrid, but the ambassador was more concerned with reaction in London. Granville passed along his compliments on Enid's courage, while Gladstone had lunch with the Layards when they returned to London for their summer holiday. They were, in fact, the talk of the town for a while, with even Queen Victoria and the Prince of Wales warming up more to Layard.

But Layard was never going to completely win over Britain's queen or for that matter the British establishment. Even in middle age, his conscience and passions could drive him to being impetuous. He stormed out of the ancient Roman Catholic ceremony in which the Spanish king washed the feet of old men, and at another function in the Spanish court, Layard got into a tiff with an arrogant master of ceremonies, then lost his temper and shook the man vigorously.

He and Enid spent seven years in Spain, but the posting was never the right fit. Then in 1876, tragic events provided a new career opportunity.

• 12 •

Fading Away in the Evening Mists

$\mathcal{I}$n the summer of 1876, a bad harvest and insensitive taxes pushed people in Bosnia and Herzegovina past the breaking point. In his landmark *Ottoman Centuries*, Patrick Balfour (known as Lord Kinross) describes what happened when the rebellion spread to Bulgaria in April and May. "In Bulgaria, a rebel leader with visions of himself as a Slav Napoleon had pledged his followers to terrorist methods. They turned savagely on the Muslim Turks, whom they started to massacre." Predictably, the Ottomans exacted a terrible revenge. "Burning innumerable villages to the ground, they spared neither age nor sex in an outbreak of indiscriminate massacre, killing in a single month no fewer than 12,000 Christians. Their orgy of slaughter and arson and rape culminated in the mountain village of Batak. Here a thousand Christians found refuge in a church, to which the irregular troops set fire rags soaked in petrol, burning all to death but a single old woman. In all, so it was reported, 5,000 out of the 7,000 villagers of Batak perished at their hands."[1]

A reporter for London's *Daily News* accompanied an American diplomat to Batak and painted a vivid landscape of the horrors, as moving as any TV report today on Syrian bombings of civilians. He described how at a schoolhouse, the ground stank of putrefying flesh, and the ground was covered with skeletons. Nearby was a shallow pit, which was "at one time literally covered with corpses of men and women, young girls and children, that lay there festering in the sun, and eaten by dogs."[2] In the Commons, Disraeli made the mistake of first denying the reports and then forced into a corner, minimizing their scale. He was furious when he discovered that the Foreign Office had sat for nearly two weeks on a consul's dispatch that gave a fuller view of the situation.[3]

Outrage over the slaughter turned into cause célèbre, and Gladstone pounced on the issue, eager to adopt it as his own. While out of power, he had kept busy by indulging his Christian zealotry, writing on various religious subjects. Now he wrote a long-winded pamphlet, *Bulgarian Horrors*, and demanded, "Let the Turks now carry away their abuses in the only possible manner, namely by carrying away themselves."[4] Others agreed with him. Charles Darwin gave $50 to a relief fund for Bulgarians. A twenty-two-year old Oscar Wilde, studying classics at Magdalen College, Oxford (i.e., reading "Greats"), dashed off the Italian-style sonnet "On the Massacre of the Christians in Bulgaria"—not one of his best.

The reaction of Britain's man in Istanbul, Henry Elliott, amounted to a shrug: "We have been upholding what we know to have been a semi-civilized nation." The Foreign Office soon called him home. In sharp contrast, Russia's ambassador, Nikolai Ignatiev—infamous for his meddling and machinations—had reasons to celebrate: "The Bulgarian massacres have brought Russia what she never had before—the support of British public opinion."[5] It was true. All the goodwill towards Turkey accumulated from the Crimean War evaporated within days of the sensational reports.

Layard's perspective was more measured and with a touch of bitter cynicism. He wrote a friend, "The English have these periodical lunacies particularly when religion is involved." Where, he might well have argued, was all this self-righteous fury when Yezidis were being slaughtered? He was unmoved by Gladstone's call for the Turk to pack up and leave. To another friend, he wrote, "You cannot drive three million . . . Turks out of Europe into starvation and hopeless misery. The wild humanitarian cry about Turkey will lead to serious mischief. It is grievous to see a man like Gladstone turned into a mere vulgar pamphleteer."[6]

After Elliot was recalled to London, Disraeli needed a new man for Istanbul. Layard was the obvious choice, even though everyone pegged him as pro-Turk. Granville, of course, had managed him before and confided to Gladstone that he considered him "a very strong man with Orientals" and that "I think he will be faithful to instructions, if the latter are of the right sort."[7] Gladstone inevitably disagreed and railed against Layard's supposed Ottoman sympathies in the House of Commons. Layard, who should have understood the game of politics by now, still complained in his *Memoirs* later over how Gladstone and his clique accused him of abandoning his political principles by serving under a Tory government. He considered these petty shots embarrassing, and they made his job harder. Russia's Ignatiev didn't want Layard in Istanbul either and tried to work his main British contact, Lord Salisbury, into discouraging the appointment but to no avail.

Like Disraeli, Layard thought reports of the Bulgarian atrocities to be exaggerated. In some cases, they were. *The Daily News* had suggested the death toll was 25,000 people when it was more likely half that. In private moments of frustration, Layard sometimes displayed an uncharacteristic callousness over the Bulgarians' plight. But he still refused to meet with a high-ranking Turkish officer implicated in the war crimes; he would, in fact, warn the Turks that if the man was appointed as grand vizier, England would be outraged. "There was so much passion and misrepresentation—increased in England by party passion—that it was difficult to ascertain the extent of his complicity in the cruelties laid to his charge." Layard would continue to press the Turks to punish those guilty of the atrocities, but the Turks were intransigent, and he blamed their attitude on being offended by "Gladstonian agitation."[8]

It didn't help that Turkey was in a precarious state of revolution that summer after the Bulgarian uprising and massacres. Thousands of theological students called for the sacking of both the grand vizier and the chief mufti—and Sultan Abdul Aziz gave in. A powerful group of intellectuals, the Young Ottomans, called for the government to be reorganized along the lines of the British constitutional system, which would make the sultan himself subordinate to legislative ministers. The reformers relied on more liberal interpretations of the Koran to address the sultan's neglect of the Islamic community and its governing apparatus.

On May 30, they went beyond talk, and a couple of battalions of soldiers took control of Dolmabahçe Palace while navy ships sailed in front of the Russian summer embassy to make sure there would be no foreign mischief. Abdul Aziz was removed as sultan because of his "mental derangement" as well as general corruption. Off he went to prison, replaced by his alcoholic nephew, Murad. He later committed suicide by slashing his wrists.

Unfortunately, if Abdul Aziz was mentally ill, his heir was equally if not more unhinged. Murad was barely into his new job when he suffered a nervous breakdown, and his younger half brother, Abdul Hamid II, took over.

Abdul Hamid was a complex personality. A man who never expected to rule, he cultivated other interests. He learned carpentry and built exquisite furniture. He translated opera librettos. He was even a good competitor in Turkish oil wrestling. But now he made it clear that he would accept the role of sultan only if he really *were* sultan. Intelligent and deeply sensitive, he had a streak of paranoia that would widen over time and dominate his character. While visiting Paris in 1867, he hid the fact that he understood French, which turned out to be useful for learning what was really going on around him. Ten years later, he was willing to collaborate with the Young Ottomans on a new constitution, one that he promulgated in December but had skillfully defanged of any clauses or stipulations that checked his power.

★   ★   ★

After a brief visit home to London, the Layards sailed off on the royal yacht *Osborne*—loaned by the Queen—and reached the Dardanelles on April 20, 1877. At first, there was little to see but mist and rain, but early in the afternoon, the weather cleared up as the yacht rounded Seraglio Point and approached Istanbul. As the diplomat and his wife were taken by carriage through the streets to their embassy, they attracted a curious crowd of both Muslims and Christians. For Enid, this was an exciting and exotic new world. Passing by the Tower of Galata and through the narrow streets, she was "astonished and bewildered" by the people in various costumes, men smoking hookahs, and women in bright silk garments.

Their official home for the next three years would be Pera House, an unimaginative, three-story block that's still used as a British consulate today in the city's modern district of Beyoğlu. A fire in 1870 caused devastating damage, and the embassy hadn't been fully restored by the time the couple moved in. Layard never thought much of the place, calling it in his memoirs "a monument to that lavish expenditure of public money, which combined with false economy, ignorance and bad taste, has not infrequently characterized the British Treasury and Office of Works." The Layards spent more time at the embassy's summer residence at Therapia, a large wooden house that overlooked the Bosporus.

The Turks, masters of protocol and ceremony, wanted to forgo the niceties and talk to Layard as soon as they could over the crumbling international situation. He met in the middle of the night with Edhem Pasha, the grand vizier at the time, an honest yet irritable official whom he considered "a dangerous man to be at the head of affairs at so critical a moment." He warned the vizier "not to be under any illusion as to the state of public opinion in England." If Russia went to war with Turkey, the Porte couldn't look for help to the British government.

The very next morning, he had to pass along the same sentiments to the country's foreign minister, Safvet Pasha, a dignified man who suffered a nervous facial twitch "which caused him to make incessant grimaces." Safvet Pasha argued that the top perpetrators of the atrocities against Bulgarians couldn't be executed because this could provoke Muslims, but they could serve long prison sentences; at the same time, imprisoned Christian Bulgarians would soon receive a general pardon. Layard had to break it to him that events had gone too far for that, and British sympathies wouldn't change.

His next stop was to the sultan himself to formally present his credentials. On April 24, a state carriage and four others rode up to the embassy's doors to take Layard to the supreme ruler of the Ottoman Empire. The four other carriages were for the diplomat's entourage of sixteen staff (brought along for the purpose simply to impress). He was going to the sultan's Kiosk of Yildiz, his "star palace." The long diplomatic caravan went up and down a rugged and steep road, so that anything that came after must have been a mild relief. Layard was done the honor of a special presentation of arms and music by the Imperial Guard's military band and then inside a waiting room was served coffee and sherbet. Then he was handed a long tobacco pipe, a *chibouk*, with an amber mouthpiece set with large diamonds.

Finally, with all the elaborate pomp over, he was led upstairs to meet the sultan, with Safvet Pasha acting as interpreter. Layard knew enough Turkish by then that he could follow what the two men said to each other and of more importance, if Safvet Pasha was correctly passing along what he said. Abdul Hamid appeared nervous and anxious, and Layard wrote in his report to the foreign minister that the sultan "was almost in despair. He insisted upon his desire for peace in a very touching way, and with tears in his eyes. There could be no doubt as to his perfect sincerity. At times, his countenance was lighted up with a most pleasant and winning smile. On the whole, he gave me the impression of a very amiable, well-intentioned, honest, thoughtful and humane man, truly desirous of doing his utmost for the welfare of all classes of his people, but wanting in physical and moral energy, and likely to yield to the influence of stronger and more determined natures." When he met the sultan a second time, Abdul Hamid made the unusual step of allowing Enid to stay during the audience.

In his *Memoirs*, Layard offered a more detailed portrait and conceded that he had to revise his assessment of the man over time but attributed the gradual, darkening changes to Abdul Hamid's character to a string of assassination attempts and the steady intrigue around him. His summation is telling about both Layard and the sultan: "One could scarcely help having a kind of personal affection mingled with pity for him—a feeling which my wife and I entertained to the last, notwithstanding the many reasons he gave me for distrusting him in public matters and for condemning his conduct."

In this, their first meeting, Layard stuck to the official line and pushed for concessions Turkey would need to make, but then, like the convenient turn of events in a movie, a telegram literally arrived at that moment from the Turkish ambassador in Moscow. Russia had declared war.

★   ★   ★

Only days before, the railway bridge that linked Moldova with Romania had been rebuilt to a design by Gustav Eiffel (famous for his tower) after spring flooding of the Prut River had destroyed the first one. With Romania wanting its independence and granting permission to pass through its territory, Russian troops could leisurely cross over to Ungheni and then prepare to invade the Ottoman Empire.

Great Britain was neutral, yet the sultan and the Turkish military kept turning to Layard for advice. At the same time, there was a lack of leadership from Whitehall and the prime minister. Disraeli's assessment of his ambassadors and of diplomats in general—as one of his best biographers, Robert Blake, has pointed out—could be idiosyncratic to the point of bizarre. He considered Layard's predecessor in Istanbul, Henry Elliott, as pro-Russian when, if anything, he was pro-Turk. And while Layard was still in Madrid, Disraeli considered him "prejudiced and passionate, and always—I will not say misleads, but certainly misinforms us." As Blake once asked, why then did he ever put Layard in the Near East? Why defend him then when the Queen expressed doubts? Perhaps he conceded like others that Layard was still the most knowledgeable for the job, but his own attitude and views on the so-called "Eastern Question" were complicated. As the crisis had first developed, Britain's prime minister had no qualms about Istanbul being made a "free port" under the "guardianship of England" following an invasion of the Ottoman Empire by Russia and Austria-Hungary.[9]

At the same time, Disraeli's foreign minister, Edward Stanley, known as Lord Derby, was firmly in the Russian camp and shared secret information from Cabinet meetings with Russia's ambassador to London, Count Pyotr Shuvalov. Disraeli, Lord Salisbury, and the Queen apparently referred to this as Derby's "indiscretion"—today, of course, we'd call it treason. And yet Derby's personal motives were peaceful.[10] Meanwhile, Victoria was in a mild panic, fearing that when the armies of the tsar inevitably captured Istanbul, the political fallout would force her to abdicate. Disraeli also understood the ramifications, but instead of yanking firmly on the leash of his foreign minister, he chose to write Layard in secret.

"Are there no means," he asked, "notwithstanding the paralyzing neutrality in vogue, which might . . . place England in a commanding position when the conditions of peace are discussed?" Disraeli's idea was to get the Turks to invite the British fleet into their waters and be willing to allow 20,000 British soldiers to occupy Gallipoli. He would back the proposal in the Cabinet, but it had to look as if it had originated within the Turkish government. It was an idea that Layard had already put to Derby, his immediate superior, who had poured cold water on it. Now he wrote back to his prime minister that "you must remember that my position here is a most difficult one, with much to ask and nothing to give, and what has passed has given the Porte great suspicion and distrust of us." Yes, of course, Britain could move into a better position—if it gave up being neutral.

It never would, but Britain's military attaché in Istanbul helped Turkish army engineers shore up the fortifications at Gallipoli. Later, during World

War I, British soldiers would be hopelessly beaten by these defenses when they faced the Turks as enemies.[11]

On June 20, Layard wrote a long and emphatic letter to Disraeli, reminding him of the stakes involved. If the Ottoman Empire fell to Russia, was London ready for the change in the balance of power? Was it ready to accept the north of Persia and an alternative route to India falling into Moscow's hands? If not, it was time to do things. He left the issue of corralling public opinion up to his prime minister, but he strongly suggested sending the Turks money and troops. The British fleet should move in. Gallipoli should be occupied. He also recommended bringing the Hungarians in as an ally, especially if Austria chose to throw its weight around on Russia's behalf and, in the same vein, appeal to Muslims in Central Asian states under control of Moscow. And he thought London should warn Greece to stay out of the conflict.

Days later, the Russians crossed the Danube, and in July, they moved deep into northern Bulgaria. In their wake, scattered refugees returned home and unleashed their fury on the resident Turkish population. Given these new massacres, the sultan told Layard that Europe should now decide who the real barbarians were. Abdul Hamid even wrote to Queen Victoria, asking her to communicate directly with the tsar to put an end to the reprisals. Whatever her perennial reservations about Layard, the Queen was outraged by events. On July 20, she wrote of how she was distressed over Disraeli taking no action. "And the language—the insulting language used by the Russians against us! It makes the Queen's blood boil!" She supported the idea of occupying Gallipoli.[12] Layard sent home reports of "a war of extermination on both sides," though he put much of the blame on the Russians.[13] On the Opposition side, Gladstone, ever stubborn, refused to accept that Christians had racked up their own butcher's bill and claimed that Layard had misinformed the government on what was really going on.

Layard has been portrayed ever since as blindly sympathetic to the Porte's interests, but his view was more nuanced and conflicted. Istanbul, he would complain for years, had few statesmen of backbone and integrity in an environment of almost total corruption; meanwhile, the Russians were reducing Turkish regions to anarchy. "The truth is that one side is as barbarous as the other," wrote Derby in early September, "but that there is really more excuse for the Turk who sees his country wantonly invaded, and his wives and children outraged and massacred." He was quick to remind others that Bulgarian rebels using terrorist methods had set everything in motion, though he recognized the Turks were exacting brutal reprisals.[14] Then as now, biases favoring either the Christians or the Muslims seem to dictate how harsh the historian's verdict is on Layard's conduct and opinions.

The Russians made early gains in the war, but at Pleven in Bulgaria, the Ottoman forces dug in. The Russians had overwhelmingly greater numbers but were armed with old-fashioned, muzzle-loading muskets. For all the condescending chatter about the "backward" Turk, the Ottomans were smart enough to buy American-made breech-loading rifles. Still, the siege dragged on into a cold and bitter winter, one in which Turkish soldiers were reduced to eating dogs and rats while Russian officers dined on caviar.[15] In December, Pleven fell, and as Turkish prisoners of war were marched away from the town, their wounded—forlorn in their cots back at the defeated base—were slaughtered by vengeful Bulgarian soldiers.

The Russians were now free to capture Sofia and fight a set of brutal battles with their Bulgarian volunteers to take Shipka Pass in the Balkan Mountains. In January 1878, Turkey's defeat at the pass sparked panic in Istanbul, and the sultan wrote in desperation again to Queen Victoria. Victoria wrote in turn to Disraeli that she couldn't remain the sovereign of a nation "that is letting itself down to kiss the feet of the great barbarians, the retarders of all liberty and civilisation that exists. . . . She is utterly ashamed of the Cabinet. . . . Oh, if the Queen were a man, she would like to go and give the Russians, whose word one cannot believe, such a beating!"[16]

On the day he received this letter, Disraeli was under the weather but not prevailing over his Cabinet, which still didn't want to help Turkey. Despite this, his open show of sympathy led the Turkish ambassador to believe—and worse, let his superiors back home believe—that any day now, the British would come to the Ottomans' rescue.

When they didn't, it was Layard who felt the pressure. Germany's ambassador in Istanbul was determined to exploit the situation, and with Bismarck finding common ground with Russia, the Germans were happy to shield in their embassy Russians who had been identified as spies. At first, Layard got word the British fleet would sail into the Dardanelles (on the flimsy pretext of protecting British citizens in the capital), but when the order was canceled from London, the British legation suffered massive embarrassment. Meanwhile, the Russians kept marching toward Istanbul and put off any negotiations on terms to end the war so that it could capture more territory. In this context, Layard's continued exasperation with London is understandable. Back in November, he had written Disraeli, "I do not despair of holding my own and maintaining the honour and interests of England, *if I could only know what the intentions and objects of my government were* [emphasis in the original]."[17]

Layard and his wife bore witness to a refugee crisis with horrifying similarities to the ones today. Tens of thousands arrived daily on trains. "As the trains arrive at the stations, the bodies of men, women and children frozen to death, or who have succumbed to illness are dragged out of the wagons," Layard wrote in a dispatch on January 16. "Even the tops of the closed carriages are occupied by the women and children who in some instances, numbed by the cold, roll off and are killed." Long streams of refugees had abandoned everything they owned and were dying by the dozens. "A panic has seized the population of Adrianople, Philippopoli, Tatar-Bazardjik and other towns. The railway stations are invaded by vast crowds, who attempt to enter the trains and overpower the officials, who are unable to keep them back."

Layard asked the Turkish authorities to give his legation a large building near the Istanbul railway station, and it soon filled up with 1,500 "of the most destitute and suffering fugitives." The building was just a stopover before people were moved to other quarters around the city and villages on the Bosporus. Mosques were already full. Layard also dipped into the legation's accounts to spare what he could to open soup kitchens on the railway between Istanbul and Adrianople.

In his dispatches, he praised how his embassy's military attaché, a Major de Winton, helped in the crisis, while the major's wife and Enid Layard spent their hours supervising hospitals, finding new places of refuge, visiting the sick, and distributing food. At night, Enid and Mrs. de Winton made clothes that could be sent to those in need.

When the Russians offered their initial terms for the armistice with the Turks, Layard examined them carefully and reported back to Derby in the Cabinet. In his professional opinion, the terms "broke up the Ottoman Empire, practically gave its European provinces and probably a part of the Asiatic territory to Russia." They were, he summed up, "disastrous to Turkey, dangerous to England and injurious to the interests of England." The Russians bullied the Turkish delegates at the negotiations, used delaying tactics to enable their troops to get closer to Istanbul, and at one point, Layard was sure they had sabotaged the telegraph lines to interfere with Turkish communications.

The armistice was signed on January 31, 1878, and the Turks did their best to obsessively keep the final terms as secret as possible, fearing they could spark a massive revolt not only in the Turkish parliament but against the sultan himself.

Days later, Layard and his wife visited the Hagia Sophia, where the "pavement and galleries of that vast and magnificent building were covered by a mass of human beings, crouching together in the utmost squalor and misery."

Layard noted in his memoirs that "smallpox and other diseases had already begun to wreck ravage amongst them." People lined up for bread, soup, and charcoal for fires. "There were between four and five thousand human beings almost perishing from cold and hunger, gathered together in this one edifice, and yet the imam of the mosque, a respected and venerable old mullah, assured me that not a quarrel had occurred, not a blasphemous or angry word had been uttered, and not a theft committed. How different would the case have been if the same number of Englishmen or any other Europeans had been collected together under similar circumstances. It was impossible not to feel what a noble and much sullied race were these Ottoman Turks, and how great was the contrast between them and their Christian fellow subjects for whose prospect they had been made to endure such infinite sufferings and misery."

Russians on the march shocked the British public and prompted jitters on the London Stock Exchange. The British Cabinet, having posed as neutral all this time, now woke up to the ramifications of Russian troops strutting around Istanbul and what this could do to its sphere of influence in the Middle East. But it kept promising the fleet and then changing its mind, forcing Layard to waste time "telegraphing in different directions" and reassuring the sultan and his ministers—who now thought British ships would provoke the Russians further into a harsh occupation of their capital.

Very early in the morning of February 12, the ships prowled into the sea during a severe snowstorm, and the Turks went through the empty gesture of making a formal protest—but not firing on the British. Nothing could demonstrate so clearly how the Ottoman Empire was hobbling and gasping its way towards its final years.

When Turkey's foreign minister, Server Pasha, called on Layard that evening, he pointed out that even a temporary occupation by the Russians would have an "incalculable effect" on the entire Muslim world. What would the Muslims of India say, he asked Layard, when they learned the Russians had entered the "Capital of Islamism in the very presence of the English Fleet, which was unable or unwilling to interfere to prevent this great humiliation?"

Server Pasha also had a point that if 30,000 Russians marched in, they would probably help themselves to provisions, engage in open looting, and pull down Muslim homes for firewood. Russian agents provocateurs could start incidents that would lead inevitably to widespread bloodshed. Layard tried to calm his fears, but there was little he could do at this point. His moment, however, was coming, one in which he would arguably save Europe from another Crimean War.

The next few weeks saw a flurry of activity and were charged with international tension. Among the humiliating concessions Russia demanded of Turkey were a substantial landgrab, including de facto control of Bulgaria, a practical giveaway on terms for the issuing by the Porte of £40 million in bonds, and while they were at it, the Russians wanted the Turkish fleet. Pressure was mounting. The sultan was racked with agitation and despair, often saying he'd perish with his children before seeing the Russians enter Istanbul, but Layard knew it was an empty threat. Meanwhile, his government officials grew suspicious of Britain's intentions and carried on secret negotiations, sharing information indiscreetly with other diplomats, including the German ambassador, who was a conduit for the Russians.

During all this, Layard walked the razor's edge, haggling to buy four of Turkey's ironclad ships to give the British fleet an advantage in the Straits. Back in London, his every move was second-guessed by the newspapers and members of Parliament in the Commons. But at a time of "immense anxiety and toil," Layard was grateful to receive a boosting letter from Disraeli, who wrote, "Amid the torrents of disasters which nearly overwhelm us, I write this line that you should at least know that your sovereign and her ministers entirely approve of your conduct and fully appreciate the energy and resource which have distinguished your management of affairs."

While the treaty negotiations went on, the Russians did their best to drive a wedge between the Turkish and British camps, and their officials now openly threatened that if they had to force their way into the capital, their soldiers would go on a spree of pillaging and destruction—with the British embassy at Pera as a target. Layard took the threat seriously enough to have the legation's archives and some of its other property moved to a British battleship.

But his purchase of the ironclads paid off, and the Russians were furious that they were checked at the Bosporus. Even as arrangements were set for the Treaty of San Stefano, the Russians captured more ground along the shores of the Sea of Marmara, while Cossacks had been seen heading towards Belgrade. The Russians claimed their soldiers were on the coast of Marmara to prepare to disembark because they were supposed to withdraw from Turkey once the agreement was signed. It was clear, however, that they weren't going anywhere until the British left.

It's not overstating it to argue that Layard played a major role in keeping the tsar's troops out of Istanbul and changing the fate of the Middle East forever. Besides his ironclad deal, he had helped the sultan stiffen his resolve. The terms of the treaty were closely guarded, but Layard managed to get his hands on a copy and telegraphed the details to London.

The treaty's greatest significance was perhaps in creating the principality of Bulgaria, and, in fact, Bulgarians still celebrate the date of its signing—March 3—as their Liberation Day. It also paved the way for Romania, Serbia, and Montenegro to become autonomous. Layard recognized correctly that the Russians intended to use these new principalities as their satellites, and the other powers of Europe—France, Italy, Germany—soon insisted on having their say. San Stefano was treated as a first draft, while the finishing touches went into the Treaty of Berlin in July. It's worth noting that thanks to Russian pressure, the Bulgarians didn't even get a seat at the table.

⋆ ⋆ ⋆

March was an ugly, tumultuous month for Layard in terms of his political career. The Russo-Turkish War had focused Britons' attention on Istanbul, which gave his enemies a good excuse to spill a tempest out of its teacup. It came to be known as the Negroponte affair, and it had been dragging on for about a year. Now it would come to a climax. As with so many political scandals, the root and the various twists and turns are absurd. Had Layard been more careful, he could have avoided the trap altogether.

The essentials of the complicated tale boil down to this. A Greek merchant in Istanbul named Menelaeus Negroponte apparently wrote to Gladstone, looking for sympathy over his views on Greek grievances in the Ottoman Empire. What Gladstone wrote in his reply wasn't clear. *The Daily Telegraph* chose to run a story on August 27, 1877, that Gladstone was urging Greeks in Istanbul to "unite with the Slavs in an attack upon the Turks."[18] It didn't matter that he was out of office; even a private letter could harm the British government's position of neutrality. It's entirely plausible that Gladstone would have expressed such a view; to the end of his days, he would thunder in speeches and statements over "superior" Christianity and human rights abuses by the Turks. It's interesting that neither he nor Negroponte ever produced Gladstone's reply.

About a week after the *Telegraph* story, Negroponte wrote to *The Times*, denying that Gladstone had ever urged a common rebellion between the Greeks and Slavs. Now the story began to pick up steam, and Gladstone felt compelled to issue a denial in a letter to *The Telegraph* on September 25. There was "a Polonius behind the curtain," and he demanded this string puller "come out and make himself known." Interestingly, the Istanbul correspondent for *The Standard* claimed that he saw the correspondence, found nothing in it very provocative against Turkey, and that it amounted to a great deal of fuss.[19]

This is where Layard enters the picture. It turned out that Negroponte had approached *him* in August, trying to persuade him that the time had come for a general uprising by Greeks in Ottoman territory. When it was clear Layard didn't agree, Negroponte bragged about his correspondence with Gladstone and made the claim that Gladstone supported a Greek–Slav rebellion. At an embassy reception on August 20, 1877, a *Times* correspondent showed Layard one of the Gladstone letters, supposedly under "a pledge of secrecy." But Layard didn't honor the bargain.

In correspondence with Lord Derby, he admitted that "I mentioned its contents to a gentleman connected with the embassy, adding that if he saw the correspondent of the *Daily Telegraph*, he could mention it to him." This was how *The Telegraph* picked up the trail. Unfortunately for Layard, in February

1878, a set of Parliamentary Papers was published with the correspondence, and an indignant *Times* reprinted its revelations.

Layard claimed that if the letter reached a journalist, it was public property, but it's clear he intended the leak to embarrass his old rival. He had also broken his promise to the *Times* correspondent, which damaged his relations with the most important newspaper in London; no reporter forgives a source who hands a juicy scoop to a competitor. And on top of that, he leaked this supposed bombshell without any corroboration. If Gladstone did express such thoughts, Layard was within his rights as Britain's ambassador to report his concerns directly to the Foreign Office, which probably would have had a private talk with Gladstone, urging him to knock it off and stop suggesting Greek insurrection. Layard had forfeited the moral high ground.

The whole matter escalated, and Layard tried to fob off the blame on Negroponte, an obvious crank associated with minor revolutionary groups. But important questions never got asked. How is it that correspondents for *The Times* and *The Standard* both got their hands on one of Gladstone's letters? It's reasonable to assume Negroponte circulated it, trying to accomplish something. Why is it then that the man for *The Times* thought it worthwhile to show Layard but the reporter for *The Standard* dismissed its contents as nothing? Where was the letter? Why didn't Gladstone face greater scrutiny over his views on the Greeks given his public statements?

Instead, it was Layard's feet held to the fire for being a bully, and he narrowly escaped a vote of censure in the House of Commons on March 12.

Layard weathered the storm because he was far from London, and the fate of the Ottoman Empire gripped his attention. It says something about the ephemeral nature of political scandals that by the end of March, he received the news that Victoria had bestowed on him the Grand Cross of the Order of the Bath.

★   ★   ★

While negotiations for the Berlin agreement carried on, a new incident in May threatened everything. Layard was talking with the prime minister in a government office when he suddenly received a summons to the palace but couldn't tell Turkey's own prime minister what was going on. Layard decided to go home, and along the way, he passed the Palace of Tcheragan occupied by troops and noticed boats were patrolling the Bosporus. Before he even left the Golden Horn, his own sources filled him in. There was an attempted coup with the goal of replacing the sultan with his brother, Murad.

The attempt was poorly planned and almost pathetic in its execution. Its mastermind was one of the reform-minded "Young Ottomans" and a Muslim radical—radical in this context being more political than religious. His name was Ali Suavi, and he argued that Turkey should be left alone to its own devices without European interference. But he pinned his hopes on Murad, and with only about seventy men, he forced his way into the Tcheragan Palace to free him. Murad's own mother was sympathetic to the cause and helped them find her son. The problem was that a bewildered Murad didn't want to leave, and even while Ali Suavi was personally trying to drag him out of the harem, a group of police stormed in and stabbed him with bayonets and cut down his supporters. As for Murad, he was whisked off to Yildiz, where he was kept under guard but was treated well.

Layard's verdict on the episode was shrewd, noting that nobody important had been involved in the conspiracy and that the whole thing was "a foolish and ill-planned affair which had no prospect of success." There were bigger matters to deal with, and London was pushing hard for them. England would pay Turkey to take Cyprus off its hands, and this would allow officials in the Foreign Office to keep an eye on the Middle East. Layard's instructions were to persuade Abdul Hamid to sign off on the deal and soon.

But the coup attempt was the tipping point that unbalanced the sultan's mind. His courtiers and spies had poisoned his delicate mental state by claiming the conspiracy was larger than it was, which defied reality. By the time Layard turned up at Yildiz to talk about Cyprus and the Russian withdrawal, Abdul Hamid was so delusional, he believed the Englishman might be there to assassinate him or have him kidnapped and taken away on a British battleship with Murad once again placed on the throne. A detail of Circassian guards stood armed and close by to keep him safe. When Layard began talking in a low voice to be discreet and approached him, the sultan shrank away "with an expression of terror."

Abdul Hamid soon excused himself, saying he was too ill to continue, and Layard worked out acceptance of the deal with government ministers. After some time, the sultan recovered his senses to a degree but careened in another emotional direction. Layard was again his most valued personal ally and friend, and he wanted to confer on him the first class of the Order of Osmaniniyeh with a portrait in diamonds (government policy wouldn't allow Layard to accept).

The next day, Layard got word the sultan was anxious to speak with him, and he found Abdul Hamid stretched out on a sofa with a Greek doctor hovering over him. The sultan was agitated again, thinking there was another plot to kill him and that he had only "a few hours to live." He had heard about the Englishman's heroic rescue of the marshal in Spain—couldn't Layard do the same for him and his family? As Layard tried to calm him down, they heard a trumpet and then marching feet at a distant camp. Abdul Hamid leapt up from the couch "with a look of terror, exclaiming that the trumpet was the signal agreed upon by the conspirators, and that they were approaching to assassinate him." Layard pointed out it was only the changing of the guard.

He stayed long into the night, along with the doctor, trying to reassure a delusional head of state. By the time he got home at four in the morning, a messenger brought a fresh note from Yildiz in French, asking the Layards to take the sultan and his family either into the embassy or onto a British battleship. Though Abdul Hamid recovered his sanity again, his intense paranoia would continue to warp his behavior.

If Layard had any remaining influence on him, he wouldn't be allowed to use it. Gladstone was back in power. The new prime minister struck a pose that he didn't bear a grudge over the Negroponte affair and claimed it would be a Cabinet decision whether Layard should be recalled. But there shouldn't have been any doubt which way he wanted them to lean.

In late April, Layard wrote a secret dispatch to make the government "fully acquainted with the state of Turkey."[20] The most enlightened and patriotic Turkish statesmen, he argued in his conclusion, believed the only thing that could save their country was a check on the sultan's power, dismissal of the corrupt stooges who surrounded him, and constitutional reforms. But "the Sultan and his present ministers will only continue to seek to deceive Europe by making a show of listening to her counsels. I share their views to a great extent. Unfortunately, there are apparently no men in Turkey capable of imposing these measures upon the Sultan."[21]

Just as in office politics today, the person getting fired is often the last one to hear about it. Layard had to learn in the newspapers that he'd been sacked, and on May 6, Granville sent him a private telegram that noted Layard himself had conceded how ineffectual he had become in his post. "This was a great blow," Enid wrote in her diary, "as I feel sure we shall never return here." On the same day, a second telegram arrived from Granville: "Inform the Porte that the Queen has approved the Rt. Honble J.G. Goschen MP to be H.M.'s special ambassador to relieve you of your duties on quitting Constantinople."

The telegram hadn't been encrypted, which meant the Turkish Telegraph Office could report its news to the sultan even before it was delivered to Britain's lame-duck ambassador. Word of the humiliation could circulate through the capital. But it also didn't follow proper diplomatic etiquette—normal protocol demanded that a country's leader have a chance to approve a country's choice for a representative before acknowledging him in his post. The Foreign Office expected the Sublime Porte to accept Goschen, and that was that.

The final knife twist came in the form of a strange request. Gladstone and Granville had asked Layard if they could publish the dispatch, which was highly unusual for a diplomatic communiqué. Layard felt he couldn't refuse, and he at least got the chance to redact from the proof some of his more incendiary personal observations of the sultan. He might have also thought it would shut up all the chatter that he was pro-Turk once and for all. When the dispatch came to light, it only served his critics in suggesting he'd never been effective at his job, and Abdul Hamid was hurt, accusing him of being a "false friend." Gladstone had exacted his final revenge.

On June 2, the Layards boarded the royal ship *Helicon* with Goschen riding along with them on the Bosporus until the ship dropped anchor in the Golden Horn. There were plenty of goodbyes to friends, and originally, Layard was supposed to present Goschen formally to the sultan, but the various delays made things too awkward. "We set off at six o'clock," Enid wrote in her diary. "A lovely evening with hardly a breath of wind, and we sat on deck and saw the fairy-like city fade away gradually into the evening mists."

This parting vision must have reminded Layard of so many years ago when he rowed in a little boat to Pera to deliver letters to Stratford Canning. His long career in diplomacy had really begun on this ancient strait, and now it would end. Enid had been correct. They would not return.

★   ★   ★

After Layard's departure and the sultan's disillusionment with him over the April dispatch, Abdul Hamid wasn't inclined to listen to Englishmen again— or any other Western diplomat. The Treaty of Berlin was supposed to guarantee the safety of the Armenians from the Kurds; in fact, the Sublime Porte was obligated to report to the European powers on the progress of reforms for them. But Abdul Hamid ignored the collective appeals in 1880, and as the years passed, he developed a truly vicious tactic for quashing Armenian and Assyrian protest.

Desperate to cling to power over his vast holdings, he collected the dregs of Kurdish tribesmen, Circassian and Arab bandits, and organized them into cavalry units known as the Hamidiye, the "men of the Sultan." They became instruments of terror, and from 1894 to 1896, they raped, robbed, and slaughtered scores of innocents. *The New York Times* used the word "Holocaust" in 1895 to refer to massacred Armenians, and Abdul Hamid earned the nickname "The Red Sultan."

Layard mercifully wouldn't live to read the most lurid reports of atrocity that filled the British and American newspapers. But he knew catastrophe awaited. "The war with Russia gave the fatal blow," he wrote in his memoir. "The doom of the Turkish Empire is now sealed." He recognized that the Treaty of Berlin would hasten its downfall, which was "a mere question of time." The long reign of the Ottomans only survived him by less than thirty years.

A Last Quiet Battle . . . in Court

*W*hen the couple returned to London in 1881, Henry Layard was at loose ends. He spent a lot of his time on writing the memoir of his years representing Britain in Istanbul, which would stay unpublished for more than a century. Perhaps his lack of interest in publication was because he knew there was more that he could do. The Foreign Office still sought him out occasionally for his opinions on Middle East affairs.[1]

There was talk that he was up for the job of Britain's ambassador in Rome, a position he would have relished. Granville, who tried to be objective to others about his old friend, worked behind the scenes on his behalf, but Gladstone was still the master of passive-aggressive string pulling. The Cabinet should have its say, just as it had with getting Layard sacked. Months passed, and Granville, though getting Layard's hopes up and suggesting the appointment was inevitable, warned him to be patient. Inevitably, word came that he had been turned down.

Layard humiliated himself by writing a long letter to Gladstone, asking for a meeting. When the two finally sat in the same room, nothing was really accomplished, but Layard clung to faint hope. "It is very gratifying to me to receive your assurance that nothing that has passed between us remains on your mind as a cause, in any degree, for resentment."[2] Gladstone told him he was even willing to tell the Commons that he held no grudge—but of course, he could follow through with this empty gesture, as the decision had been made.

This pose also drove a wedge between Layard and Granville, who tried later to secure an ambassadorship for Layard in Berlin. This time, Gladstone was more direct in arguing that Layard wasn't right for the posting. It was clear that as long as his nemesis was in power, there was no hope of returning to diplomatic life. Granville did achieve one thing for Layard, making sure he would get his Foreign Service pension of £1,700.[3] This money, along with inheritances and other income, ensured that Henry and Enid could live in relative comfort. But Layard never forgave Granville.

The couple moved to Venice and settled into a quiet life of entertaining friends and Enid pursuing her hobbies of painting and playing the guitar while her husband spent the days writing and reading in his study. These were the years when Layard was an invaluable trustee for Britain's National Gallery, and its collection of Italian paintings owes a lot to his recommendations. Layard built up a collection of minor masters that included the Renaissance's Vittore Carpaccio and Gentile Bellini.[4]

He helped popularize the methodology of his friend, the art historian Giovanni Morelli. Morelli, who had studied medicine, figured out that you can determine the true authorship of works by the Masters by studying original drawings and sketches—the clues are in how a great painter rendered the fingers, drew an ear, worked out the folds of a garment. Layard and Morelli would often visit galleries and churches together to admire paintings. Layard wrote a friend, "I am leading the life which from my earliest days I aspired to lead—what more can I want?"[5]

But there was something else he wanted: to stay relevant. In February 1885, he wrote to *The Times* and offered a perspective that flew in the face of the British anger and grief pervading the country at the time. Charles "Chinese" Gordon had failed in his mission in Sudan to avenge British and Egyptian soldiers slaughtered by the Mahdi's rebellion. Gordon was now a national martyr, but Layard asked, "Why are we going to Khartoum? No one, it seems, can answer that question, and yet the soil of the Sudan is reeking with the blood of our soldiers and with that of the wretched Arabs we are pleased to call 'rebels.' Why 'rebels?' They are not our subjects and have done us no wrong. Gordon, betrayed by his own government, has fallen in a war brought on by ourselves, while holding a fortified place to which we had no right. . . . Our only course is to allow the Sultan, who is the legitimate owner of the Sudan, to occupy it once we have retaken it."[6]

By 1888, he decided that he deserved a peerage. "I have no desire to be 'a Lord,' and nothing would induce me to ask for that or for any other distinction," he wrote to his friend Lord Duncannon. "But I should like to have employment during the remainder of my days, which cannot in the nature of things be very much prolonged."[7] Though he claimed he wouldn't ask, eventually he did just that, writing directly to Salisbury, who was now prime minister, and rattling off his credentials. But deserving had nothing to do with it. Too many enemies didn't want to see him in the House of Lords, where he would have a forum for his views.

Now in his seventies with a full white beard, he looked like a biblical sage. In 1890, Enid arranged to have the Austrian artist Ludwig Passini paint his portrait, which Layard considered "a piece of senseless extravagance, but it will be the last record of me."[8] In the picture, he appears at his cluttered desk, writing, looking up as if curious over an interruption. The subject quipped that the portrait made him look "very much like an old jew-dealer in his bric-a-brac shop."[9]

From Venice, he checked the English newspapers, which were inevitably behind events because of shipping, and he enlisted friends to tell him the latest news of British politics. But he was seldom impressed. "I have read Gladstone's last speech with even more disgust and indignation than usual. If he should, unhappily, succeed in getting back to power, it will, I fear, be a disastrous day to England."[10]

The great sage of archaeology decided he should pull out the many stories from long ago that were never included in *Nineveh and Its Remains*. But in 1884, his old travel companion, Edward Mitford, had beaten him to the punch, bringing out his own account, which he called *A Land March from England to Ceylon Forty Years Ago*. It was published by Murray's competitor, W. H. Allen. Unfortunately, Mitford's book is as dry as its title, and no doubt Layard's *Early Adventures* sold more copies when it was released three years later. It's the story of a young man, hungry for the excitement of travel and fascinated by the cultures he encounters. Within a few short pages, he introduced the reader to the horrible torture of the bastinado, the cliff-hanger of being sick in an exotic backdrop and his dangerous encounters with bandits.

It's one of those mysteries of publishing that *Nineveh and Its Remains* should be Layard's literary monument to this day, even though like many classics, it's seldom read cover to cover. Long sections of it are devoted to detailed descriptions of his finds, which can only interest an archaeological historian. There is none of such minutiae in *Early Adventures*. It crackles with episodic drama and observations on Arab, Kurdish, and Bakhtiari life.

It was inevitably a time for looking back rather than forward. Writing to his friend William Gregory, he casually mentioned how he had been reading a biography of Canning. "I saw a spiteful notice of the book by Arabian Nights Burton[11] . . . in which notwithstanding the ill nature and evident vindictiveness, there was some truth. Lord S., like other men, was in the habit of taking credit for the work of others—political as well as archaeological. Judging from his letters, etc., he discovered Nineveh, and I was only his 'agent.'"[12]

He and Enid entertained friends and the acquaintances who knew that the Layards should be their first social call in Venice. The art critic John Ruskin visited, as did the poets Robert and Elizabeth Barrett Browning. William Henry Smith, an heir to the W. H. Smith bookselling chain, arrived on his yacht *Pandora*.[13] And Layard still had fans. A letter in late June 1890 came all the way from Copenhagen from "one of your most enthusiastic admirers here in the cold north." Olaf Halvorsen, who volunteered his age as eighteen, wrote, "I beg to ask you for your monogram. You are not able to imagine the delight it would give me to have your handwriting."[14] But Layard also suffered occasional bouts of depression. "The fact is that I feel myself suddenly a very old man, with no 'go' left in me."[15]

Months later, he seemed to reconcile himself to not gaining a peerage. "I am now too old to take part in public affairs . . . and am very happy and contented as I am. I live here to avoid the turmoil of English life and to escape the London fogs. Had I been put into the House of Lords, I should have considered it my duty to reside in England—which certainly would not have contributed to my health or happiness."[16]

Time and age also sometimes made him less gracious and nourished a streak of conservatism. Asking Gregory if he had read Tolstoy's racy (for the time) short novel *The Kreutzer Sonata*, he declared, "It is worse than Zola!" He called it a "mischievous book—not to be left about. . . . I cannot understand its object."[17] Isabella Bird, a pioneer in travel writing and who was elected as the first woman fellow of the Royal Geographical Society in 1890, was inspired by his *Early Adventures*. She gallivanted off to Persia and Kurdistan to have adventures and produce her own book, but Layard refused to review it; he argued to John Murray that ladies shouldn't go on journeys among wild peoples lest they lose their virtue.

There was, however, one last crusade for Henry Layard: to rush to the defense of an old friend.

★   ★   ★

Layard's discoveries of Assyrian artifacts had unintentionally given birth to a brisk trade in stolen Assyrian antiquities, a phenomenon that mortified him. By this time, Hormuzd Rassam was digging around Abu Habba, again on a limited budget and with only the guards he could afford—his excavation sites were easy prey for thieves. The British Museum was annoyed by valuable finds turning up in bazaars in Baghdad and Istanbul, so it sent Wallis Budge off to Mesopotamia to find out what was going on.

If the name rings a faint bell, it's because Budge would later be known for his prolific writings on ancient Egyptian religion and hieroglyphs. Only twenty years ago, you could still walk into any well-stocked bookstore and find Dover Publishing's brightly colored paperback reprints of Budge's translation of *The Egyptian Book of the Dead* or his work *The Gods of the Egyptians*. But at the time, he was an operative, tracing the network of stolen antiquities and building a network of dealers the museum could rely on to make purchases. Budge began his studies focusing on Assyriology rather than Egyptology, so it's not implausible to think he may have been jealous of both Layard and Rassam.

Whatever the reason, he chose to complain about Rassam in his reports to museum officials: "Other people got all the whole tablets; we got the fragments—mere rubbish. The overseers who carried on the excavations were his relations, and they picked out all the good tablets and sold them to the Germans, Americans and others."[18]

He spread these accusations for years in museum circles, which eventually got back to Layard, who duly informed his old friend. With all the talk behind his back from other quarters as well, Rassam now had grounds to sue Budge for libel. Layard first tried to mediate between the two and get Budge to apologize, while Rassam demonstrated to museum officials that besides not stealing, he didn't have any relatives at Abu Habba or within hundreds of miles. In a long "Statement of Services & Complaints against Mr. Budge," Rassam laid out his side of the story to the Trustees.[19]

As he wrapped up his arguments, he quoted two damning pieces of correspondence between Layard and the museum's principal librarian. Layard's letter to the librarian of November 30, 1891, read, "I remember that you complained to me in my house that Mr. Rassam had sent to the museum several cases of mere fragments of tablets which were absolutely useless; but as I considered our conversation as strictly private, I have never alluded to it either to him or to others." The principal librarian, Edward Maunde Thompson, wrote Layard back on December 21, "If Mr. Rassam will follow your advice (meaning that I should not move any further in the matter), I think we need have no more of these stories. Mr. Budge will on this side be kept quiet."

"It is a mystery to me to understand," Rassam asked, "what Mr. Thompson means by the words *keeping Mr. Budge quiet*, unless he thought that he was going to tell more lies about me!" He also noted that "Sir Henry Layard had not promised *never* to inform me of the calumny when he found it necessary for me to know it [emphasis in the original]."[20]

Budge then offered an apology, one that Layard judged "mean, shuffling and untruthful." Layard may have been naturally biased, but even a court of law decided later that Budge's apology was "insincere, ungentlemanly and shabby."[21] Rassam chose to see Budge in court. Museum officials and the elites, however, informed Layard they would rally to Budge's side. Layard being Layard, he stuck by his old comrade and protégé. From Venice, he wrote his friend, William Gregory, that Budge's gossip was intended to "supplant Rassam, one of the honestest [*sic*] and most straightforward fellows I ever knew, and one whose great services have never been acknowledged—because he is a 'nigger' and because Rawlinson, as is his habit, appropriated to himself the credit of Rassam's discoveries."[22]

Over five days across June and July 1893, the case was heard, and Budge's lawyers tried to argue that their client's conversation with Layard had somehow been privileged, meaning he shouldn't have repeated the remarks to Hormuzd Rassam. The logic was ridiculous. Layard had never practiced law and certainly wouldn't think of himself as Budge's professional confidante, nor was he a full-time employee with the museum.

When Layard got his chance to testify, he related how he once visited the museum in 1891 and Budge had pushed a tray towards him, saying, "This is the sort of rubbish Rassam sends us. He allowed his overseers [meaning his relatives] to collect good tablets and sell them to other museums." When later confronted on the stand, Budge dug in his heels: "I may be wrong about the overseers being his relations, but there is no doubt he connived at their robberies."[23]

All this might sound to us today like small beer, but Rassam's reputation was at stake, and the case did have its dramatic, even mildly salacious moments. Peter Renouf, who had retired from running the Egyptian and Assyrian department for the museum, was called to testify and told how on one occasion he was busy reading about military men in the East, including Henry Rawlinson. Budge, noting this, commented, "Oh, yes, Rawlinson and Sir H. Layard used to lead rather loose lives in Baghdad, and Rassam used to pimp for them." There were excited murmurs in the courtroom.

When it was his turn, Budge's barrister asked Renouf, "What led you to carry this bit of stale gossip to Sir Henry Layard relating to what happened forty years ago?"

"Because," Renouf replied coolly, "shortly before leaving the museum, things came to my knowledge which entirely changed my opinion of Mr. Budge and proved to me that his stories were not simply those of artless credulity, but the utterances of a very cowardly, mendacious, dishonorable scoundrel."

The barrister tried to wrestle control back over his cross-examination. "Well, now that you have been able to express your feelings, perhaps you will answer this question. What led you to carry that miserable bit of gossip to Sir Henry Layard?"

"I mentioned it very naturally to show the persons whom we had to deal with," snapped Renouf.[24]

The court sided with Rassam, but it was a hollow victory. Rassam had asked for £1,000 in damages; the case was appealed, and the court eventually awarded him a mere £50. Worse, the old guard of the museum covered Budge's court costs. "It is understood," reported a Yorkshire paper, "that this is not merely an expression of sympathy with a popular colleague, but that the action of the museum officials was prompted by a strong feeling that as Dr. Budge has acted throughout in the interests of his department, it would be most unfair to allow him personally to suffer."[25]

Budge's colleagues continued to treat him as a hero, and he was soon promoted to head of the British Museum's Assyrio-Egyptian department. He outlived both Layard and Rassam, so that he could pick apart errors in Layard's work at Nineveh and refight his lost court battle by quoting all supportive news stories in his book *By Nile and Tigris*. With his legitimate contributions to archaeology and the study of cuneiform, he inspired giants like James Joyce, William Butler Yeats, and his friend H. Rider Haggard, who wrote the Allan Quartermain stories. But in time, Hormuzd Rassam's career would be reassessed, while Budge lost a measure of prestige. By 1963, Richard Barnett, in charge of the Western Asiatic Antiquities department at the museum, could write, "In effect, the young Budge was really attacking the then ageing Layard, Rassam's life-long protector and friend, and knew what he was doing."[26]

A final note on Budge's character. Whatever the controversies over where priceless artifacts belong today, consider again that Layard and Rassam invested the effort, time, and honest commitment to obtain antiquities *legally* via the firmans from the Ottoman authorities. In *By Nile and Tigris*, Budge recounts proudly how he and his colleagues provided a "substantial supper" for police and watchmen to distract them so they could steal the Papyrus of Ani without permission from the Egyptian government in 1888.[27]

★ ★ ★

Layard's help in defending Rassam was his last battle. Life in Venice went back to quiet reflection in his study and socializing with good friends. In March 1894, he and Enid celebrated their silver wedding anniversary, and Layard declared happily that he had never spent a single day separated from his wife; he also claimed they had never argued. He was now seventy-seven years old.

By April, however, his health was failing, and his Italian doctor urged him to return to London and see a specialist. The problem was diagnosed as a malignant tumor in his groin. The news came as a shock to both Layard and to Enid, who could "hardly believe in this dreadful thing just as we were so happy with our silver wedding! . . . and Henry seeming so very well!"[28] The arduous journey back to Britain seemed to only hasten Layard's decline. Soon, he could no longer walk, reduced to being carried up and down flights of stairs. "I think this is going to finish me," he confessed to his nurse.

For the man who opened his eyes to other cultures and ways of life thousands of miles away and who urged others to see, the world was now reduced to the bedroom of a house at One Queen Anne Street in Marylebone. In late

June, a clot reached his lung, causing him trouble, but Layard's spirits stayed up. On July 4, his condition worsened, and Enid was "terribly anxious." She recorded in her diary, "He knew me, and liked to hold my hand and twice raised my hand to his lips and tried to kiss it. But it was a terrible night, so restless and his breathing terrible."[29] He died the next day, his doctor telling Enid he hadn't suffered. "The suffering has passed to me," she wrote in her diary, "and at 8:15, he left me forever."[30]

His death made the English papers around the world. *The Times* of London mistakenly wrote in his obituary that his mother was Spanish and that he had come to London for the purpose of being called to the bar. It also claimed he was "somewhat brusque and curt in demeanor, except in cases where his intellectual interests were touched or his sympathies moved." While the paper found him "wanting" in qualities as a diplomat, it conceded that "he was a man of determined courage and perseverance, and he has left a name deservedly high on the list of the archaeological investigators and discoverers."[31] One of his friends who no doubt didn't find him brusque quickly wrote to *The Times* to set its facts straight.

Enid survived her husband by another eighteen years. When she ventured abroad, she often visited Turkish embassies, and at their official functions, she wore the order of merit given her by the sultan. After learning that the Layards' old acquaintance and former grand vizier, Midhat Pasha, had been arrested, she raised money for the financial relief of his family. All these actions and more were, as scholar Sinan Kuneralp puts it, "genuine expressions of her feelings for a country and a people she had loved."[32] She died in 1912.

After her passing, Layard's nephew, Arthur, fought in court to get his hands on the couple's works of art, but he accepted a settlement for £17,000 in March 1917, and the collection of paintings by British, Dutch, and Italian artists all found homes in the National Gallery and the Tate Gallery in London.[33]

Layard was known best for uncovering ancient sculptures in the biblical dust, but he had begun his life and spent his final days with beautiful paintings from Renaissance Italy. Now curious strangers could roam the exhibits and appreciate them for long, contemplative stretches in the same way he did. No doubt, Mr. Bull would have approved.

· *14* ·

After Layard

A Modern Epilogue

$\mathscr{I}$n late February and early March 2015, news media around the world reported—but sadly didn't dwell on—the fact that ISIS militants took sledgehammers and drills to ancient statues in Mosul and used bulldozers to demolish priceless ruins in Hatra. Here were the treasures and sites that Henry Layard had found, to be enjoyed and contemplated by the whole world, and the one comfort out of the tragedy was that *some* priceless artifacts had been moved to distant museum facilities. In fact, in the militants' self-congratulatory video sent online, archaeologists noted that in several cases, the hammers swung down on mere plaster cast replicas of pieces in the British Museum.

Still, the damage was enough to prompt the head of UNESCO, Irina Bokova, to label the acts a war crime. "There is absolutely no political or religious justification for the destruction of humanity's cultural heritage," said Bokova.[1]

Back when the world was shocked by the first wave of barbarian vandalism at Palmyra in 2015, I spoke to Clemens Reichel, assistant professor for Mesopotamian archaeology at the University of Toronto. I mentioned to him how surprising it was to hear certain pundits suggest the ruins weren't worth the expense of lives, and he immediately grasped my point. "No one seems to have a problem with the fact that people defend oil fields or strategic roads or even flags." Ordinary people might think of antiquities in terms of material value, but for archaeologists, "material value of cultural heritage means nothing to most of us. It's the intrinsic connection between the cultures and the people, of course, that are living in that part of the world that makes them valuable to us. It's the history, basically, that we are learning about. The definition of identity. It's what we learn about our own past that makes it meaningful."[2]

And there are those who have understood what's at risk—and have been willing to give their lives for the sake of these treasures.

Khaled al-Asaad was born in Palmyra and spent most of his life protecting its unique archaeological finds. He was instrumental in getting Palmyra its status as a UNESCO World Heritage site, and even when retired and in his eighties, he was still active and celebrated as the man who knew the ruins best and had made important discoveries. When ISIS captured the city, his family and friends begged him to flee, but he told Syria's minister of antiquities who was also a personal friend, "Whatever happens, I cannot go against my conscience."[3]

ISIS fanatics arrested him twice. The second time, they held him for a month, demanding to know where certain archaeological works were hidden. Khaled al-Asaad was a tough old bird and told them nothing, and for his refusal, they dragged this gentle academic into a public square in August 2015 and beheaded him. But instead of erasing an enemy, ISIS created a martyr to all that's good about secular education and civilization. It took only two days for the story of Khaled al-Asaad's defiance to leak out of a town held hostage and spread through the global media.

Sadly, within a few months, a leading German archaeologist, Hermann Parzinger, charged that Syrian troops were looting Palmyra just as the terrorists had.[4] And as late as January 2017, ISIS still managed to damage important sections of Palmyra after recapturing the city again in the brutal back-and-forth with Syrian forces; it destroyed a tetrapylon and part of a Roman theater.[5]

★   ★   ★

I couldn't get to Syria—far too dangerous. But I did find my way to Iraq, choosing to spend part of my vacation staring at a mine-laced road in a lonely patch of open valley in northern Iraq as the war with ISIS was still going on.

Northern Iraq, yes, but it's really Kurdistan, the semiautonomous province that managed to win part of its freedom from Saddam Hussein's regime in 1991. The Kurds have their own language, their own music, their own traditional clothing, and the regional government even keeps its own consulate in Washington, D.C. Kurdistan's capital, Erbil, just happens to be an hour's drive from Mosul in Iraq's province of Nineveh.

In June 2015, I flew to Erbil from Amman, Jordan, with an insane plan. I had hoped to sneak across to the surrounding countryside near Mosul to see if there were any smaller archaeological sites that ISIS had abandoned; after all, there would be little strategic or tactical point in holding on to them. I thought if I could get in, I might discover some treasures that had been overlooked for mutilation and annihilation. This wasn't foolish bravado; I really did feel that I couldn't write this book thoroughly without getting to some key locales in Layard's story, and war had been getting in the way of this task for fifteen years. I also firmly believe, as I've written elsewhere, that no work of history should be read without considering the context of the times, not only of the era which it covers but in which it was written.

It was a blistering 50° Celsius when my flight landed; about a week later, the news was full of reports of how people in Pakistan were dying in a heat wave with the same temperature. On the afternoon I met my affable and resourceful fixer, Khasraw Hamerashid Ahmed, I told him my idea in an embarrassed tone, trying to dispel any impression that I was an adrenaline junkie. He listened politely, chuckled, and said, "Let me ask you something: do you want to be beheaded?" Days later, I got the chance to see for myself why my scheme was ridiculous and impossible.

Khasraw and his twin brother, Khoshnaw, drove me out to the front, taking me to a base of the Kurdish Defense Forces, known as the Peshmerga. We trudged our way along a bed of gravel within sight of a couple of armored cars, and then inside a large tent, I met Najim Abdullah Kedo, the deputy commander of the Peshmerga forces in the Bashik area—"Bashik" in this case being the Kurdish term for the countryside near the Iraqi village with the Arabic name of Bashiqua. On the day of our appointment, it was still being held by ISIS and sat only about fifteen miles from Mosul. But the Kurds gave the militants the hardest fight of the war.

"We don't want to have any more suffering like the kind we had in the past," Kedo told me through Khasraw, acting as my interpreter.

Kurdish people often have the rugged looks of their tribal ancestors depicted in old black-and-white photographs, and at fifty-four years old, Kedo was the same; a man with a square face, wearing a modern-looking jacket with the traditional baggy trousers called shalwar held up by a cummerbund. He had already lost a piece of himself to history. His right hand was missing a finger from when units of the Peshmerga joined the uprising of their people against Saddam Hussein. He also knew what it was like to be a refugee, having fled with his family to Iran in the 1970s. "Even now," he pointed out, "there are villages destroyed by Saddam that haven't been rebuilt yet."[6]

But in 2015, he and his men were fighting a different war, and he admitted the tactical situation was "difficult." That was clear enough from an observation post a short drive from the base. Over a wall of sandbags, the hilly landscape baked by the sun stretched out, and a village under ISIS control was less than two kilometers away. Anyone who approached could be seen coming, and the road was mined with improvised explosive devices. Until the liberation two years later, the war here was a stalemate. There were enemy snipers but no major offensives, especially in the melting heat of the day. ISIS preferred to attack at night or just before dawn.

As the Ahmed brothers and I trudged back to our car to return to Erbil, Khoshnaw, who was obviously a brave and levelheaded sort who had done his own military rotations, exclaimed, "Too close!" Khasraw teased me about my original scheme to sneak into the enemy's territory. Did I see now why it was hopeless? I certainly did.

But even if Mosul and Hatra were still inaccessible, the trip offered modest but useful insights. It's astonishing how we're still captives of history from Layard's era and how he remains significant. Bandits were still preying on the treasures and people of Nineveh, just as they did in his time. The two key differences were that these organized criminals—for that is what they were—took on the camouflage of nihilistic religious fanaticism, and they grew more sophisticated in their business dealings than any previous terrorist group.

Some of what Henry Layard found in his youth in the Nineveh province has now been lost forever, and there is no doubt that he would be horrified by the destruction. It is a bitter irony that the Yezidis were obscure to the West in Layard's time and won attention only because of their suffering—and so it is again today. For who had heard of them in North America and Europe before the recent slaughter?

In 2014, a Yezidi member of the parliament in Iraq, Vian Dakhil, made a tearful appeal to the international community: "Save us! Save us!"[7] Though ISIS was driven out of Mosul and much of Iraq, many Yezidis remain in refugee camps and temporary shelters, while some have been accepted into the United States, Canada, and other nations. In August 2017, Cathy Otten, a freelance writer based in Kurdistan, spoke to a young woman who escaped a nightmare of rape and torture under ISIS. "The Yezidis will never recover," she told Otten. "Even if we marry or fall in love, there will still be this thing inside that is broken."[8]

★ ★ ★

Kamal Rasheed Raheem, the director of antiquities in Sulaimani, is a man with leonine, regal features and an animated personality. In 2015, we sat in his office at his big conference table, where he occasionally slammed his hand down on the wood for emphasis. In the background, several men—some in traditional Kurdish dress—sat and chatted on the plush couch. Every museum official in Kurdistan seems to have a massive office that serves as part café for senior employees and guests and part town hall.

"As you know, *Daesh* are not human," he told me, using the pejorative Arabic name for ISIS, which the group hated. "They are butchers." I asked him about the smuggling trail of antiquities, and he insisted it didn't run from Mosul to Erbil, what would normally be a short drive without the war. Kurdish authorities, he claimed, were quite efficient in that regard, but he conceded that no one knew exactly what and how much had been taken given that some museum and antiquities officials were trapped behind ISIS lines. "They're hiding themselves, and if they are lucky, they survive."[9]

Instead, he argued that smuggled works made their way north and east along the same route that brought ISIS volunteers to the war. "All the fighters from the European countries, they come through Turkey," said Raheem. "Through Turkey . . . they support them, and they open the border for them. And from *Daesh* (ISIS), it's easy to sell everything in Turkey or maybe in Gulf area, or in Europe. Also, they have foreign people, they buy it with them."

Mark Altaweel, a lecturer in Near East studies at the UCL Institute of Archaeology in London, told me later that he was sure that Turkey was a "big supplier" and that "stuff is also going to Beirut, Lebanon. Lebanon in general has a long history in the antiquities market, and key middlemen have been there in the past, moving things out of the region." Syria has also long served as a smuggling route. [10] Altaweel strolled into a few dealerships in London with a reporter from Britain's *Guardian* newspaper and easily picked out items, such as glassware and statuary that likely came from the region.[11]

Abdullah Khorseed Qadir, the director of the Iraqi Institute for the Conservation of Antiquities and Heritage, wouldn't come out and bluntly accuse Turkey, but he pointed to the aftermath of the liberation in June 2015 of Tal Abyad—the town is called Grespi in Kurdish. It's interesting, he noted, that Turkey seemed to hardly care about Tal Abyad before, but then it complained to the U.S. and coalition forces about territorial integrity and "incursions" by Kurdish forces.

And the ongoing political division between Iraq and Kurdistan must also be kept in mind. Baghdad used to insist on keeping the lion's share of major antiquities for itself, but the Peshmerga demonstrated during the war that it was often the most effective protector of the region's legacies.

As in Layard's era, the Kurds have proved as stubborn as the impressive mountain ranges that seem to flank every road. In a restaurant in Sulaimani, you only had to watch the TV mounted on the wall to get a quick history lesson through a music video. As the patriotic pop tune warbled on, old photos flashed by. There was one of the Kurds' hero who fought the British, Mahmud Barzinji. Another showed Mustafa Barzani, who fought the Iraqis during the 1960s.

And yet in 2015, it was sometimes difficult, in fact, to tell there was a war going on at all in Kurdistan. At various checkpoints in the countryside, Peshmerga soldiers casually waved drivers through after a quick "*Slaw*" (hello).

Even when ISIS was breathing down Erbil's neck, having taken the nearby town of Makhmur fifty kilometers away, residents in the regional capital didn't evacuate. Such was their complete faith in the Peshmerga. The market arcade near the historic Citadel was busy with shoppers and men sitting in plastic chairs, socializing, smoking, and sipping tea.

Still, Erbil was not immune. People complained about the war hurting the economy, and the city had scores of abandoned construction sites around town. On a Thursday night at Abu Afif, a patisserie which boasted out front "Sweets Since 1974," a front door slammed too loudly, and everyone turned, startled. At a UN educational event, a balloon popped because of the oppressive heat, and folks ducked. People were jittery because in the mainly Christian district of Ankawa where many Western expatriates lived, a car bomb went off outside the U.S. consulate and killed two people. It was a credit to the efficiency of the Kurdish authorities that they scooped up five suspects a mere ten days later. But in this case, faith trumped nationalism. Four of the alleged perpetrators were Kurds themselves—Sunni militants—and a fifth, who was Arab, admitted according to a Reuters report that they had targeted the consulate "because Erbil has become the source of the decision to fight against the Islamic State."[12]

No sooner was ISIS driven out of the ruins of Mosul than the Kurds held an independence referendum in late September 2017. To no one's surprise, the "yes" vote won by an overwhelming margin. Baghdad then claimed it was nonbinding and illegal, while Erbil replied that yes, of course it was. Tensions exploded into what now is called the Battle of Kirkuk, with Iraqi forces plowing into the Kirkuk Governate and clashing with Peshmerga units, prompting the Peshmerga to fall back. That led to more chaos as Masoud Barzini, who had been president of Kurdistan for twelve years, announced in Erbil at the end of October that he would step down, accusing his political rivals of abandoning Kirkuk and arguing that "without the help of Peshmerga, Iraqi forces could not have liberated Mosul."[13] This was certainly true.

Dozens of Barzini's supporters broke into the region's parliament building and attacked lawmakers and reporters while a crowd waved Kurdish flags outside. Yet such is his political power that ambassadors to Iraq for Britain and Canada were still willing to meet with him only two years later.[14]

In early November 2017, an Iraqi federal court ruled that no province could secede, and the Kurdistan Regional Government (KRG) announced it would respect the court's decision—while also hoping the decision would "become a basis for starting an inclusive national dialogue between Erbil and Baghdad to resolve all disputes."[15] And so the uneasy relationship goes on.

The region's misery goes on as well. In the summer of 2020, Turkey launched more ground and air offensives into Kurdistan to attack its nemesis, the militant nationalist group, the Kurdistan Workers' Party (more famously known as the PKK). What made the attacks especially disturbing was that Iran's Revolutionary Guard shelled the border area, helped by Turkish drones. As human rights activist John Lubbock put it at the time, while the KRG government could ask Turkey and the PKK to respect the region's sovereignty, "the KRG government certainly knows that there is little it can do to persuade either Turkey or the PKK to give up their decades-long conflict."[16] Meanwhile, Turkey had already begun air strikes in January 2018 against Syrian Kurds who were fighting ISIS in the Afrin region; it considers them PKK as well despite their having worked with U.S. forces.[17]

And from North America and Europe? Little more than a polite hand covering up a yawn. The bogeyman of ISIS had been driven out—who cared about the aftermath? For a while, some of the so-called Brides of ISIS were fascinated because of the question, what was to be their fate now? Could these once-dedicated enemies of Britain, France, the United States, and other nations have their old nationalities back and go home? It depended on the Western country each woman originally came from, whether willing or not. But a new story soon eclipsed theirs, what seemed to be a devil's bargain made between President Donald Trump and Turkey's Recep Erdogan. Trump finally got what he had wanted for a long time, announcing that U.S. forces were pulling out of Syria, a place he had tactlessly written off in front of reporters as "sand and death."[18] As for Turkey, it was free now to pummel America's old ally the Syrian Kurds, with no risk of complaint from Washington.

It was an appalling betrayal. Kurdish fighters had to rush to the front, abandoning their duties of guarding more than 10,000 ISIS prisoners—many of whom soon escaped. And under the relentless pressure of bombings and invasions, the Kurdish militias cut a deal with the regime of Bashar al-Assad, the man behind some of the worst war crimes of the young twenty-first century.[19] The Assad who used chemical weapons against his own people. The Assad who is backed by Iran and Vladimir Putin's Russia.

The dynamics would make Layard's head spin. But then again, perhaps not. He had seen enough inexplicable and frustrating pro-Russian lobbying in his own time. As with the Yezidis, his sympathies would be—as always—with ordinary innocents, Kurdish and Syrian civilians forced to endure gauntlets of death again and again, on the run as refugees. Yet he would also perhaps take comfort and hope from other developments. As should we.

★ ★ ★

Mosul has lamassu again—of a kind.

In October 2019, two lamassu replicas created fifteen years before by Factum Arte of Madrid were transported by the Spanish air force and given to the University of Mosul, where they now guard the entrance of the main student building.[20] And in the summer of 2020, UNESCO began work to bring much of the old city back to life, including restoration of the Al-Aghawat mosque and the Conventual Church of Our Lady of the Hour, known as Al-Saa'a. A Dominican priest, now Mosul's archbishop, had "kept an archive of thousands of ancient and rare manuscripts including Christian, Muslim and Yezidi texts as well as scientific documents."[21] When ISIS came, he managed to rescue more than 800 of them, leaving many in the hands of Christians evacuating Mosul. Now the church's district would get a new school, and houses would get repairs. Shops could once more accept customers.

And work has started as well . . . slowly . . . to bring back the Mosul Museum, where ISIS stole priceless treasures, used explosives to destroy two winged bulls, and sledgehammered a lion statue from the Temple of Ishtar at Nimrud. When the facility does eventually reopen, as Tom Westcott reported for *Middle East Eye*, "it will be a shadow of its former self."[22]

But even with perhaps 70 percent of the museum's collection stolen or demolished, it is something of a minor miracle that it should be reborn at all. More than five years ago, to stand in the hot sun by sandbags as I did and overlook an ISIS-held village was to consider a vulgar, shameless enemy that boasted its permanence. Mosul seemed lost forever. The green highway signs to it appeared to be a dark joke. And yet now they serve a purpose again, and in 2020, floor space at the museum was "taped into a two meter-squared grid as part of a laborious process to gather and label each [Assyrian] statue fragment to help accurate future reconstruction."[23]

Full restoration will not happen tomorrow, and it will not happen soon. It will take years. But one day, there will be a winged lion and two winged bulls again at the Mosul Museum. Reminders of the lesson that Henry Layard knew well: stone can be smashed, buried, left to sleep underground, but its pieces can be found, rediscovered, gathered up to share their secrets once more—and to keep an ancient legacy alive.

Notes

The most extensive source on Henry Layard is Layard himself, through his books and the more than 240 volumes of correspondence, official papers, memos, and memoirs that make up the so-called "Layard Papers" in the British Library. After visiting several locales important in his life, I spent most of December 2017 in the chilly Manuscript Room of the British Library, leafing through the thick books, their pages often crackling—literally—with age. I often had to rely on a borrowed magnifying glass to parse the baffling loops of Rawlinson; the schizophrenic, sometimes indecipherable curves of Layard; and the near unintelligible scrawls of Stratford Canning.

If *Nineveh and Its Remains*, *Early Adventures*, or Layard's *Autobiography* is quoted in a specific chapter, I list it as a major source for that chapter, saving the reader from endlessly repetitive citations. When one of Layard's letters is quoted without a reference, it can be found in his autobiography. Endnotes most often reflect where I have hunted down particular sources myself, such as in the British Library (BL in citations). In the case of Layard's years as a diplomat in Istanbul, Sinan Kuneralp and Isis Press have saved many researchers time and trouble by publishing his *Memoirs* of those years as well as reprinting Enid's diary entries for that period; again, the originals can be found in the British Library.

Gordon Waterfield was Layard's first biographer, and he deserves much credit for mapping all this territory first. But while he was admirably thorough in his research, he lacked the literary flair of his subject, and I find questionable his dwelling on certain aspects of Layard's life at the expense of others (for instance, Waterfield spends considerable time on the soap opera of the aunt and mother's concerns over young Henry's adventures rather than the adventures themselves, and he's completely mute on Layard's attitude to the American Civil War and his efforts to keep Britain out of the conflict).

It was impossible in the time available to me to conduct original research while simultaneously rechecking Waterfield's citations, but except for a couple of instances where I'd second-guess his truncating of quotations, I've found him to be reliable. I've tried to keep my falling back on him to a minimum, but in several instances, it did prove necessary. In other instances, I relied on quotations made by Arnold Brackman, whose *The Luck of Nineveh* is delightfully accessible despite having no exhaustive endnotes.

CHAPTER 1: VICTORIAN SLACKER

Autobiography and Letters
Early Adventures in Persia, Susiana and Babylon

1. You can still find the palace there today, which is home to international students working on ancient and medieval history, arts, and environmental programs.
2. *Autobiography and Letters, Early Adventures in Persia, Susiana and Babylon*, BL MS 58149, fol. 135, letter dated August 14, 1839.

CHAPTER 2: DEBATING BLOODLUST WITH A GIANT

Early Adventures in Persia, Susiana and Babylon
Autobiography and Letters

1. Djilas, *Njegos*, p. 116.
2. Ibid., p. 206.
3. Judah, *The Serbs*, p. 77.
4. BL MS 58154, fols. 3–4, letter dated September 15, 1839.
5. Ufford, *The Pasha*, p. 16.
6. Ibid.
7. Ibid., p. 29.
8. De Bellaigue, *The Islamic Enlightenment*, pp. 20–21.
9. http://mideasti.blogspot.ca/2013/05/weekend-nostalgia-when-talaat-harb.html.
10. Montefiore, *Jerusalem*, p. 343.
11. Ibid., p. 344.
12. Mitford, *A Land March from England to Ceylon Forty Years Ago*, p. 201.
13. Ibid., p. 203.

CHAPTER 3: CAMPING NEAR DESOLATION

Nineveh and Its Remains
Early Adventures in Persia, Susiana and Babylon

1. Fraser, *Mesopotamia and Assyria from the Earliest Ages to the Present Time*, p. 247.
2. Marozzi, *Baghdad*, p. 247.
3. Ibid., p. 249.

CHAPTER 4: LIVING AMONG THE BAKHTIARI

Early Adventures in Persia, Susiana and Babylon

1. Garthwaite, *Khans and Shahs*, p. 72.

CHAPTER 6: BEGINNER'S LUCK

Nineveh and Its Remains

1. BL MS 38939, fol. 22, letter dated April 15, 1843.
2. BL MS 38939, fol. 31, letter dated June 14, 1847.
3. BL MS 38939, fol. 23, letter dated April 15, 1843.
4. Brackman, *The Luck of Nineveh*, p. 121.
5. BL MS 38976, fols. 231–233, letter dated October 9, 1845.
6. Ross, *Letters from the East*, p. 41.
7. Larsen, *The Conquest of Assyria*, p. 72.
8. BL MS 58154, fols. 139–140, letter dated November 10, 1845.
9. Lane-Poole, *The Life of Lord Stratford De Redcliffe*, p. 227.
10. BL MS 40637, fol. 21, letter dated December 1, 1845.
11. BL MS 40637, fol. 28, letter dated December 15, 1845.
12. BL MS 38976, fol. 265, letter dated December 6, 1845.
13. BL MS 58149, fol. 210, letter dated November 29/December 1, 1845.
14. Adkins, *Empires of the Plain*, p. 135.
15. BL MS 58149, fols. 211–212, letter dated December 1, 1845.
16. Brackman, *The Luck of Nineveh*, p. 133.
17. BL MS 58154, fols. 153–154, letter to his aunt dated April 21, 1846.
18. Lane-Poole, *The Life of Lord Stratford De Redcliffe*, p. 228.
19. BL MS 58154, fol. 151, letter dated March 22, 1846.
20. BL MS 38976, fols. 359–360, copy dated May 5, 1846, translated into French.
21. BL MS 38976, fol. 363, letter dated May 10, 1846.

CHAPTER 7: DEVIL WORSHIPPERS

Nineveh and Its Remains

1. BL MS 58154, fol. 156, letter to his uncle dated June 1, 1846.
2. BL MS 38977, fols. 18–19, letter dated August 5, 1846.
3. BL MS 38977, fols. 25–27, letter dated August 19, 1846.
4. BL MS 58154, fol. 164, letter dated July 27, 1846.
5. BL MS 58154, fols. 168–169, letter dated October 5, 1846.
6. Rahman, "Little Respite for Iraqis Displaced by Mosul Fighting"; Alter, "A Yezidi Woman Who Escaped ISIS Slavery Tells Her Story."
7. Asher-Schapiro, "Who Are the Yezidis, the Ancient, Persecuted Religious Minority Struggling to Survive in Iraq?"
8. BL MS 58154, fol. 169, letter dated October 5, 1846.
9. Xinhuanet.com, "Extremist IS Militants Damage Ancient Citadel, Two Shrines in Iraq's Nineveh."
10. BL MS 38977, fol. 47, letter dated September 7, 1846.
11. BL MS 38977, fol. 52, letter dated September 22, 1846.
12. BL MS 38977, fols. 110–112, letter dated December 3, 1846.
13. BL MS 39077, fol. 17, Memorandum dated September 21, 1846.
14. Ibid.
15. BL MS 38977, fols. 119–121, letter dated December 9, 1846.
16. BL MS 38977, fols. 110–113, letter dated December 3, 1846.
17. *The Athenaeum*, October 10, 1846, p. 1047.
18. *The Athenaeum*, November 2, 1846, p. 1145.
19. Ross, *Letters from the East*, p. xi.
20. Silberman, *The Oxford Companion to Archaeology*, pp. 216–217.
21. BL MS 38977, fols. 161–165, letter dated January 20, 1847.
22. Ross, *Letters from the East*, p. xi.
23. BL MS 58154, fol. 183, January 26, 1847.
24. BL MS 58150, fol. 46, letter dated March 22, 1847.
25. Thesiger, *The Life of My Choice*, p. 443.

CHAPTER 8: NINEVEH AND ITS REMAINS

Early Adventures in Persia, Susiana and Babylon
Autobiography and Letters

1. Flanders, *The Victorian City*, pp. 272–273.
2. BL MS 47658, fols. 30–31, letter dated February 28, 1848.
3. Waterfield, *Layard of Nineveh*, p. 171.
4. Aberdare, "Introductory Notice," *Early Adventures*, 1894 abridgement, p. 11.
5. BL MS 38978, fol. 52, letter dated March 7, 1848.

6. Ross, *Letters from the East*, p. 151.

7. Ibid., p. 155.

8. Brackman, *The Luck of Nineveh*, p. 221; Waterfield, *Layard of Nineveh*, p. 188.

9. BL MS 38939, p. 36, letter dated November 12, 1848.

10. *The Times* of London, February 9, 1849.

11. Adkins, *Empires of the Plain*, p. 270.

12. Larsen, *The Conquest of Assyria*, p. 231.

13. Waterfield, *Layard of Nineveh*, p. 204.

14. *Ruins of Sacred and Historic Lands*, pp. 90–95.

15. BL MS 38979, fols. 93–94, letter dated November 28, 1849.

16. Adkins, *Empires of the Plain*, pp. 282–283.

17. Waterfield, *Layard of Nineveh*, p. 202.

18. BL MS 38979, fols. 219–220, letter dated May 13, 1850.

19. BL MS 58156, fol. 25, letter dated May 13, 1850.

20. BL MS 58156, fol. 39, letter to his uncle dated June 10, 1850.

21. Ibid.

22. BL MS 38979, fol. 260, letter to Ross dated June 24, 1850.

23. BL MS 38979, fol. 261, letter dated June 24, 1850.

24. BL MS 38979, fols. 289–290, letter dated September 2, 1850.

25. BL MS 38943, fols. 11–12, letter dated November 6, 1850.

26. Ibid.

27. Thesiger, *The Marsh Arabs*, p. 13.

28. BL MS 38943 fols. 31–32, letter dated April 14, 1851.

CHAPTER 9: FORWARD THE LIGHT BRIGADE

Autobiography and Letters

1. Ross, *Early Days Recalled*, p. 42.

2. Ross, *The Fourth Generation*, p. 80.

3. BL MS 38980, fol. 184, letter dated November 30, 1851.

4. BL MS 38944, fol. 8, letter dated February 3, 1852.

5. BL MS 38944, fol. 9, letter dated February 17, 1852.

6. BL MS 38944, fol. 13, letter dated May 20, 1852.

7. BL MS 38944, fols. 14–15, letter dated July 9, 1852.

8. BL MS 38947, fols. 53–54, letter dated December 10, 1868.

9. Figes, *The Crimean War*, pp. 104–105.

10. Royle, *Crimea*, p. 33.

11. Hansard, UK Parliament, August 16, 1853.

12. *The New York Tribune*, September 2, 1853.

13. Badem, *The Ottoman Crimean War (1853–1856)*, pp. 88–89.

14. Lytton, *The Life of Edward Bulwer, First Lord Lytton*, p. 215.

15. Hansard, UK Parliament, February 14, 1854.

16. Hansard, UK Parliament, February 17, 1854.

17. Ross, *Letters from the East*, p. 211.

18. Ross, *The Fourth Generation*, p. 356.

19. Waterfield, *Layard of Nineveh*, p. 246.

20. Hansard, UK Parliament, March 31, 1854.

21. Hansard, UK Parliament, July 24, 1854.

22. Dasent, *John Thadeus Delane*, vol. 1, p. 179.

23. Ibid., p. 184.

24. BL MS 38982, fols. 301–304, letter dated September 16, 1854.

25. Smith, *The Reason Why*, pp. 114–129.

26. Hansard, UK Parliament, March 31, 1854.

27. Figes, *The Crimean War*, p. 205.

28. Waterfield, *Layard of Nineveh*, pp. 252–253.

29. Ibid., p. 253.

30. Sawer, "Letter Sheds Light on Who Was to Blame for 'Blunder' Which Sent Light Brigade into the Valley of Death."

31. Ibid.

32. Ibid.

33. "The Charge of the Light Brigade," p. 6.

34. Spilsbury, *The Thin Red Line*, pp. 161–162.

35. Waterfield, *Layard of Nineveh*, p. 253.

36. BL MS 38982, fol. 320, letter dated October 23, 1854.

37. BL MS 38982, fol. 321, letter dated October 23, 1854.

38. BL MS 38982, fols. 321–322, letter dated October 23, 1854.

39. BL MS 38982, fol. 323, letter dated October 23, 1854.

40. Hansard, UK Parliament, December 12, 1854.

41. Otway, "The Parliamentary Life of Sir Henry Layard, 1852–1869," *Autobiography*, vol. 2, pp. 253–254.

CHAPTER 10: "WE NEVER GET THE INDIAN STORY"

Twixt Pera and Therapia: The Constantinople Diaries of Lady Layard

1. BL MS 38947, fols. 14–15, letter dated April 3, 1855.

2. BL MS 38947, fol. 17, letter dated April 7, 1855.

3. Letter dated May 14, 1855, author's private collection.

4. BL MS 38947, fol. 19, letter dated May 20, 1855.

5. "The New English Reformer," *The New York Times*, June 13, 1855.

6. Hansard, UK Parliament, June 18, 1855.

7. BL MS 58158, fol. 61, letter dated August 7, 1855.

8. Baster, "The Origins of British Banking Expansion in the Near East," pp. 76–86.

9. Paget, *Sergeant Pearman's Memoirs*, p. 27.

10. Hibbert, *The Great Mutiny*, p. 47.

11. Waterfield, *Layard of Nineveh*, p. 287.

12. *The Times* of London, August 25, 1857; Marx, *Colonialism and Modernization*, p. 226.

13. BL MS 38944, fol. 56, letter dated July 23, 1857.

14. BL MS 38944, fol. 56, letter dated July 23, 1857.

15. BL MS 58157, fol. 18, letter dated December 13, 1857.

16. BL MS 58157, fols. 18–19, letter dated December 13, 1857.

17. BL MS 58157, fol. 21, letter dated January 10, 1858.

18. BL MS 58157, fol. 24, letter dated February 1, 1858.

19. "Mr. Layard on India," *The Times* of London, May 12, 1858.

20. Ibid.

21. BL MS 38944, fol. 57, letter dated August 21, 1858.

22. BL MS 38947, fols. 27–28, letter dated December 4, 1860.

23. Connell, *Regina v. Palmerston*, pp. 341–343.

24. Ibid., p. 343.

25. Waterfield, *Layard of Nineveh*, p. 296.

26. "Our Rebellion Abroad," *The New York Times*, October 20, 1861.

27. "The American Issue in England," *The New York Times*, December 9, 1861.

28. BL MS 38988, fol. 169, note dated June 19, 1862.

29. BL MS 38988, fols. 9–11, letter dated January 17, 1862.

30. Foreman, *A World on Fire*, pp. 164, 330.

31. Walpole, *The Life of Lord John Russell*, pp. 366–367.

32. Wilson, *The Victorians*, p. 356.

33. Alvin Shuster, "Gladstone Diary: Sexual Problems," *The New York Times*, March 15, 1975.

34. BL MS 58223, fols. 24–25, letter dated June 11, 1869.

35. Kuneralp, *Twixt Pera and Therapia*, p. 91.

36. *The Times* of London, October 27, 1869.

CHAPTER 11: MR. BULL IN THE LAND OF MATADORS

1. "Velasquez," *The Quarterly Review*, October 1872.

2. Steinberg, *Bismarck*, p. 281.

3. Thieblin, *Spain and the Spaniards*, p. 156.

4. Waterfield, *Layard of Nineveh*, p. 335.

CHAPTER 12: FADING AWAY IN THE EVENING MISTS

The Queen's Ambassador to the Sultan: Memoirs of Sir Henry A. Layard's
　Constantinople Embassy, 1877–1880
Twixt Pera and Therapia: The Constantinople Diaries of Lady Layard

1. Kinross, *The Ottoman Centuries*, pp. 506–507.
2. J. A. MacGahan, *The Daily News*, August 22, 1876.
3. Blake, *Disraeli*, p. 593.
4. Gladstone, *Bulgarian Horrors and the Question of the East*, p. 38.
5. Kinross, *The Ottoman Centuries*, p. 507.
6. Waterfield, *Layard of Nineveh*, p. 352.
7. Seton-Watson, *Disraeli, Gladstone, and the Eastern Question*, p. 207.
8. Ibid.
9. Blake, *Disraeli*, p. 595.
10. Ibid., p. 623.
11. Weintraub, *Disraeli*, p. 578.
12. Monypenny and Buckle, *The Life of Benjamin Disraeli*, p. 153.
13. Seton-Watson, *Disraeli, Gladstone, and the Eastern Question*, p. 283.
14. Ibid., pp. 282–286.
15. Kinross, *The Ottoman Centuries*, p. 519.
16. Monypenny and Buckle, *The Life of Benjamin Disraeli*, p. 217.
17. Seton-Watson, *Disraeli, Gladstone, and the Eastern Question*, p. 213.
18. "The Alleged Russian Atrocities," *The Telegraph*, August 27, 1877.
19. *The Standard*, September 25, 1877.
20. BL MS 39156, fols. 72–76, dated April 27, 1880.
21. BL MS 39156, fol. 76, dated April 27, 1880.

CHAPTER 13: A LAST QUIET BATTLE . . . IN COURT

1. BL MS 39140, fols. 35–36, letter dated May 23, 1881.
2. BL MS 39140, fol. 84, letter dated March 9, 1883.
3. BL MS 39140, fol. 141, letter dated August 15, 1884.
4. "Lady Layard Dead," *The New York Times*, November 2, 1912.
5. Waterfield, *Layard of Nineveh*, p. 469.
6. *The Times* of London, February 16, 1885.
7. BL MS 38939, fol. 117, letter dated June 30, 1888.
8. BL MS 38950, fol. 158, letter dated December 9, 1890.
9. Waterfield, *Layard of Nineveh*, p. 469.
10. BL MS 38950, fols. 151–152, letter dated November 4, 1890.
11. Sir Richard Burton is best remembered today for trying to find the source of the Nile and for his journey in disguise to Mecca. He was appointed as British consul in Damascus from 1868 to 1871. Almost equally famous for his arrogance and eccen-

tricities, it was perhaps inevitable that he would clash with Canning, who would have considered Syria under his sphere of influence.

12. BL MS 38950, fol. 59, letter dated December 8, 1888.

13. BL MS 38950, fol. 59, letter dated September 19, 1890.

14. BL MS 39046, fol. 45, letter dated June 23, 1890.

15. BL MS 38950, fol. 142, letter dated September 14, 1890.

16. BL MS 38950, fol. 147, letter dated September 19, 1890.

17. BL MS 38950, fol. 160, letter dated December 28, 1890.

18. "Rassam v. Budge," appeal allowed, March 16, 1893, *The Law Reports: Queen's Bench Division*, 1893, Volume 1, pp. 571–572.

19. BL MS 39099, fols. 84–98, statement dated October 9, 1892.

20. BL MS 39099, fol. 97, statement dated October 9, 1892.

21. "Discoveries at Nineveh—Letter to the Editor by Alexander Del Mar," *The New York Times*, September 20, 1910.

22. BL MS 38950, fol. 58, letter dated December 8, 1888.

23. *The Bristol Mercury*, June 30, 1893, p. 8.

24. *The Manchester Courier and Lacanshire General Advertiser*, July 1, 1893.

25. *The Huddersfield Chronicle*, July 22, 1893.

26. Waterfield, *Layard of Nineveh*, "A Hundred Years Later," section of comments by Barnett, p. 487.

27. Budge, *By Nile and Tigris*, vol. 1, p. 144.

28. BL MS 46164, fol. 211, Enid Layard's journal entry dated April 3, 1894.

29. BL MS 46164, fols. 255–256, Enid Layard's journal entry dated July 4, 1894.

30. BL MS 46164, fol. 256, Enid Layard's journal entry dated July 5, 1894.

31. *The Times* of London, July 6, 1894.

32. Kuneralp, "Introduction," in *Twixt Pera and Therapia*, p. 14.

33. Information on the National Gallery website, www.nationalgallery.org.uk.

CHAPTER 14: AFTER LAYARD: A MODERN EPILOGUE

1. "UNESCO Director General Condemns Destruction of Nimrud in Iraq," UNESCO.org, March 6, 2015.

2. Author interview, University of Toronto, May 25, 2015.

3. Waraich, "Khaled al-Asaad."

4. Agence France-Press in Berlin, "Syrian Troops Looting Ancient City Palmyra, Says Archaeologist."

5. Shaheen, "Isis Destroys Tetrapylon Monument in Palmyra."

6. Author interview at Bashik Front base, June 20, 2015.

7. Haworth, "Vian Dakhil."

8. Otten, "Life after ISIS Slavery for Yazidi Women and Children."

9. Author interview in Sulaimani, June 17, 2015.

10. Author interview by phone to London, July 2015.

11. Shabi, "Looted in Syria—and Sold in London."

12. Crowcroft, "Isis."

13. "Iraqi Kurdish Leader Masoud Barzini to Step Down," BBC News at bbc.com, October 29, 2017; "Abadi Calls for Calm in Kurdistan after Barzini Resignation," VOA News at voanews.com, October 29, 2017.

14. Shilani, "Masoud Barzini Hosts New Canadian, British Ambassadors to Iraq."

15. Rasheed and Jalabi, "Abadi Says Iraq to Act Soon over Border Areas in Stand-Off with Kurds."

16. Lubbock, "Turkey Ramps Up War on Kurds in Northern Iraq."

17. "Syria: Turkey War Planes Launch Strikes on Afrin," BBC News at bbc.com, January 20, 2017.

18. Marcin, "Donald Trump Calls Syria 'Sand and Death,' Says 'We're Not Talking about Vast Wealth.'"

19. Turak, "Hundreds of ISIS Prisoners Are Escaping from Camps in Northern Syria amid Turkish Offensive."

20. Fleming, "How Two Colossal Assyrian Icons Were Recreated Using Digital Tech."

21. Ditmars, "Unesco's Plan to 'Revive Spirit' of Devastated Mosul Gets Under Way."

22. Westcott, "'A Shadow of Its Former Self.'"

23. Ibid.

Acknowledgments

$\mathscr{B}$lame Nicholas Rankin for the title. The author of *Ian Fleming's Commandos*, *Telegram from Guernica*, and *Dead Man's Chest* didn't like the first one I came up with, made a good case against it, and so we sat ruminating over drinks in a basement bar near London's Russell Square in 2017. Then with the bell-clear diction that comes from having worked for the BBC for about twenty years, he said, "What about *Winged Bull?*"

As a title is crucially important to a book, a tip of the hat and thanks are in order.

I must also thank Sinan Kuneralp, whom I met years ago in Istanbul when I first got down to serious work on this project and who probably knows more about Layard's life and diplomatic career than anyone else. I am greatly indebted to his brilliant scholarship. Lesley Adkins, author of *Empires of the Plain*, a biography of Henry Rawlinson, and her husband, Roy Adkins, author of *Nelson's Trafalgar*, gave me wonderful encouragement and tips through e-mail correspondence, and I must thank Lesley for allowing me to cite from *Empires*. I am very grateful to fixer Khasraw Hamerashid Ahmed and his brother, Khoshnaw, who did a brilliant job of taking me where I needed to go in Kurdistan and showing me a few places that I would have never known about; they were also wonderful company on the road. And my sincere thanks go to Clemens Reichel, Mark Altaweel, Kamal Rasheed Raheem, Abdullah Khorseed Qadir, and Najim Abdullah Kedo for giving me their time and patience with my questions.

Thanks also go to Mogens Trolle Larsen for allowing me to briefly quote and cite from his work. Twenty-five years ago, I walked into a bookshop in Toronto and saw *The Conquest of Assyria* on a display table. I was intrigued, bought it on the spot, and spent many happy hours tunneling through his

211

fascinating volume. It sparked a decades-long obsession with Layard that resulted in this modest effort.

At Prometheus Books, acquisitions editor Jake Bonar first championed this story, and so I have him to thank for my winged bull at last taking flight.

Bibliography

KEY WORKS BY LAYARD

Nineveh and Its Remains. Vols. 1–2. New York: Putnam, 1849.
The Monuments of Nineveh. London: John Murray, 1849.
Nineveh and Babylon. London: John Murray, 1853.
Early Adventures in Persia, Susiana and Babylon. Vols. 1–2. New York: Longmans, 1887.
Handbook of Painting: The Italian Schools. London: John Murray, 1887.
Early Adventures. London: John Murray, 1894 (abridged one-volume edition).
Autobiography and Letters. Vols. 1–2. London: John Murray, 1903.
Kuneralp, Sinan, ed. *The Queen's Ambassador to the Sultan: Memoirs of Sir Henry A. Layard's Constantinople Embassy, 1877–1880.* Istanbul: Isis Press, 2009.
Various articles in *The Quarterly Review,* London: John Murray, 1853–1890.

KEY WORKS ON HENRY LAYARD AND ENID LAYARD

Aberdare, Lord (Henry Bruce). "Introductory Notice." *Early Adventures,* 1894 abridgment.
Brackman, Arnold. *The Luck of Nineveh.* New York: McGraw-Hill, 1978.
Kuneralp, Sinan, ed. *Twixt Pera and Therapia: The Constantinople Diaries of Lady Layard.* Istanbul: Isis Press, 2010.
Waterfield, Gordon. *Layard of Nineveh.* London: John Murray, 1963.

OTHER SOURCES

The Layard Papers in the British Library consist of 248 volumes, plus supplementary
   volumes, identified by the reference numbers MS 38931–39164.
"Rassam v. Budge," Appeal allowed, 16 March 1893, *The Law Reports: Queen's Bench
   Division*, 1893, Volume 1. London: Clowes and Sons.
Hansard, UK Parliament.

SECONDARY BOOK SOURCES

Adkins, Lesley. *Empires of the Plain*. New York: St. Martin's Press, 2003.
Badem, Candan. *The Ottoman Crimean War (1853–1856)*. Boston: Leiden, 2010.
Blake, Robert. *Disraeli*. New York: St. Martin's Press, 1966.
Budge, E. A. Wallis. *By Nile and Tigris*. London: John Murray, 1920.
"The Charge of the Light Brigade." *Flintshire Observer*. November 4, 1897.
Christie, Agatha. *Come, Tell Me How You Live*. Reprint, London: HarperCollins, 2015.
Connell, Brian. *Regina v. Palmerston: The Correspondence between Queen Victoria and Her
   Foreign and Prime Minister 1837–1865*. New York: Doubleday, 1961.
Dasent, Arthur. *John Thadeus Delane*. 2 vols. London: John Murray, 1908.
David, Saul. *The Indian Mutiny*. London: Penguin, 2003.
De Bellaigue, Christopher. *The Islamic Enlightenment*. New York, Liveright, 2017.
Djilas, Milovan. *Njegos: Poet, Prince, Bishop*. New York: Harcourt, Brace, 1966.
Figes, Orlando. *The Crimean War*. New York: Picador, 2010.
Flanders, Judith. *The Victorian City: Everyday Life in Dickens' London*. London: Atlantic
   Books, 2012.
Foreman, Amanda. *A World on Fire*. New York: Random House, 2010.
Fraser, James Baillie. *Mesopotamia and Assyria from the Earliest Ages to the Present Time*.
   New York: Harper & Brothers, 1842.
Garthwaite, Gene R. *Khans and Shahs: A History of the Bakhtiyari Tribe in Iran*. New
   York: I. B. Tauris, 2009.
Gladstone, William. *Bulgarian Horrors and the Question of the East*. New York: Lovell,
   Adam, Wesson & Company, 1876.
Hibbert, Christopher. *The Great Mutiny: India 1857*. London: Penguin, 1978.
Judah, Tim. *The Serbs: History, Myth and the Destruction of Yugoslavia*. 3rd ed. New
   Haven, CT: Yale University Press, 2009.
Kinross, Lord. *The Ottoman Centuries: The Rise and Fall of the Turkish Empire*. London:
   HarperCollins, 1977, first edition text with minor emendations republished as *The
   Ottoman Empire*, Folio Society, 2006.
Lane-Poole, Stanley. *The Life of Lord Stratford De Redcliffe*. New York: Longmans, 1890.
Larsen, Mogen Trolle. *The Conquest of Assyria*. London: Routledge, 1996.
Lloyd, Seton. *Foundations in the Dust*. London: Penguin, 1947.
Lytton, Victor. *The Life of Edward Bulwer, First Lord Lytton*. London: Macmillan, 1913.

Marozzi, Justin. *Baghdad: City of Peace, City of Blood*. Cambridge, MA: Da Capo Press, 2014.

Marx, Karl, with Shlomo Avineri, ed. *Colonialism and Modernization*. New York: Doubleday, 1968.

Mitford, Edward. *A Land March from England to Ceylon Forty Years Ago*. London: W. H. Allen, 1884.

Montefiore, Simon Sebag. *Jerusalem: The Biography*. New York: Knopf, 2011.

Monypenny, W. F., and George Erale Buckle. *The Life of Benjamin Disraeli*. Vol. 6. New York: Macmillan, 1920.

Otway, Arthur. "The Parliamentary Life of Sir Henry Layard, 1852–1869." *Layard's Autobiography and Letters*. London: John Murray, 1903.

Paget, George, with John Pearman, ed. *Sergeant Pearman's Memoirs*. London: Jonathan Cape, 1968.

Ross, Henry. *Letters from the East*. London: J. M. Dent, 1902.

Ross, Janet. *Early Days Recalled*. London: Chapman and Hall, 1891.

———. *The Fourth Generation*. New York: Charles Scribner's Sons, 1912.

Royle, Trevor. *Crimea: The Great Crimean War, 1854–1856*. New York: St. Martin's Press, 2000.

Ruins of Sacred and Historic Lands. London: Thomas Nelson, 1851.

Seton-Watson, R. W. *Disraeli, Gladstone, and the Eastern Question*. New York: W. W. Norton, 1972 of 1935 edition.

Silberman, Neil Asher, ed. *The Oxford Companion to Archaeology*. 2nd ed. Oxford: Oxford University Press, 2012.

Smith, Cecil Woodham. *The Reason Why*. New York: McGraw-Hill, 1953.

Spilsbury, Julian, ed. *The Thin Red Line: An Eyewitness History of the Crimean War*. London: Weidenfeld & Nicolson, 2005.

Steinberg, Jonathan. *Bismarck: A Life*. New York: Oxford University Press, 2011.

Thesiger, Wilfred. *The Life of My Choice*. London: W. W. Norton, 1988.

———. *The Marsh Arabs*. Reprint, London: Penguin, 2007.

Thieblin, Nicholas. *Spain and the Spaniards*. Vol. 1. London: Hurst and Blackett, 1874.

Ufford, Letitia W. *The Pasha: How Mehmet Ali Defied the West, 1839–1841*. Jefferson, NC: McFarland, 2007.

Walpole, Spencer. *The Life of Lord John Russell*. London: Longmans, Green & Co., 1891.

Weintraub, Stanley. *Disraeli*. New York: Truman Talley Books, 1993.

Wilson, A. N. *The Victorians*. London: Hutchinson, 2002.

MODERN ARTICLES AND INTERNET REPORTAGE

"Abadi Calls for Calm in Kurdistan after Barzini Resignation." VOA News, www.voanews.com, October 29, 2017.

Agence France-Press in Berlin. "Syrian Troops Looting Ancient City Palmyra, Says Archaeologist." *The Guardian*, June 1, 2016.

Alter, Charlotte. "A Yezidi Woman Who Escaped ISIS Slavery Tells Her Story." *Time.com*, December 20, 2015.

Asher-Schapiro, Avi. "Who Are the Yezidis, the Ancient, Persecuted Religious Minority Struggling to Survive in Iraq?" *National Geographic News*, August 11, 2014.

Baster, Albert. "The Origins of British Banking Expansion in the Near East." *Economic History Review*, October 1934.

Crowcroft, Orlando. "Isis: Kurdish Student Admits Islamic State Car Bombing in Erbil on Television." *International Business Times*, April 28, 2015.

Ditmars, Hadani. "Unesco's Plan to 'Revive Spirit' of Devastated Mosul Gets Under Way." *The Art Newspaper*, June 15, 2020.

Fleming, Susan. "How Two Colossal Assyrian Icons Were Recreated Using Digital Tech." World Economic Forum, www.weforum.org, October 29, 2019.

Haworth, Abigail. "Vian Dakhil: Iraq's Only Female Yazidi MP on the Battle to Save Her People." *The Guardian*, February 8, 2015.

"Iraqi Kurdish Leader Masoud Barzini to Step Down." BBC News, www.bbc.com, October 29, 2017.

Lubbock, John. "Turkey Ramps Up War on Kurds in Northern Iraq." *New Internationalist*, July 13, 2020.

Marcin, Tim. "Donald Trump Calls Syria 'Sand and Death,' Says 'We're Not Talking about Vast Wealth.'" *Newsweek*, www.newsweek.com, January 2, 2019.

Otten, Cathy. "Life after ISIS Slavery for Yazidi Women and Children." *The New Yorker*, August 31, 2017.

Rahman, Grace. "Little Respite for Iraqis Displaced by Mosul Fighting." *The Guardian*, August 2, 2016.

Rasheed, Ahmed, and Raya Jalabi. "Abadi Says Iraq to Act Soon over Border Areas in Stand-Off with Kurds." *Reuters*, November 14, 2017.

Sawer, Patrick. "Letter Sheds Light on Who Was to Blame for 'Blunder' Which Sent Light Brigade into the Valley of Death." *The Telegraph*, December 10, 2016.

Shabi, Rachel. "Looted in Syria—and Sold in London: The British Antiques Shops Dealing in Artefacts Smuggled by Isis." *The Guardian*, July 3, 2015.

Shaheen, Kareem. "Isis Destroys Tetrapylon Monument in Palmyra." *The Guardian*, January 20, 2017.

Shilani, Hiwa. "Masoud Barzini Hosts New Canadian, British Ambassadors to Iraq." www.kurdistan24.net, December 17, 2019.

"Syria: Turkey War Planes Launch Strikes on Afrin." BBC News, www.bbc.com, January 20, 2017.

Turak, Natasha. "Hundreds of ISIS Prisoners Are Escaping from Camps in Northern Syria amid Turkish Offensive." CNBC, www.cnbc.com, October 14, 2019.

Waraich, Omar. "Khaled al-Asaad: Authority on the Antiquities of the Syrian City of Palmyra Who Was Devoted to Studying and Protecting Its Treasures." *The Independent*, August 20, 2015.

Westcott, Tom. "'A Shadow of Its Former Self': Mosul Museum and the Long Road to Recovery." Middle East Eye, www.middleeasteye.com, July 13, 2020.

Xinhuanet.com. "Extremist IS Militants Damage Ancient Citadel, Two Shrines in Iraq's Nineveh." December 31, 2014.

NEWSPAPERS AND PERIODICALS IN LAYARD'S TIME

The Times of London
The New York Times
The Athenaeum
The Bristol Mercury
The Daily News
The Flintshire Observer
The Huddersfield Chronicle
The Quarterly Review
The Manchester Courier and Lacanshire General Advertiser
The Standard
The Telegraph
The New York Tribune

INTERVIEWS BY THE AUTHOR

Clemens Reichel, assistant professor for Mesopotamian archaeology at the University of Toronto and associate curator, ancient Near Eastern art, Royal Ontario Museum, Toronto, May 25, 2015.

Kamal Rasheed Raheem, director of antiquities, in Suleimani, June 17, 2015.

Abdullah Khorseed Qadir, director of the Iraqi Institute for the Conservation of Antiquities and Heritage, June 18, 2015.

Najim Abdullah Kedo, deputy commander of the Peshmerga forces in the Bashik area, June 20, 2015.

Mark Altaweel, lecturer in the archaeology of the Near East, UCL Institute of Archaeology in London, phone interview, July 14, 2015.

Index